Language and Reason

Language and Reason

A Study of Habermas's Pragmatics

Maeve Cooke

The MIT Press   Cambridge, Massachusetts   London, England

Set in Baskerville by Maple-Vail Book Manufacturing Group.
Printed and bound in the United States of America.

Library of Congress Cataloging-in-Publication Data

Cooke, Maeve.
  Language and reason : a study of Habermas's pragmatics / Maeve
Cooke.
    p.   cm.—(Studies in contemporary German social thought)
  "Works by Habermas cited in the text": p.
  Includes bibliographical references and index.
  ISBN 0-262-03217-1
  1. Habermas, Jürgen.   I. Title.   II. Series.
B3258.H324C66   1994
193—dc20   93-6412
                                                                   CIP

for my parents

Contents

Preface

The project of modernity—the realization of rational forms of individual and social life—has been accompanied since its inception in the Enlightenment by a counter-reckoning consisting of two independent strands: the critique of the capitalist model of modernization (here the name of Karl Marx has come to be representative) and the critique of reason as the will to instrumental power (here the name of Friedrich Nietzsche springs to mind). With the collapse of the socialist states of Eastern Europe, one might suppose that the first strand had come to a dead end; but there is a good argument to be made that now more than ever we need a critical theory of Western capitalism—a *differentiated* critique, however, that acknowledges the positive potentials of market-based *economies* while drawing attention to, and explaining, the pathological development of modern *societies*. The current intellectual atmosphere is dominated, though, not by attempts to rethink Marx but by the heirs of the second strand, namely postmodernism and poststructuralism. In their wake, the charge that the Enlightenment conception of reason is repressive has become an intellectually respectable commonplace.

Refusing to abandon the first strand of the critique of Enlightenment or to give in to the second, Jürgen Habermas has explored another alternative: the possibility of a nonrepressive conception of reason—that is, a conception that provides standards for the critique of irrational or unjust forms of individual and social life while avoiding possibly repressive metaphysical projections. Habermas's project is neither politically nor philosophically fashionable. It takes its impetus from the critical theory of the "Frankfurt School" as developed since the 1930s by such theorists as Max Horkheimer, Theodor Adorno, and Herbert Marcuse, but it strives to rescue that theory from the theoretical impasse into which Habermas argues Horkheimer and Adorno led it in the 1940s. Habermas regards it as no accident that the critique of the Enlightenment presented in Horkheimer and Adorno's *Dialectic of Enlightenment* has since been appropriated by postmodernism and poststructuralism.

Habermas remains convinced that it is possible to continue the project of the Enlightenment. In this he is guided by the spirit of Karl Marx, whose coupling of a critique of capitalist modernization with an emancipatory intention places him in the traditions of both the Enlightenment and the Counter-Enlightenment. Despite Habermas's commitment to democratic ideals and his faith in the potentials of the democratic institutions and practices that have developed in bourgeois society, and despite his recognition that we may not wish to or be able to dispense with the capitalist mode of production completely, he is impressed by Marx's overall emancipatory intention and convinced by Marx's basic strategy. Marx takes as his starting point a two-level model of society, distinguishing between an economic base and a symbolically structured and normatively regulated superstructure, and he explains the deformation of the latter in terms of the violence inflicted upon it by the former. Speaking generally, Habermas criticizes Marx for his narrow focus on the capitalist economic system as a threat to the symbolically structured and normatively regulated spheres of society and for his neglect of the emancipatory potentials implicit in the latter spheres. Nonetheless, Habermas also finds it useful to operate with a two-level model. Where Marx refers to a base and a superstructure, however, Habermas distinguishes between a *system* and a *lifeworld* as the dimensions of material and social reproduction, respectively. He argues that the pathologies of modern societies can be traced back to the one-sided development of the system at the expense of the lifeworld.

Habermas hopes to continue the project of a critical theory of society without relying on the various kinds of metaphysical projections to which he believes his forerunners in the tradition succumbed. He recognizes the truth of the critique of the Counter-Enlightenment (from Hegel through Nietzsche, Horkheimer, and Adorno to poststructuralism) with regard to metaphysical notions of reason, but he refuses to give up the idea of reason altogether. He insists on the possibility of a conception of reason that is *postmetaphysical yet nondefeatist*. Indeed, he argues that such a conception is already operative in the everyday linguistic practices of modern societies. This communicative rationality falls prey neither to the repressive objectivism against which the critics of the Enlightenment have warned nor to the perils of a relativism that would undermine the very basis of a critical theory of society.

What is communicative rationality? Where does it come from, and what does it imply? In what sense does it represent a "postmetaphysical yet nondefeatist" conception of rationality? Can it really avoid metaphysical speculation, and does it have a genuinely critical thrust? What is its role within Habermas's critical theory of society? The two volumes of *The Theory of Communicative Action,* published in 1981, offer the most systematic presentation of his critical social theory, and I propose in this book to discuss the notion of communicative rationality in the context of this and subsequently published texts.

The concept of communicative rationality invokes a voice of reason that appears in the everyday linguistic activities of members of modern societies. It is based on "strong idealizations" that are implicit in the general presuppositions of communication in such societies. It is by reconstructing these presuppositions—which are the universal conditions of possible understanding—that Habermas shows that a concept of communicative rationality is already operative in everyday communicative practices. The name he gives to this undertaking is "the program of formal pragmatics."

The concept of communicative rationality makes sense only against the background of Habermas's theory of communicative action, which in turn must be placed within the context of his critical theory of the developmental processes of modern societies. In chapter 1 I sketch the outlines of the theory of communicative action and introduce certain concepts that are necessary to the subsequent discussion. In chapter 2 I offer a preliminary specification of the idea of communicative rationality as a postmetaphysical yet nondefeatist conception of reason. In chapters 3 and 4 I go into the details of Habermas's account of the connection between language and validity. The concept of communicative rationality is based on the thesis that the basic

units of everyday linguistic activity raise various kinds of intersubjectively criticizable validity claims. Habermas uses this thesis to argue
that linguistic understanding is connected with the idea of reaching
agreement with others with regard to the validity of a disputed claim.
My discussion of Habermas's formal pragmatic investigations thus ne-
cessitates examination of his theory of validity claims (chapter 3) and
his account of meaning and understanding (chapter 4). In chapter 5
I return to the implications of the notion of communicative rationality
and look in more detail at Habermas's account of the pathologies of
modernity. This leads me into a more general discussion of the critical
thrust of the concept of communicative rationality, which concludes
the book.

Acknowledgements

A postgraduate scholarship from the Deutscher Akademischer Austauschdienst (DAAD) marked the first important step on the path that, many years later, led to this book. The DAAD sent me to the University of Konstanz, where I encountered Professor Albrecht Wellmer and his colleagues. I would like to thank the DAAD for financial assistance, and Professor Wellmer and all the members of his Wednesday Colloquium for stimulating discussions and invaluable help and support over the years. Thanks are also due to the Swiss government, from which I was, once more, the happy recipient of a scholarship; this enabled me to spend two years at the University of Zürich and to make use of the excellent research facilities there. I would like to express my gratitude to Professor Emeritus R. Meyer, of the University of Zürich, for his support during this time. I would also like to thank my colleagues at University College Dublin—in particular, Professor Hugh Ridley, for taking time to read the first chapters of the manuscript at a crucial stage in its revision, and Dr. Maria Baghramian, who, despite her initial suspicions of "continental philosophy," devoted a great deal of time to reading chapters 3 and 4 and made a number of very helpful suggestions. Finally, I am indebted beyond words to the tolerance, patience, and unfailing encouragement of my husband, Martin Sauter, who has accompanied me on this path from the beginning.

Author's Notes

A Note Concerning Translations

I have as a general rule not relied on the existing English translations, although page numbers for these are given where available. Unless otherwise stated, all translations from the German are my own.

Abbreviations of Works by Habermas

TCA: The Theory of Communicative Action
TKH: Theorie des kommunikativen Handelns
Discourse: The Philosophical Discourse of Modernity
Diskurs: Der philosophische Diskurs der Moderne
Erläuterungen: Erläuterungen zur Diskursethik
"Questions": "Questions and Counterquestions"
"Remarks": "Remarks on the Concept of Communicative Action"
"Reply": "A Reply to My Critics"

Language and Reason

1

Communicative Action: An Overview

1

The Theory of Communicative Action, published in two volumes in 1981, is Habermas's most systematic presentation to date of his critical social theory. It decisively marks his shift from the theory of knowledge to the theory of language as the basis for this theory. It has been well documented how Habermas, in his attempt to ground a critical social theory, moved in the course of the 1970s from a theory of knowledge—his well-known theory of anthropologically deep-seated cognitive interests[1]—to a theory of communicative action.[2] This has become known as Habermas's "linguistic turn."[3]

As part of this shift in theoretical strategy, Habermas moved from the *critique* of ideology[4] to the *reconstruction* of the presuppositions of the universal conditions of knowledge and action. For Kant and his successors, reconstruction took the form of a search for the transcendental ground of possible theoretical knowledge and moral conduct. Habermas maintains that in the meantime reconstruction, as a mode of reflection, has taken the form of a rational reconstruction of generative rules and cognitive schemata.[5] Here he is thinking of endeavors such as Chomsky's generative grammar, Piaget's theory of cognitive development, and Kohlberg's account of moral development. According to Habermas these are examples of reconstructive sciences, for they set out to reconstruct, or make theoretically explicit, the pretheoretical, implicit knowledge and competencies of acting and speaking subjects.

Two differences between Habermas's strategy of reconstruction and the Kantian project of transcendental knowledge should be noted in particular.

First, Habermas demotes philosophy and promotes the reconstructive sciences in the construction of his critical social theory. The task of reconstruction can no longer be carried out by philosophy, for philosophy has had to give up its claim to be able to explain the foundations of all knowledge and must now cooperate with the various empirical (and, in particular, reconstructive) sciences.[6]

Second, the reconstructive sciences are empirical sciences, to the extent that the status of their reconstructions of general structures and universal conditions is *hypothetical* and these hypotheses must be subjected to the usual methods of testing. This means, for instance, that Habermas's reconstructions of the universal presuppositions of communication in modern societies must be open to checking against speakers' intuitions, scattered across as broad a sociological spectrum as possible.[7] Habermas also makes the point that the confirmation of reconstructive hypotheses often relies on indirect substantiation through *other* empirical theories; their plausibility is defined on the basis of their *coherence* within a set of theories that work together cooperatively and overlap productively. Habermas speaks of fitting together individual pieces of theory like a puzzle and quotes one of his commentators approvingly:

. . . Habermas practices (a mode of theory whereby) . . . claims articulated in one domain can be checked for their consistency, or more permissively, consonance, with assumptions accepted in others. Judgements reached with confidence in one area can be brought to bear on issues posed in more problematic or mysterious areas of a theory.[8]

Habermas has continued to affirm the methodological pluralism of his theory of communicative action—a pluralism that he claims is often not recognized.[9] In view of this, it is hardly surprising that his most recent work on legal and political theory warns against fixation on any one theoretical perspective.[10] It is a further characteristic of the reconstructive sciences that they do not claim validity once and for all for the knowledge they produce; rather, they understand it *fallibilistically*. A fallibilistic (as opposed to foundationalist) understanding of validity takes into account that claims to validity are raised in actual, historical contexts which do not remain stationary but are subject to change, and also that no one can predict whether changes in context will have an effect on what is accepted here and now as sufficient justification in support of the validity of a given claim.[11] A fallibilistic perspective recognizes that validity claims, even where there seem to be good grounds for regarding them as justified or true, are always in principle open to revision in the light of new evidence and insight. Consequently, Habermas believes that his reliance on a strategy of reconstruction will help him to avoid the charge of foundationalism.[12]

The theory of communicative action relies in particular—although by no means exclusively—on a reconstructive theory that seeks to identify the universal presuppositions of everyday communication in modern societies.[13] This science is referred to by Habermas as "universal" or "formal" pragmatics.[14] It can be described as a quasi-transcendental[15] analysis that reconstructs the universal pretheoretical and implicit knowledge that makes possible practical processes of understanding *(Verständigung)*.[16] It contrasts with *empirical* pragmatic research to the extent that the latter is concerned not with the reconstruction of general competencies but with the description and analysis of specific elements of language use.[17] It is *pragmatic* to the extent that it focuses on the *use* of language, and hence on speech acts or utterances, in contrast to semantics (which is concerned with the properties of isolated sentences).[18] As I will explain, the theory of formal pragmatics should be understood, in the first instance, as part of the theoretical underpinning of Habermas's critical social theory. It supports his sociological theory of communicative action and must be seen as part of this broader context. However, the program of formal pragmatics also yields a notion of communicative rationality that is of interest philosophically. In the following discussion I am concerned primarily with two things. First, I examine the *details* of Habermas's formal pragmatic analyses. In view of the central place occupied by formal pragmatics within Habermas's critical endeavor, there is a need to be clearer about which parts of his theory are convincing, which parts are implausible, and which parts are in need of minor modification. Second, I direct my discussion *both* toward consideration of the implications of Habermas's formal pragmatic analyses for the construction of a concept of communicative rationality *and* toward consideration of the implications of this concept of communicative rationality, in particular within the framework of Habermas's critical theory of society. Habermas argues that his analyses of the general structures of everyday communication, in addition to producing insights useful for his theory of communicative action, point to a potential for rationality that is implicit in the validity bases of everyday speech. He calls this potential "communicative rationality," and he maintains that it provides a basis for a postmetaphysical yet nondefeatist (and thus distinctively modern) conception of reason. I attempt to elaborate the precise shape of the conception of reason that can be extracted from Habermas's formal-pragmatic analyses. In the final chapter, I will consider whether this conception can live up to the claims that Habermas makes for it.

My main focus in this volume is the notion of communicative rationality. I want to consider whether Habermas's attempt to extract such a concept from the validity bases of speech is convincing, and to evaluate the scope and the critical power of the concept of rationality that he constructs. The latter, in particular, will necessitate some discussion of Habermas's theory of communicative action. Thus, I begin my inquiry with a very brief sketch of this, and I return to some of the aspects touched on here in the final chapter. (My main concern is not with the details or the implications of Habermas's sociological theory. I deal with this theory in the present chapter only insofar as is necessary to set the scene for the subsequent discussion, and I come back to it in the final chapter only to the extent that it is relevant to the question of the critical thrust of the concept of communicative rationality.)

2

As the subtitles to *The Theory of Communicative Action* make clear,[19] this theory is concerned with rationality, rationalization, and the critique of one-sided or foreshortened conceptions of reason. Such problems can be dealt with from either a philosophical or a sociological point of view: Habermas's concern is less philosophical than sociological. Since my main concern in the present context is with the *philosophical* conception of rationality that emerges from Habermas's analyses, it is important to remember that the development of such a conception is not the primary intention of the theory of communicative action. Although this theory has repercussions for the solution of some philosophical problems (most notably in the areas of the theory of meaning and the theory of rationality), Habermas's analyses of action, meaning, speech acts, etc. are tailored to the needs of social theory.[20] Habermas's main concern is with such questions as "How is social action possible?" and (connected with this) "How is a social order possible?"[21] These questions must be seen as part of an attempt to develop a comprehensive theory of social (in the sense of "societal") rationalization; this theory, in turn, is part of a critical theory of modernity.

What is a theory of societal rationalization? As Richard Bernstein points out, the term "rationalization" could cause problems for English-speaking readers, who "frequently think of rationalization as an activity that disguises or conceals underlying motives and intentions."[22] In contrast, Habermas uses the term "rationalization" to refer to the development of the internal logic of a particular mode of societal action coordination. His theory of rationalization is comprehensive in the sense that it recognizes *two* kinds of rationalization process and does not remain fixated on just one (as most theories hitherto have done).[23] At the heart of Habermas's theory of communicative action is a categorial distinction between two modes of societal rationalization, corresponding to two categorially distinct modes of societal integration. Habermas distinguishes between "system" and "lifeworld" as two aspects of societal integration that must be kept *analytically* distinct.[24] In the lifeworld, coordination of action takes place primarily by way of communicative action[25] and depends on the action orientations of individuals in society.[26] System coordination, in contrast, operates by way of the functional interconnection of action consequences and bypasses the action orientations of individual agents. The basis for Habermas's distinction between social (lifeworld) and functional (system) integration (and thus between "system" and "lifeworld") is whether coordination of action depends on or bypasses the consciousness of the individual in her capacity as an agent. Rationalization processes are possible in both dimensions of societal integration. In the lifeworld, rationalization takes place in the domains of cultural reproduction, social integration, and socialization and takes the general form of an increasing independence of procedures of justification from traditional normative contexts of validity and an increasing reliance on action oriented toward understanding (*Verständigung*).[27] The rationalization of the system, in contrast, refers to increasing complexity and increasing capacity to take on steering functions (including functions of material reproduction) in society.

Habermas moves from an account of the historical separation from one another of distinct mechanisms of social (lifeworld) and functional (system) integration to an account of the uncoupling of (functionally integrated) subsystems of economic and administrative activity from the lifeworld. He argues that the latter results in the "colonization" of the lifeworld by the system (or, more accurately, by modes of system integration). Habermas's thesis of the colonization of the lifeworld puts forth the view that in modern societies the communicatively structured spheres of the lifeworld have become increasingly subject to the imperatives of functional (system) coordination. Rationalization of the system takes place increasingly at the cost of the lifeworld. This uneven or selective development of societal rationalization processes gives rise to deformations within the various domains of the lifeworld, and these deformations manifest themselves in social pathologies such as loss of meaning, anomie, and pyschological disorders. Habermas's critical theory attempts to explain such social pathologies as the effects of the colonization of the lifeworld, which effects are claimed to result from the unbalanced (selective) progress of rationalization in modern societies.

On a methodological level, Habermas asserts that a two-level theory of society is needed in order to take account of the development of modern societies.[28] Habermas claims that up to now most attempts to explain the pathologies of modernity have been deficient to the extent that they have explained these *either* in terms of the rationalization of the lifeworld *or* in terms of the rationalization of the system.[29] Since its beginnings in the late eighteenth century, bourgeois cultural criticism has attempted to attribute the pathologies of modernity *either* to the fact that secularized worldviews have lost the socially integrating power of (religious or other) tradition *or* to the fact that the increasing complexity of the societal system overtaxes individuals' power to coordinate their actions. According to Habermas, neither perspective is adequate on its own. For this reason he finds a Marxist line of critique more fruitful, for Marxist critique already operates with a two-level model. Although Habermas criticizes Marx on a number of counts, he praises him for his basic strategy of attempting to explain the pathologies of the lifeworld as the results of its deformation through the conditions of material reproduction (the system). However, Marx's approach must be rethought and developed to the extent that Marx (a) clamps system and lifeworld together too rigidly, (b) has no criteria by which to distinguish the destruction of traditional forms of life from the reification of post-traditional lifeworlds, and (c) focuses only on how the economic system encroaches on the lifeworld, failing to recognize that the administrative system does this in equal measure.[30] Habermas believes that he can develop a Marxist line of critique productively by means of a theory that brings together two methodological perspectives: that of action theory and that of systems theory. The perspective of action theory is necessary in order to give an adequate account of social (lifeworld) integration and rationalization, and the perspective of systems theory is necessary in order to give an adequate account of functional (system) integration and rationalization. However, a conceptualization of society that develops a concept of the lifeworld in terms of action theory and supplements this with borrowings from systems theory opens itself to the charge of being an "eclectic fusion of heterogeneous approaches, models, and procedures."[31] And, indeed, Habermas's two-level model of societal rationalization is the aspect of his theory of communicative action that has attracted some of the sharpest criticism.[32] Habermas acknowledges the criticism but continues to justify the need for a combined methodological perspective.[33] Although I cannot deal with this debate in the present context, it tends to merge two questions which I find it helpful to keep apart: the question of whether the distinction between system and lifeworld is useful, and of how one is to understand it, and the question of whether one needs an action-theoretic perspective to give an account of the lifeworld and a system-theoretic perspective to give an account of the system. It could be argued that there are good reasons for upholding the distinction between system and lifeworld but that, for example, one does not need to use *systems theory* in order to give an account of functional (system) integration and rationalization. The distinction between system and lifeworld as two distinct modes of societal integration in modern societies does not itself say anything about which methodological approaches one needs to give an account of the expansion of the latter at the expense of the former. In the following

I leave aside the question of the appropriate methodological perspective, as the distinction between system and lifeworld is to a certain extent independent of it; furthermore, nothing of crucial importance for the discussion of communicative rationality turns on this debate. I simply accept Habermas's distinction between system and lifeworld, interpreting this, as I have indicated, as a distinction between two categorially distinct modes of societal integration.

Even the foregoing very brief sketch has made clear that Habermas's theory of communicative action is intended as a critical theory of modernity. This theory identifies social pathologies such as loss of meaning, anomie, and pyschological disturbances and sets out to explain these as the effects of the one-sided or selective (and therefore pathological) development of rationalization processes in modern societies. In the final chapter I will take a closer look at Habermas's account of the uneven development of modern societal rationalization processes in order to consider where the concept of communicative rationality fits into his critical theory of modernity. In the remainder of the present chapter I examine what Habermas has to say about social (lifeworld) integration, for this is the background against which his theory of communicative rationality becomes intelligible.

3

As part of his theory of communicative action, Habermas wants to answer the questions "How is social action possible?" and "How is a social order possible?" In order to do so, he investigates those mechanisms of action coordination that make possible a regular and stable network of interactions in a given society. Habermas argues that only mechanisms of social (lifeworld) integration, not those of functional (system) integration, are relevant to an account of the conditions that make possible an intersubjectively shared social order. In the following I focus on *communicative action* as a mode of action coordination in the lifeworld; on the *lifeworld* itself as the background to, resource for, and stabilizing factor in the face of communicative action; on the contribution of communicative action to the *reproduction* of the lifeworld; and on the distinction between communicative and strategic action and Habermas's claim that communicative action is the primary mode of action coordination within the lifeworld.

Habermas identifies two mechanisms for coordinating social actions: consensus (*Einverständnis*) and influence (*Einflußnahme*). He argues, however, that these are mutually exclusive—at least from the perspective of the agent. A participant in everyday processes of communication cannot simultaneously intend to reach understanding (consensus) with another participant and to influence (have a causal effect on) that participant. For our purposes, Habermas's more important—and stronger—thesis is that consensus is the fundamental mechanism of social coordination in the lifeworld.

The notion of "consensus" and that of the "lifeworld" are both of crucial importance to Habermas's project. For Habermas, "consensus" as a mechanism of social coordination is connected with the idea of *Verständigung*. A notoriously difficult word to translate, *Verständigung* refers both to linguistic understanding and to the process of reaching agreement, thus extending across a spectrum of meanings ranging from comprehension to consensus. The English translations of Habermas tend to favor "understanding" as a translation, presumably because the English term may also be used to imply both comprehension and agreement (although its use in the latter sense is far less common in everyday English than it is in everyday German).

Communicative action is a form of social interaction in which the plans of action of various agents are coordinated through an exchange of communicative acts—that is, through a use of language (or of corresponding extra-verbal expressions) oriented toward understanding (*Verständigung*).[34] Habermas also refers to such a use of language as the use of language oriented toward consensus (*Einverständnis*).

According to Habermas, the use of language oriented toward understanding or consensus[35] rests on the presupposition that participants in interaction have developed what Habermas (borrowing from Piaget[36]) refers to as a decentered view of the world. By this he means that the decentering of consciousness in the modern age has enabled participants in communication to take up different attitudes toward the world. Participants in modern processes of understanding have learned to take up different attitudes—objectivating, norm-conformative, and expressive—toward the elements of three (formally conceived) "worlds"—the objective, the social, and the subjective.[37] The distinction between "worlds," or the object domains of understanding, is conceived formally to the extent that it is derived from the three basic attitudes identified by Habermas. When we adopt an objectivating attitude we relate, in the first instance, to the objective world of facts and existing states of affairs; when we adopt a norm-conformative attitude we relate, in the first instance, to the social world of normatively regulated interactions; when we adopt an expressive attitude we relate, in the first instance, to the subjective world of inner experience.[38] Although it is possible to adopt varying attitudes toward elements of one and the same world, (for instance, an objectivating attitude toward elements of the normatively regulated social world or a norm-conformative or expressive attitude toward elements of the objective world of facts and states of affairs),[39] for participants in communicative action this is always a *secondary* operation:

> . . . facts, norms and and subjective experiences have their *originary* locus in "their" corresponding worlds (objective, social or subjective), and, *in the first instance,* are accessible, or identifiable, only from the perspective of an actor who takes a corresponding attitude (be it objectivating, norm-conforming, or expressive)."[40]

Failure to recognize this leads to the respective dangers of *objectivism* (adopting, in the first instance, an objectivating attitude toward all three worlds), *moralism* (adopting, in the first instance, a norm-conformative attitude toward all three worlds), and *aestheticism* (adopting, in the first instance, an expressive attitude toward all three worlds).[41]

Habermas is not denying that it may be productive to adopt (as a secondary operation) different attitudes toward different worlds[42]; he acknowledges, moreover, that participants in everyday communication often adopt, without any trouble, different attitudes toward one and the same world. Within communicative action, this movement between worlds is regulated by what Habermas calls "the performative attitude."

For Habermas the performative attitude has a double aspect, referring both to a capacity for transition *between* worlds and to the ability to adopt a reflective relation toward elements *within* any one world. I will have more to say about this reflective relation very shortly. With regard to the capacity for transition *between* worlds, Habermas claims that the performative attitude (which participants in communicative action must adopt) regulates transition between worlds while retaining consistency of meaning.[43] Habermas uses this as a basis for distinguishing communicative from strategic action.[44]

If reference to "worlds" is confusing, one may prefer to speak of "validity dimensions." Put in this way, Habermas's thesis is that, with the decentering of consciousness in the modern age, participants in communication have developed an ability to distinguish various validity dimensions—to recognize, for instance, that the validation of an empirical truth claim ("It is raining outside") requires different methods and procedures than the validation of a claim to subjective truthfulness ("I have a headache"), and that the validation of either of these is distinct from a claim to normative validity ("Abortion is morally wrong"). One could also say that the ability to distinguish between "worlds" is nothing more than the ability to distinguish between types of validity claims. It is thus not surprising that a theory of validity claims plays an important role in Habermas's theory of communicative action.[45] What Habermas seems to be saying is that the modern—decentered—understanding of the world has opened up different dimensions of validity; to the extent that each dimension of validity has its own standards of truth and falsity and its own modes of justification for determining these, one may say that what has been opened up are dimensions of rationality.

Habermas claims that the ability to adopt different attitudes toward corresponding worlds is the precondition for a reflective relation to the world.[46]

A reflective relation to the world is present when participants in communication raise validity claims that can be reciprocally accepted or denied. Formal pragmatic reconstruction of the conditions of possibility of everyday linguistic communication identifies a mode of linguistic communication (communicative action) in which participants reciprocally raise and acknowledge (or reject) various kinds of validity claims. According to Habermas, a speaker raises a validity claim with a given utterance when the success of the interchange depends on the hearer's ability to respond to the claim with a "Yes" or a "No." In raising a validity claim, the speaker relativizes her utterance against the possibility that it will be contested by other agents.[47] The possibility of rejecting, on the basis of reasons, the validity of a given claim is the defining characteristic of this mode of communication. The very notion of a validity claim thus seems to imply a reflective relation to the world, for in order to recognize a given utterance as a validity *claim* a participant in communication must recognize that other participants may have reasons for challenging the utterance's validity. To be sure, different degrees of reflexivity are possible.[48] Habermas also describes this reflective relation to the world as an indirect one: An agent relates to something in the world (or in any of the three "worlds") indirectly when she relativizes her utterances against the possibility that their validity will be contested by other agents.[49] The relationship is indirect because it is mediated; it is mediated by the need for intersubjective recognition of the validity claim raised with the utterance. From this it is (for Habermas) an easy step to the thesis that communicative action is characterized—from the perspective of the participants—by an orientation toward understanding (consensus).[50] To say that participants in communication aim to come to an agreement regarding the claimed validity of their utterances is the same as saying that they aim to achieve intersubjective recognition of the validity claims they raise. From this we can also see that participants in communicative action can pursue their aims only cooperatively. The means of success are not at the disposal of the individual agent; she is dependent on the cooperation (more precise, the recognition) of others.

In its simplest terms, communicative action—that is, action oriented toward understanding *(Verständigung)*—is action in which a speaker carries out a speech act whereby the success of the interaction depends on the hearer's responding to the validity claim raised with the speech act with a "Yes" or a "No." The speaker must be able to supply reasons to support the validity of the claim, if challenged, and the hearer must be able to provide reasons in support of his "Yes" or "No." To raise a claim is thus to undertake to show, if challenged, that this claim is justified. This assumption of responsibility on the part of the speaker (in the first instance) is described by Habermas as a "warranty" *(Gewähr)*. This warranty is the source of the coordinating power of speech acts. With every speech act, by virtue of the validity claim it raises, the speaker enters into an interpersonal relationship of mutual obligation with the hearer: The speaker is obliged to support her claim with reasons, if challenged, and the hearer is obliged to accept a claim unless he has good reasons not to do so. The obligation in question is, in the first instance, not a moral one but a rational one—the penalty for the failure to fulfil it is (in the first instance) the charge not of immorality but of irrationality—although clearly the two will often overlap.[51] Furthermore, although this way of characterizing communicative action points to an internal connection between such action and processes of argumentation, these processes may be very rudimentary ones. What counts as a good reason may be fixed and given by the traditions of a particular society, for instance, and the validity of these reasons may be regarded as beyond dispute. This suggests that it is useful to distinguish between *conventional* and *postconventional* modes of communicative action. Only the latter are connected with forms of argumentation that are open-ended and critical. Habermas does not take adequate account of this distinction, which is a crucial one in the context of the present discussion.[52]

Habermas acknowledges that some cultures are more practiced in the ability to distance themselves from themselves—that is, to take up a critical, questioning attitude toward their traditions, their norms, their conventions and their conceptions of personal identity. He goes on to say, however, that all languages make possible a distinction between what is true and what we regard as true.[53] This is misleading if it implies that all languages show a connection between communicative action and open-ended and critical argumentation. This is clearly not the case. The connection between everyday communicative action and argumentation is of vital importance to Habermas's account of communicative rationality, but—as will become clear in the next chapter—what is required is not just a connection between everyday linguistic practices and argumentation but a connection between the former and open-ended and critical forms of argumentation. In this regard, Habermas may be guilty of running together a number of senses of "reflective." As we have seen, Habermas characterizes "modern" societies as those in which a decentering of consciousness has taken place; this, in turn, has given rise to the ability to take up different attitudes toward the world—that is, to distinguish different dimensions of validity. It will be recalled that Habermas refers to this as a "reflective" relation to the world.[54] However, although this kind of reflective relation to the world may be a necessary precondition for taking part in any kind of argumentation, it by no means implies the ability or the willingness to take part in forms of argumentation that are reflective in the sense of open-ended and critical. Indeed, the issue is further confused by the fact that we can find a third sense of the term "reflective" in Habermas's writings. Habermas occasionally distinguishes between "naive" and "reflective" forms of communicative action; here, however, he is referring to the distinction between the thematization of validity claims in everyday communicative practice and the development of institutionalized, specialized forms of argumentation ("expert cultures"). Discourse is the reflective form of communicative action in this sense of "reflective."[55]

Thus, while Habermas's account of communicative action is restricted to modern societies (as characterized above), his account of communicative rationality makes most sense in connection with those modern societies in which postconventional forms of communicative action have developed.[56] As the distinction between "conventional" and "postconventional" modes of communicative action makes clear, the concept of communicative action does not itself presuppose that processes of open and critical debate exist in a given society. The concept of communicative action has only a critical potential; as we shall see, the idea of communicative rationality expresses this potential.

Habermas introduces the notion of the lifeworld as a necessary complement to the notion of action oriented toward understanding. The concept of communicative action must be understood against the background of the lifeworld. We have already encountered Habermas's use of the term "lifeworld" to refer to the symbolically (and, in the final instance, communicatively) structured spheres of society as distinct from what he calls the "system." More precise, he uses "lifeworld" to refer to the stock of implicit assumptions, intuitive know-how, and socially established practices that functions as a background to all understanding. The lifeworld is "the horizon-forming context of communication"[57] and functions both as a restriction and as a resource. As communicative action becomes increasingly rationalized, the lifeworld also takes on important stabilizing functions.

To begin with, the lifeworld has a context-forming function: "Subjects acting communicatively reach understanding with one another [both linguistic comprehension and consensus are implied here—MC] against the horizon of the lifeworld."[58] The idea of a horizon indicates that the lifeworld limits the action situation, and that it itself is not accessible to interpretation; it is made up of background convictions which are more or less diffuse and which are unproblematic to the extent that they remain unarticulated and unthematized. These background convictions constitute a form of implicit, holistically structured knowledge that we cannot make explicit and call into question at will. Participants in communicative action find themselves in situations, and the elements of situations can be thematized readily, but a situation is never more than a segment of the lifeworld that is delimited momentarily with respect to a topic or a problem (what Habermas calls a "theme"[59]). The lifeworld *as a whole* can never be thematized.

The lifeworld as a background to everyday processes of communication also functions as a resource. It provides a reservoir of intuitively certain interpretations upon which participants in communication can draw. As a resource, the lifeworld is one of the conditions that enable communication, specifically the kind of communication that is characteristic of communicative action. The relationship is a dialectical one. Habermas claims that the lifeworld, as an enabling condition of communicative action, is itself reproduced by the integrative mechanisms of communicative action. In coming to an understanding with one another, participants stand in a cultural tradition which they simultaneously use and renew; furthermore, as members of social groups they reinforce existing bonds of solidarity while at the same time creating new bonds; finally, they internalize the value orientations of the social group while acquiring competencies that are essential to the development of their personal identities. The three domains of the lifeworld identified by Habermas are thus the domains of cultural reproduction, social integration, and socialization, which correspond to the three functional aspects of communicative action: reaching consensus, coordinating action, and socialization (the formation of personal identities).[60]

Although there may be some grounds for claiming that communicative action functions to reproduce the symbolic structures of the lifeworld,[61] one could argue that it also has a potentially destructive function.[62] As we have seen, communicative action is conceptually linked with the idea of argumentation, whereby the latter can take a more or less rudimentary form. However, in at least some societies (in fact, in those which Habermas considers most advanced), communicative action is linked to an idea of argumentation that denies that any claim to validity is, in principle, exempt from critical examination. As we have seen, we can distinguish such postconventional modes of communicative action from conventional ones. Although (as Habermas rightly points out) the lifeworld as a whole can never be called into question, it seems as though its fabric could be worn away through constant critical examination and rejection of its traditions, practices, and fixed patterns of personality development. Communicative action cannot in itself *renew* this fabric. Of course, critical examination, through argumentation, of traditions, practices, and patterns of socialization by no means implies the rejection of these; nonetheless, it often does lead to rejection, and the possibility that it may do so cannot be excluded in principle. Habermas recognizes the problem of the cultural impoverishment of the lifeworld, but he sees it as the result of the increasing encapsulation of learning processes in various areas within specialist cultures that are split off from everyday communicative practice.[63] He rarely regards increasing reflexivity itself as a threat; on the contrary, he argues that it contributes to a reinforcement of the kinds of continuity that are necessary to the reproduction of the lifeworld.

Habermas acknowledges that the gap between communicative action and the lifeworld widens to the extent that conventional modes of communicative action are increasingly replaced by postconventional modes—that is, to the extent that action oriented toward understanding increasingly relies on "Yes" or "No" responses to validity claims that cannot be traced back to a prevailing normative consensus but are the reflective result of critical and open processes of interpretation.[64] This, in turn, leads to the pluralization of (overlapping) forms of life: Participants in highly reflective (in the sense of critical and open) modes of communicative action achieve understanding against the background of a plurality of overlapping *lifeworlds*.[65]

Nonetheless, Habermas believes that the continuity of ways of thinking and behaving (which is necessary to the reproduction of the lifeworld) is not threatened by increasing reflexivity in the above sense.[66] Indeed, he claims that it strengthens the processes of social (lifeworld) reproduction in all three domains. He argues that increased reflexivity *reinforces* the continuity of post-traditional cultural

traditions; that abstract-universal procedures of discursive will formation *strengthen* solidarity between individuals in contexts that are no
longer legitimated in a traditional way; that increased scope for individuation and self-realization *intensifies* and *stabilizes* a process of socialization that no longer progresses according to fixed patterns.[67]

However, even if Habermas is correct in asserting that increasingly
reflective (in the sense of critical and open) modes of communicative
action strengthen rather than threaten the kinds of continuity necessary to the reproduction of the lifeworld, he has not thereby addressed the problem of the impoverishment of the *substance* of the
lifeworld through continual critical challenges to received ways of
thinking and behaving. The only challenge to the substance of the
lifeworld acknowledged by Habermas is its impoverishment due to
the development of increasingly esoteric "expert cultures" in which
questions of validity (such as truth, justice, and taste) are dealt with
only by specialists. For Habermas, therefore, the problem of the impoverishment of the lifeworld amounts to no more than the question
of how the knowledge produced in these expert cultures can be fed
back into the practices of everyday life.[68] In answer to this, Habermas
points to the mediating roles of philosophy, art criticism, and literary
criticism.[69] However, even if this could be rendered plausible (and
Habermas admits that the logic of the mediation between expert cultures and lifeworld has not yet been adequately explained[70]), what is
at issue is less a problem of successful mediation than one of semantic
renewal. Unless the substance of the lifeworld can be regenerated in
some way (and it is not clear how the input of specialist knowledge
can do this), we are faced with the counter-intuitive prospect of a fully
rationalized but barren lifeworld. Although we can find no more than
a few hints in his recent writings that this might be a problem,[71] Habermas acknowledged this possibility in an essay written as far back as
1972. In the context of a discussion of Walter Benjamin, who emphasized happiness as well as social progress and freedom, Habermas is
for a moment beset by doubt:

Benjamin saw the experience of happiness, which he called secular illumina-
tion, as being bound to the redemption of tradition. We need those rescued
semantic potentials if we are to interpret the world in terms of our own needs,
and only if the source of these potentials does not run dry can the claim to
happiness be fulfilled. Cultural goods are the spoils which those who rule

carry along in triumphal procession; therefore, the process of tradition must be wrenched from myth. Now it is true that the liberation of culture is not possible without overcoming the repression anchored in institutions. Yet, for a moment, one is beset by suspicion: wouldn't it be just as possible to have an emancipation without happiness or fulfillment as it is to have a relatively high standard of living without the abolition (*Aufhebung*) of repression?[72]

At the end of this remarkable passage, Habermas concludes that this question (posed at the threshold of *post-histoire,* when symbolic structures are spent and threadbare) is not a safe[73] question but not a totally idle one either. Twenty years on, it seems even less of an idle question; indeed, in the context of Habermas's own thought, with its postmetaphysical utopian vision of a rationalized lifeworld, its force has, if anything, increased. Habermas himself, however, appears to have been distracted from this particular source of unease by the prospect of other dangers. Recently he has mentioned the threat of social instability that accompanies the increasing reflexivity[74] of communicative action a number of times.[75]

This brings us to the third main function of the lifeworld. In addition to acting as both horizon and resource, the lifeworld acts as a safeguard against the threat of social disintegration that accompanies increasingly reflective processes of communicative action. Anticipating the objection that linguistic processes of consensus formation may be more disruptive than cohesive, Habermas admits that communicative action does not appear to be a very reliable mechanism for social integration.[76] The idea that every explicit agreement to a speech-act offer rests on a double negation (i.e., that in agreeing to something we reject the possibility of saying "No") is one of Habermas's favorite formulations. It underscores the precarious character of communication oriented toward understanding. In the face of the ever-present risk of dissensus—which increases with increasing reflexivity—there are a number of alternatives: for instance, undertaking simple repairs, passing over or leaving aside controversial validity claims, initiating discourses, breaking off communication, and going over to strategic action.[77] Since none of these possibilities is unproblematic, stabilizing and regulatory media are necessary. The lifeworld, with its stock of implicit assumptions, intuitive know-how, and firmly rooted social practices, is one such medium.[78]

4

We have seen that Habermas gives an account of communicative action as action oriented toward understanding and that this has three functional aspects—reaching understanding, coordinating action, and the socialization of individuals—which contribute to the reproduction of the lifeworld. This indicates that the reproductive processes of the lifeworld are based on—and may even be dependent on—communicative action. Habermas's critical theory of modern society, with its thesis of the colonization of the lifeworld by mechanisms of functional integration, requires him to show a dependency; his colonization thesis makes sense only to the extent that it can be shown that the integrative mechanisms of communicative action are essential to the reproductive processes of the lifeworld. Habermas pursues a language-theoretic strategy in order to show this: He argues that the use of language oriented toward understanding is the original or primary mode of language use, and that other modes (such as the indirect and the instrumental) are parasitic on it.[79] This has been seen as the most fundamental claim of the entire corpus that constitutes the work of the later Habermas.[80] Whether or not it rests on an assumption that communicative claims are somehow emancipatory, as David Rasmussen contends,[81] Habermas certainly appears to regard it as central not only to his theory of language but to his entire theory of communicative action. The primacy of the communicative over the instrumental (more specific, the strategic) mode of language use is supposed to provide a basis for asserting the primacy of communicative action over strategic action.

I begin this section with a characterization of strategic action. I then consider Habermas's thesis that the strategic mode of language use is parasitic on the communicative mode, pointing out that Habermas has not shown this conclusively. Finally, I suggest that a language-theoretic argument can show no more than the *conceptual* priority of the communicative mode of language use. Thus, even if the conceptual priority of the communicative use of language could be shown conclusively, this would not be sufficient to show the *functional* primacy of the communicative use of language (and hence of communicative action) over the strategic use of language (and hence over strategic action). However, other kinds of argument are available to Habermas in his attempt to show that communicative action is the primary mechanism of social (lifeworld) integration; I conclude by drawing attention to one of these arguments.

Habermas claims that consensus (*Einverständis*) is the fundamental mechanism of action coordination in the lifeworld. Since, as we have seen, Habermas identifies two mechanisms of social (lifeworld) coordination, it is clear that he will have to both give an account of influence (*Einflußnahme*) as a mechanism for coordinating actions and explain why it fulfils functions of social (lifeworld) integration only in a secondary way. Since Habermas's theory of communicative action has been accused of being blind to the role of power within the lifeworld, it is worth emphasizing that strategic action is a mechanism of action coordination *within* the lifeworld.[82] As we have seen, both communicative and strategic action represent modes of action coordination within the lifeworld, in contrast to the functional regulation of action consequences (the mechanism of action coordination that is characteristic of the economic and administrative subsystems). Habermas's shorthand for the administrative subsystem as a subsystem of "power" may be one source of confusion. The administrative system does indeed represent a mechanism of action coordination external to the lifeworld. Strategic action, in contrast, represents power *internal* to the lifeworld.[83]

Where actions are coordinated through influence rather than consensus, the agents are oriented toward success rather than toward understanding. Whereas Habermas describes action oriented toward understanding (consensus) as communicative action, he describes action oriented toward success as instrumental action. Strategic actions are instrumental to the extent that participants in strategic action instrumentalize one another as a means for achieving their respective success.

Strategic action is best characterized by contrast with communicative action. Both strategic and communicative action have a teleological structure to the extent that in both cases participants act purposively, pursue aims, and achieve results,[84] but otherwise they differ radically both from the point of view of their structural characteristics and from the point of view of the attitudes of the individual agents concerned.

Strategic action can be distinguished structurally from communicative action with regard to the aims of the agents and with regard to the agent-world relations that participants in modern processes of communication are able to adopt. Participants in communicative action adopt a "performative attitude"[85] whereby they take up one of three possible attitudes toward the elements of one of three formally conceived worlds from within a framework that allows them to adopt (but only as a *secondary* operation) either of the other two attitudes as well. In contrast, in strategic action, agents do not operate within this three-world reference system. The strategic agent confronts the world, rather than worlds, as though only one agent-world relation were possible. The three possible attitudes toward three corresponding worlds are reduced to just one attitude and one world—the objectivating attitude to the objective world. The agent relates to the social world of normatively regulated interactions and the subjective world of inner experience in an objectivating way as though they were the objective world of facts and states of affairs. Translating this into the language of validity dimensions, one might say that agents who act strategically recognize only one dimension of validity: that of propositional truth and efficacy. They deal with other persons and with their own inner nature as though these were states of affairs, or entities in the physical world, for which criteria of propositional truth and efficacy are appropriate. They recognize no other modes of validity and, hence, no other modes of rationality than the cognitive-instrumental mode.

We have also seen that participants in communicative action adopt a reflective relation to the world.[86] This means that they do not relate *directly* to something in one of the three worlds; rather, they relativize their utterances against the possibility that their validity will be contested by others. Their relation to the world is mediated by the need for intersubjective recognition of the criticizable validity claims that they raise; to this extent, participants in communicative action can achieve their aims only cooperatively. The means of success are not at the disposal of the individual agent, so she is dependent on the cooperation of others. In contrast, agents who act strategically are not dependent on the recognition of others. They can treat other persons as though they were objects or entities in the physical world. This is a further dimension of the "objectivating attitude" that has freed itself from the three-world reference system of communicative action.

Yet another way of distinguishing between communicative action and strategic action is in terms of the aims of the agents. The aims pursued by participants in communicative and strategic action are conceptually distinct. The aims of action oriented toward understanding cannot be defined independent of the conceptual means of their realization; the relationship between the means of communication and the aim of communication is a constitutive one. As such, the aims of communicative action are situated conceptually within the linguistically constituted lifeworld.[87] In contrast, the aims of strategic action must be conceptualized as part of the objective world of facts and existing states of affairs. They can thus be described adequately in terms of their *effect* qua causal interventions in the objective world. In other words, a description of an action oriented toward understanding that described only its results would be an inadequate characterization, whereas this is not necessarily true of a similar description of a strategic action.

Habermas argues that communicative action is the primary mechanism of social integration (in modern societies) and that strategic action is merely a secondary one. His attempt to prove that the use of language oriented toward understanding is the original mode of language use, and that other modes of language use are parasitic on it, appears to be an important part of this argument. The other (parasitic) modes of language use include the figurative, the symbolic, in general the *indirect* mode of language use, on the one hand, and the strategic or more generally the *instrumental* mode of language use on the other.[88] Within the strategic mode of language use Habermas distinguishes further between the *manifestly* and the *latently* strategic use of language and, as subdivisions of the latter, between the *conscious* and the *unconscious* latently strategic use of language. Habermas has to show that *all* these forms of strategic language use are parasitic on the communicative mode of language use.

In *The Theory of Communicative Action* Habermas attempts to show that the strategic mode of language use is parasitic on the use of language oriented toward understanding by drawing on Austin's distinction between illocutions and perlocutions.[89] However, Habermas's use of this distinction is distinctive and, as numerous critics have pointed out, problematic. Habermas has since revised his terminology while insisting that these terminological concessions have no bearing on his original argument.[90] Even more recently, Habermas has introduced three distinct types of "perlocutionary effect."[91] He now acknowledges, in contrast to his earlier position, that not all kinds of perlocutionary effect are instances of the strategic use of language. Since this aspect of Habermas's argument has often been criticized, and since it is often seen as central to his argument for the primacy of communicative action, it is worth clarifying his present position.

According to what appears to be Habermas's latest position, the notion of illocutionary success refers both to understanding (IS^1) and to the acceptance of a speech-act offer (IS^2).[92] The first type of perlocutionary effect that he identifies (PE^1) refers to all aims and effects that go beyond illocutionary success in either of these senses. The second type of perlocutionary effect (PE^2) results *only in a contingent way* from what is said. For example, I understand a request to give Y some money (IS^1) and then accept a request to do so (IS^2); I give Y some money (PE^1) and thereby give pleasure to Y's wife (PE^2). The latter kind of perlocutionary effect (PE^2) is usually one that can be declared *openly* without this having a negative effect on the course of action. In contrast, one can distinguish a third type of perlocutionary effect (PE^3) that could not be achieved if the agent were to declare her aim openly from the outset. We can imagine a case where Y asks me for some money, which he wants to use for a criminal purpose. He presumes that if he were to say what he intends to do with the money I would not give it to him, so the success of his request (IS^2) depends on his concealing his motive. Only with this type of perlocutionary effect (PE^3) do we have an instance of (latently) strategic language use (and action).

In order to show that the strategic mode of language use is parasitic on the communicative mode, Habermas must show that not just the *latently* strategic use but also the *manifestly* strategic use of language is parasitic on the communicative mode. However, Habermas, in attempting to justify his claim that the communicative mode of language use is the primary one, makes his case with regard to only *one* type of strategic language use: the latently strategic mode. Even if we can take it that both conscious and unconscious modes of latently strategic language use are included here, the fact remains that Habermas has also undertaken to show that *manifestly* strategic linguistic activity is parasitic on the communicative use of language.

Habermas has clarified what the manifestly strategic use of language would look like.[93] We learn that in manifestly strategic action the orientation toward validity claims is suspended; language loses its potency and shrinks to a medium of transmitting information. The bank robber's saying "Hands up!" while aiming a gun at the cashier is an example of the manifestly strategic use of language.[94] Other examples are threats ("Give me the money or I will shoot you") and certain kinds of insults or curses ("May your children die before you"). But to what extent is the manifestly strategic use of language *parasitic* on the communicative use? There is no evidence that Habermas has adequately addressed this issue.[95]

Habermas does show that the latently strategic use of language is parasitic on the use of language oriented toward understanding. This is hardly surprising, however. If we consider a few of Habermas's examples, we can see that his thesis is tautological. The latently strategic use of language is *per definition* a use of language that simulates the communicative use. Its success depends on the success of the pretense; it is thus by its very nature parasitic.

A brief glance at some of Habermas's examples of the latently strategic use of language makes this clear.[96] In one example, an officer gives a command to attack in order to get his troops to rush into a trap. Habermas claims that this action is successful only if the troops understand the command as a genuine communicative offer. Further examples include someone's proposing a bet in order to embarrass others and someone's telling a story late in the evening in order to delay a guest's departure. In each case, the success of the strategic action depends on the successful creation of the illusion that the actors are using language with an orientation toward understanding.

I have suggested that Habermas attempts to show that communicative action is the primary mechanism of social integration in modern societies through showing that the communicative mode of language use is the primary one. I have already drawn attention to a gap in his argument: He has undertaken to show, but has not in fact shown, that manifestly strategic language use is parasitic on communicative language use. It could be argued, however, that it does not matter very much whether Habermas manages to fill this gap and demonstrate the derivative status of the manifestly strategic use of language. The reason for this is as follows: Even if his thesis that the use of language oriented toward understanding is the primary mode of language use is successful, the most Habermas can show is its *conceptual* priority. He cannot use this to assert the *functional* primacy of communicative action over strategic action in the integrative and reproductive processes of the lifeworld. Since the primacy for which he argues in the case of communicative action is a *functional* one, he would have to show that the communicative use of language is not just *conceptually* prior to the strategic use but that it also has a *functional* primacy. The functional primacy of a certain mode of language use does not follow from its conceptual priority. We can see this quite easily if we recognize that the claim to conceptual priority of a given mode of language use is in the first instance a claim about how we *learn* language; it does not refer to how we *use* language. Habermas uses his analyses of everyday communication to show that we can understand language when it is used strategically *only* because we *already* understand language when it is used communicatively. This is similar to arguing that we can understand the nonliteral use of language only because we already know what it is to use language literally. Just as the nonliteral use of language is conceptually dependent on the literal use, the strategic use of language may be conceptually dependent on the communicative use. However, the conceptual priority of the literal use of language does not say anything about its functional primacy—for instance, it does not tell us what proportion of literal language use is necessary to the functioning of a given linguistic community—or whether this question is a meaningful one. It tells us that we must have the capacity for using language literally before we use it nonliterally, but it does not tell us that we should not use it nonliterally or that our linguistic practices will run into difficulties if too much of our language use is nonliteral. Additional arguments are necessary if the functional primacy of the literal use of language is to be shown. Exactly the same can be said with regard to the strategic use of language. Even if Habermas could show that the communicative use of language is conceptually prior to the strategic use, he would need additional arguments in order to show that it has functional primacy.

I have expressed reservations as to whether Habermas can use language-based arguments to show the primacy of communicative over strategic action as a mechanism of social integration. This by no means implies, however, that his thesis collapses. Other lines of argument are open to him. I will conclude this chapter by drawing attention to one of these.

In his major essay on discourse ethics published in 1983,[97] Habermas does in fact make use of a different type of argument to suggest that communicative action is an indispensable mechanism of social integration.[98] He claims that all modern socio-cultural forms of life depend for their reproduction on processes of communicative action. That is, the symbolic structures of modern lifeworlds—cultural traditions, social integration in groups, and the development of personal identities—can be reproduced only through communicative action. The forms of argumentation connected with these processes of communicative action may be very rudimentary. In certain communities or societies, what counts as a good reason may be determined by tradition and exempt from critical scrutiny; in such cases, action oriented toward understanding may not progress beyond the initial "Yes" or "No" response to the validity claim raised with a speech act.[99] Nonetheless, although practices of argumentation may be underdeveloped in many communities or societies, members of every modern community or society participate in action that can be described as communicative, and this is the medium through which cultural traditions are reproduced and through which social integration (membership of groups) and individual socialization are effected.

As a result, in modern societies the possibility of *choosing* between communicative and social action is abstract to the extent that this option is available only from the perspective of individual agents and not from the perspective of the lifeworld as a whole. Moreover, individual agents may choose not to act communicatively only in particular cases—no agent can choose to withdraw from contexts of communicative action completely. To withdraw from contexts of communicative action completely is possible, ultimately, only at the cost of schizophrenia or suicide.[100] However, even if this argument seems convincing, its limitations should be recognized. To begin with, it holds, if at all, only for *modern* societies (as defined in section 2 above). It is hard for us, as members of modern societies, to imagine that societies might exist in which cultural traditions reproduced themselves independent of communicative action (or in which there were no cultural traditions); that societies might exist in which group solidarities were maintained and reproduced independent of communicative action (or in which there were no memberships of social groups); and that societies might exist in which individual personal identities developed independent of recognition from others in communicative action (or in which there were no personal identities). Nonetheless, no matter how difficult it is for us to imagine this, the possibility of such societies cannot be excluded in principle.

Furthermore, Habermas's argument is limited in that the claim to the functional primacy of communicative over strategic action says nothing about *how much* communicative action is necessary for the reproduction of the lifeworld. The question of the extent to which modes of strategic action can take over the lifeworld (or of the extent to which modes of functional integration can penetrate into the lifeworld) before cultural interpretation and transmission, the maintenance and creation of normatively regulated social practices, and the development of personal identities are irremediably threatened remains an open one.[101]

Finally, Habermas's argument is limited in that the claim to the functional primacy of communicative over strategic action has nothing to say about the question of *what sort of* communicative action is necessary for the reproduction of the lifeworld; it is not in itself a claim that postconventional forms of communicative action are superior to conventional ones or that the former are the necessary outcome of historical development.

2

Communicative Rationality: An Initial Specification

1

The term "communicative rationality" refers to the rational potential of action oriented toward understanding, the structural characteristics of which Habermas identifies by means of his formal pragmatic investigations into everyday language. In this chapter I introduce the concept of communicative rationality as a postmetaphysical yet non-defeatist conception of reason. After discussing the relationship between language and validity in chapters 3 and 4, I will return, in the final chapter, to the question of the critical thrust of the concept of communicative rationality.

As we have seen, communicative action, in its simplest terms, is a form of interaction in which the success of the interaction depends on a hearer's responding "Yes" or "No" to the validity claim raised with a given utterance.[1] With every speech act the speaker takes on an obligation to support the claim raised with reasons, if she is challenged by the hearer, while the hearer takes on a similar obligation to provide reasons for his "Yes" or "No." This means that communicative action is conceptually tied to processes of argumentation. Of course, these processes of argumentation may be very rudimentary. What counts as a good reason may be determined in advance, and inflexibly, by the traditions and the normative consensus prevailing in a given society or community, and in such cases argumentation will hardly progress beyond the initial "Yes" or "No" response. As I have indicated,[2] forms of communicative action that depend on such rudimentary processes of argumentation can be called "conventional." In what I refer to as "postconventional" forms of communicative action, in contrast, argumentative processes are critical and open-ended; in such processes of argumentation, no validity claim is exempt in principle from critical examination.

Although we should bear in mind the distinction between conventional and postconventional communicative action, Habermas contends that *all* forms of argumentation, no matter how rudimentary, are based on a number of "idealizing suppositions" which are rooted in the very structures of action oriented toward understanding. Even the most rudimentary forms of validity-oriented discussion point implicitly to ideal forms of argumentation. Habermas demonstrates, by way of formal pragmatic analysis of the presuppositions of everyday communicative action, that the appeal to validity claims that characterizes this form of action makes reference to a number of "strong idealizations."[3] Among these strong idealizations is the presupposition that the participants in the communicative exchange are using the same linguistic expressions in the same way.[4] This presupposition of consistency of meaning is a necessary one if comprehension is to be possible, but clearly it is often counterfactual. It is precisely because it is often counterfactual that Habermas identifies it as an idealization. Habermas's point seems to be that we could not regard ourselves as engaging in a communicative exchange at all if we did not assume consistency of meaning; indeed, it is only *because* we assume this that we can—indeed must—treat as a problem the discovery, in given instances of communication, that this assumption was unwarranted. In the same way, participation in even the most rudimentary forms of argumentation presupposes other strong idealizations. If we are to regard ourselves as participating in argumentation, we must presuppose that certain idealizing suppositions have been at least approximately satisfied; once again, it is only because we must assume that our argumentations satisfy, or come close to satisfying, such exacting conditions that we can—indeed must—treat as a problem the discovery, in actual cases of argumentation, that they do not.[5]

Some of the strong idealizations specific to argumentation that Habermas frequently mentions include the presupposition that no relevant argument is suppressed or excluded by the participants, the presupposition that no force except that of the better argument is exerted, and the presupposition that all the participants are motivated only by concern for the better argument.

Habermas sometimes suggests that the strong idealizations implicit in argumentation include presuppositions such as the idea that everyone capable of speech and action is entitled to take part in the argumentation and the idea that everyone is equally entitled to question any assertion, to introduce new topics, to express attitudes, needs, and desires, and so on.[6] This is more controversial, for these presuppositions appear to be moral intuitions shared, not by all participants in communicative action, but only by those who are already convinced by universalist moral thinking. These intuitions—referred to by Seyla Benhabib as the principles of "universal moral respect" and "egalitarian reciprocity"—are necessary presuppositions of argumentation only for the members of modern ethical communities, "for whom the theological and ontological bases of inequality among humans has been radically placed into question."[7] For this reason, it is useful to distinguish between those strong idealizations that are necessarily supposed in *all* forms of communicative action and those that are necessarily supposed only in *some*.

In earlier works,[8] Habermas used the term "ideal speech situation" (*ideale Sprechsituation*) to refer to the hypothetical situation in which the strong idealizations implicit in everyday communicative action would be satisfied; however, he now dissociates himself from this formulation and claims to regret ever having used it.[9]

Forms of argumentation that come sufficiently close to satisfying these strong idealizations are called "discourses" by Habermas. A qualification is necesary here, however, for in *The Theory of Communicative Action* Habermas reserves the term "discourse" for forms of argumentation that not only satisfy (or come sufficiently close to satisfying) certain strong idealizations but in which the participants are conceptually required to suppose that a rationally motivated consensus on the *universal* validity of a contested validity claim is possible in principle (if only the argumentation could be carried on long enough).[10] Habermas singles out claims to propositional truth and normative rightness[11] as validity claims that are conceptually linked to the idea of *universal* agreement on the *universal* validity of what is agreed.[12] Universal validity claims are thus universal in a double sense: They are conceptually linked to the idea that *everyone* would agree that what is agreed to be valid is valid *for everyone*.[13] To this extent, this idea is an idealizing supposition that is necessarily presupposed by only *some* forms of argumentation: the forms that Habermas calls "theoretical discourses" (discourses that thematize claims to propositional—empirical or theoretical—truth) and "practical discourses" (those that thematize claims to moral validity[14]).

Aesthetic or evaluative or ethical validity claims, in contrast, remain bound to particular local contexts, and are valid, if at all, only for the members of particular spatially and temporally circumscribed forms of life. They are thus distinguished from universal validity claims by virtue of their context-specificity.[15] As a result, Habermas originally[16] wished to reserve the term "critique" for types of argumentation in which these kinds of claims are thematized. He spoke, for example, of aesthetic critique.[17] Despite this explicit terminological distinction, Habermas himself has not always been consistent in his use of the term "discourse." In more recent texts he quite clearly refers to pragmatic, ethical, and moral *discourses,* although he regards neither pragmatic nor ethical questions as universal validity claims in the double sense of "universal" that I have indicated.[18]

Whether we understand discourse as referring only to theoretical and practical discourses or somewhat more generally, it is important to note that discourses are ideal (or, perhaps better, improbable) forms of argumentation. As Habermas puts it, "Discourses are islands in the sea of practice, that is, improbable forms of communication; the everyday appeal to validity claims implicitly points, however, to their possibility."[19]

What is noteworthy in the discussion so far is Habermas's implied distinction between those strong idealizations that are implicit in *all* everyday forms of communicative action and those that are necessary presuppositions of only *some* forms of communicative action. The former are thus implicit in even the most rudimentary forms of argumentation; the latter are implicit only in some more demanding forms of argumentation. As we have seen, the former category contains (*inter alia*) the presuppositions that participants are using the same linguistic expressions in the same way, that no relevant argument is suppressed or excluded, that the only force used is that of the better argument, and that all participants are motivated only by concern for the better argument. The latter category, as we have seen, contains (*inter alia*) the idea that everyone would agree to the universal validity of the claim thematized; presumably, it would also contain moral intuitions such as the idea that everyone capable of speech and action is entitled to participate, as well as the idea that everyone is equally entitled to query any assertion, to introduce new topics, and to express attitudes, needs, and desires. In the category of strong idealizations that are necessary presuppositions of only some forms of communicative action we must also include the idea that no validity claim is exempt in principle from critical evaluation in argumentation, for this idea is implicit only in what I have referred to as postconventional modes of communicative action. At the same time, the idealization that no argument is in principle immune to critical evaluation in argumentation appears to have its roots in an idealizing supposition that is implicit in all forms of argumentation. It appears to be a postconventional interpretation of the idealizing supposition, implicit in all forms of argumentation, that no relevant argument is excluded or suppressed by the participants. Whereas in conventional forms of argumentation what counts as relevant is narrowly and rigidly defined according to fixed prevailing conventions, in postconventional forms no argument is regarded as irrelevant in principle. Indeed, there are a number of idealizations that, although implicit in all forms of argumentation, take on a special meaning in postconventional modes. For instance, the presupposition that participants are willing to reach an understanding (*Verständigungsbereit*). This too is an idealization that, although implicit in all forms of argumentation, gains a special force in postconventional modes, for only in the latter case does it take on the sense of a willingness to continue discussion indefinitely and an openness to the arguments of others. (I will have more to say about this particular idealizing supposition in section 4 of chapter 5.)

It would seem, therefore, that we can distinguish between conventional and postconventional modes of argumentation as corresponding roughly to conventional and postconventional modes of communicative action. The correspondence is only approximate, for the foregoing suggests that we can further distinguish various types of postconventional argumentation on the basis of which of a number of possible strong idealizations they implicitly refer to. All forms of postconventional argumentation refer to the idea that no validity claim is exempt in principle from critical evaluation in argumentation, only some of these refer to the idea that everyone would agree to the universal validity of the outcome and others again (or possibly even all[20]) refer to what Benhabib calls "universal moral respect" and "egalitarian reciprocity." Clearly, any typology one might wish to construct would have to take account of many overlaps.

This distinction between conventional and postconventional modes of argumentation has implications for the notion of communicative rationality. Up to now, this has been defined very generally as the rational potential of language oriented toward understanding. We are now in a position to be more precise. Communicative rationality is the mode of dealing with validity claims that is practiced by participants (primarily[21]) in *postconventional* forms of communicative action. Participants necessarily suppose not only that all taking part are using the same linguistic expressions in the same way, that no relevant opinions have been suppressed or excluded, that no force is exerted except that of the better argument, and that everyone is motivated only by the desire for truth but also that no validity claim is in principle exempt from the critical evaluation of the participants.[22] As I explain below, the latter idea is important if Habermas is to maintain the critical, "nondefeatist" thrust of his concept of communicative rationality. However, as should now be clear, the idea that no validity claim is exempt in principle from critical evaluation in argumentation is, at best, only a strong idealization implicit in the argumentative practices of participants in postconventional modes of communicative action. Such modes of communicative action presuppose specific learning processes that are features of only certain sorts of modern societies— or, indeed, certain sections of certain sorts of modern societies. To this extent, Habermas's notion of communicative rationality gains its critical thrust only in certain contexts—specifically, in the context of post-traditional lifeworlds. It is situated firmly within those theoretical, moral, legal, political, ethical, and aesthetic practices of modern lifeworlds in which all ultimate sources of validity external to human argumentation have been called into question.[23]

2

Habermas tells us that communicative reason raises its voice in validity claims that are both context-dependent and context-transcendent.[24] Validity claims are always raised by flesh-and-blood individuals in actual socio-cultural and historical situations, but they always at the same time also transcend all given contexts. This transcendent power is tied to the strong idealizations to which all forms of argumentation, and hence all forms of communicative action, refer. Indicating its subversive potential, Habermas describes the transcendent power of validity claims as a "thorn in the flesh of social reality."[25]

We can understand this context-transcendent power in a number of different ways, depending on which of the various strong idealizations implicit in everyday communication we focus on. We should bear in mind that some of these idealizations are implicit only in postconventional forms of communicative action (or, at least, gain a special meaning in postconventional forms).

One possible way of interpreting the notion that validity claims have a context-transcendent power is in terms of their potential for calling into question established notions of validity (beliefs that something is true or false, right or wrong, and so forth). Validity claims are subversive to the extent that they rely on (in principle) disputable reasons that are potentially subversive of all spatio-temporally defined local agreements. The idealization (implicit in postconventional modes of argumentation) that no argument is in principle exempt from critical evaluation means that every actual process of postconventional argumentation opens up the possibility that what is accepted as valid in a given area may be called into question by means of the critical arguments of the participants. To this extent, validity claims raised in processes of postconventional argumentation always have the potential power to call into question, and thereby move beyond, what is accepted as valid in existing contexts of validity. Clearly, this particular kind of context-transcendent power is not a property of validity claims in conventional modes of communicative action and is, as such, a thorn in the flesh only of post-traditional social realties.

On a second possible interpretation, when Habermas refers to the context-transcendent power of validity claims he wants to draw attention to the special power of truth claims and moral-validity claims to call into question, and point beyond, what is regarded as true or morally right in particular, local contexts.[26] This special power derives from the asserted internal connection between truth and moral claims, on the one hand, and the idealizing supposition that everyone would agree to the universal validity of an agreement reached concerning them in a process of argumentation, on the other. As we have seen, Habermas believes that only claims to propositional truth and claims to moral validity make reference to this idealization. If it could be shown that they are internally connected with an idea of argumentatively reached universal agreement (in a double sense of "universal"), truth and moral claims would have a special context-transcendent power. This would reside in the tension between the idea of a universal agreement on the universal validity of a particular claim to propositional truth or moral validity and the non-universality of a given consensus with regard to the validity of that claim. The thesis that claims to truth and moral validity have a special context-transcendent power stands or falls with the thesis that they are internally connected with the idea of an argumentatively reached universal agreement (in a double sense of "universal").

In chapter 5 I will examine, respectively, Habermas's theories of truth and moral validity. With regard to the former I will point out that Habermas himself acknowledges that not all truth claims are internally connected with the idea of discursively achieved universal agreement; with regard to the latter I will suggest that in post-traditional societies the class of normative validity claims for which it is possible to assert an internal connection with the idea of a discursively achieved universal consensus is so small that it can, at best, constitute no more than one element in an account of moral validity.

A third way of interpreting the context-transcendent power of validity claims is possible if we focus on some of the other idealizations implicit in communicative action. Once again, we should bear in mind the distinction between conventional and postconventional forms of this. On the third interpretation, the subversive power of validity claims resides in the tension between the normative promise contained in the implicit strong idealizations and what actually happens in everyday practices of argumentation. This tension is potentially present in every form of communicative action, but its critical thrust is greater in postconventional forms. The idealizing supposition (common to all forms of argumentation) that participants are motivated only by a concern for the better argument provides a critical standard for the assessment of actual practices of argumentation: It allows us to criticize those who unavoidably must profess to, but do not in fact, share this motivation; it thus provides us with a standard for the critique of latently strategic action.[27] The idealizations supposed by some forms of postconventional communicative action have an even greater critical thrust. For example, the necessary presupposition in at least some kinds of postconventional argumentation (for instance, moral discourses) that everyone is equally entitled to query any assertion, to introduce new topics into the discussion, and to express attitudes, needs, and desires provides us with a standard for critically assessing actual processes of these kinds of postconventional argumentation. We can criticize these for their failure to allow certain agents capable of speech and action to participate, or for their failure to allow certain participants equal rights or opportunities within the discussion. On such an interpretation, the strong idealizations implicit in communicative action have a potential critical (and thus context-transcendent) power; however, in contrast to the first interpretation I proposed, this is only indirectly connected with the claims themselves. As a result, although it allows us to criticize certain *procedures* of argumentation as dishonest or unjust, communicative rationality in this sense has nothing to say about the validity of *claims*.[28]

3

Habermas maintains that the concept of communicative rationality expresses a conception of rationality that does justice to the most important impulses of twentieth-century philosophy while escaping relativism and providing standards for critical evaluation (for instance, of social pathologies, questions of moral validity (justice), and practices of communicative action). This double aspect allows him to regard his conception of reason as a distinctively modern one and to describe it as postmetaphysical yet nondefeatist.[29] If, to begin with, we consider communicative rationality as a postmetaphysical conception of reason, we find that this characterization embraces a number of aspects.

Postmetaphysical thinking is one of the most important impulses of twentieth-century philosophy, in Habermas's view[30]: (a) It has called into question emphatic (substantive) conceptions of rationality and put forward procedural or formal conceptions instead. (b) With regard to the question of valid knowledge and how it may be achieved, it has replaced foundationalism with fallibilism. (c) It has cast doubt on the idea that reason should be conceived abstractly, beyond history and the complexities of social life, and has contextualized or situated reason in actual historical practices. (d) As part of this contextualization of reason, it has replaced a focus on individual structures of consciousness by a concern with pragmatic structures of language and action. (e) As part of this orientation toward practice and away from abstract or "pure" theory, it has given up philosophy's traditional fixation on theoretical truth and the representational functions of language to the extent that it also recognizes the moral-practical and expressive functions of language.

Habermas asserts that the conception of communicative rationality he proposes is in tune with all these impulses of twentieth-century postmetaphysical thinking:

(a) Communicative rationality is not a substantive conception of reason; it is defined procedurally by way of purely formal characteristics. Rationality in the various validity dimensions of the lifeworld is conceived in terms of (or, in the case of moral rationality, as the result of) a formally defined procedure of argumentation. Rationality refers primarily to the *use* of knowledge in language and action rather than to a property of knowledge.[31] One might also say that it refers primarily to a mode of *dealing with* validity claims and that it is, in general, not a property of these claims themselves. Furthermore, although (as we shall see) the notion of communicative rationality contains a utopian perspective, this perspective suggests no more than formal specifications of the structural characteristics of possible forms of life and life histories; it does not extend to the concrete shape of an exemplary form of life or an individual life history.[32]

(b) Foundationalism is the attempt to establish the absolute, universal validity of some conception of knowledge or morality. Habermas identifies two aspects to Kantian foundationalism and seeks to avoid both of them.[33] Kant attributed to philosophy, on the one hand, the role of "usher" (*Platzanweiser*) and, on the other, the role of "supreme judge" (*oberster Richter*). Kant believed that philosophy can establish the foundations of all knowledge once and for all and is therefore in a position to show the other sciences their (subordinate) places in the theater of human knowledge. Against this, Habermas argues that philosophy must assume the role of a "placeholder" (*Platzhalter*), or stand-in, for, in particular, the reconstructive sciences. (As we have seen, the knowledge produced by such sciences is hypothetical, not absolute; it is subject to empirical testing, and it often relies on indirect substantiation through coherence with the findings of other empirical theories. In addition, the reconstructive sciences understand the validity of the knowledge they produce *fallibilistically*—as subject to modification in the light of future new evidence and insight.) Kant also attributed to philosophy the role of supreme judge, not just with regard to the foundations of possible knowledge but with regard to culture in general. Instead of upholding a substantive (metaphysical) conception of reason, Kant differentiates metaphysical reason into three moments of rationality (theoretical, practical, and aesthetic) and ascribes to philosophy not only the task of ultimate adjudicator of validity within each dimension of rationality but also the task of maintaining the unity of these dimensions. Against this, Habermas acknowledges the independent logic of the three dimensions of rationality and recognizes no more than a formal, procedurally defined unity between them; he allows philosophy no more than the task of a mediator that feeds back the knowledge gained in the specialized discourses within each dimension into everyday communicative practice.

(c) Communicative rationality is not a conception of reason that stands abstractly above history and the complexities of social life; it is conceived as a conception of rationality that is *already operative* in the everyday communicative practices of modern societies, To this extent, it is temporally and historically situated. Correspondingly, communicative rationality does not operate from the extra-mundane standpoint of an extra-mundane subject and refer to a context-independent ideal language in order to produce infallible and definitive statements.[34] On the contrary, communicative rationality is a conception of situated reason that raises its voice in validity claims that are at once context-bound and context-transcendent.[35] Although (as we have seen) validity claims transcend given contexts of validity in various ways, they are always raised in specific temporally and spatially defined contexts of communicative action. On a general level, Habermas situates communicative rationality within the communicative practices of *modern* societies—that is, societies that have undergone certain processes of differentiation necessary for the emergence of a reflective relation to the world (the decentering of consciousness).[36] Communicative action functions as the primary mechanism of social (lifeworld) reproduction only in such societies. In addition, I have suggested that we further distinguish between conventional and post-conventional contexts of everyday communicative practice in order to take account of, and acknowledge, the greater critical thrust of the concept of communicative rationality in postconventional contexts of communicative action.

(d) The situation of communicative rationality in historically defined practices of linguistic activity is evidence of a change in paradigm from the philosophy of consciousness to the theory of communication. Habermas replaces the conceptual framework of earlier critical theory, which had at its center a subject-object model of cognition and action, with a conceptual framework that is centered around social interaction through communication. Instead of taking as its starting point the isolated individual consciousness in its relation to an external world, Habermas's critical theory emphasizes the social constitution of the self through the relationships of mutual recognition into which she enters on the basis of her involvement in processes of communicative action.

(e) Habermas's conception of communicative rationality overcomes the logocentric bias of Western philosophy, and to this extent it rethinks the traditional philosophical belief in the primacy of theory over practice. On Habermas's conception, rationality comprises theoretical *and* practical (and, indeed, aesthetic and expressive) elements, and these relate to one another not hierarchically but on an equal footing. Formal pragmatic analysis of the everyday practices of communication reveals a network of validity dimensions, *all* of which must be taken account of by the notion of communicative rationality. The Western philosophical tradition has remained fixated on a single di-

mension of validity—that of propositional truth and theoretical reason—and this has laid it open to the charge of logocentrism.
Habermas overcomes logocentrism to the extent that the notion of
communicative rationality refers to a complex interplay of the three
validity dimensions—propositional truth, normative rightness, and
subjective truthfulness or authenticity—that formal pragmatic analyses of language show to be effective in the lifeworld. The multi-di-
mensionality, as opposed to logocentricity, of Habermas's notion of
communicative rationality requires a few more words. Habermas believes that formal pragmatic analysis of everyday communication suggests that we can distinguish three types of validity claim,
corresponding to three dimensions of validity, which, although distinct, interact in complex ways. This leads Habermas to put forward
a postmetaphysical idea of the unity of reason as the interpenetration
of the three logically distinct spheres of reason. In conceiving reason
as multi-dimensional, Habermas does not simply rely on formal pragmatic investigations into language. He also draws on Max Weber's
diagnosis of cultural modernity in terms of the historical differentiation of three cultural spheres of value, each with its own internal logic.
On Habermas's reading of Weber, this assertion can be plausibly de-
fended with regard to modern Europe on two levels: on the level of
ideas that can be transmitted in traditions (scientific theories, moral
and legal beliefs, aesthetic productions) and on the level of cultural
action systems (which are organized around questions of truth, justice, and taste, and in each of which the relevant set of questions is
dealt with professionally by experts and given an institutionally organized form; this gives rise to the three "expert cultures" of science,
law and morality, and art). To this extent, modern reason has fragmented (or, more neutrally, differentiated) into its constitutive moments, and Habermas believes that to attempt to reunite these into a
substantive totality is to fall prey to metaphysics: "Only at the cost of
Occidental rationalism itself could we rescind the differentiation of
reason into those rationality complexes to which Kant's three critiques
of reason refer. Nothing is further from my intention than to make
myself an advocate of such a regression, to conjure up the substantial
unity of reason."[37] Habermas replaces the substantive unity of reason
with a tentative notion of a *formal* unity. The spheres of science, law
and morality, and art have become differentiated from one another;

now they must also communicate with one another. What is required is the noncoercive interplay of the differentiated moments of reason—an interpenetration of spheres of validity that allows the productive insights gained through argumentation in one sphere to be applied to problems in the other spheres while at the same time respecting the distinctive internal logic of these other spheres. As Habermas puts it, "the unity of reason must be conceived in the plurality of its voices."[38] What Habermas has in mind here is the application in the sphere of the sciences (in particular, the human sciences—history, sociology, etc.) of nonobjectivistic modes of inquiry that bring to bear moral and aesthetic points of view without violating that sphere's primary orientation toward questions of truth—indeed, he claims that only through such an interpenetration of viewpoints does a critical social theory become possible in the first place. The sphere of law and morality can profit just as much if cognitive or expressive points of view (such as the calculation of consequences or the interpretation of needs) are brought to bear on moral or legal problems. Finally, Habermas thinks that the development of post-avant-garde art has been characterized by the influence of cognitive elements (realism) and moral-practical elements (committed art) on the strictly aesthetic laws of form.[39] It would be easy to dispute the examples that Habermas suggests (for instance, by suggesting a different interpretation of the aesthetic point of view, or by challenging his interpretation of the development of modern art), but it would be equally easy to come up with other ones. The basic idea of a productive interpenetration of forms of argumentation is interesting and plausible. The problem, of course, as Habermas has recently recognized, is that there is no *metadiscourse* to which we can refer in order to justify a choice between different forms of argumentation.[40] There is no forum for deciding when we should bring to bear arguments from other spheres of validity or for deciding which kinds of argument are relevant. Habermas raises the possiblity that this might be a matter for the practical judgement (*Urteilskraft*) of individuals, only to dismiss it immediately as unacceptable. This is not only due to his suspicion of the "vague Aristotelian conception of practical judgement"; it is also because he does not think an Aristotelian type of reflective judgement is what is required here—what is required is a feeling (*Gespür*) for sorting (in the sense of ordering) problems.[41] Habermas does not elaborate on this, nor does he give any hints as to how we might solve the problem.[42]

4

If Habermas's concept of communicative rationality is postmetaphysical to the extent that it is (a) defined formally and procedurally, (b) construed fallibilistically, (c) situated historically, (d) derived from everyday practices of communication and thus nonsubjectivistic, and (e) multi-dimensional, in what sense can it be said to be nondefeatist?

Communicative rationality can be defined as a nondefeatist conception of rationality in at least two interconnected ways.

First, in contrast to all varieties of relativism, it asserts a context-transcendent notion of validity. This itself has two aspects: the refusal to reduce validity to that which prevails in a given form of life, and the assertion of standards for the critique of dishonest and unjust practices of communicative action and for the injustice of moral norms and principles. These two aspects were apparent in the three ways of interpreting the idea of a context-transcendent power to which I drew attention in section 2 above. On the first interpretation that I suggested, communicative rationality is nondefeatist to the extent that it steadfastly insists on a sense of validity that goes beyond the "provincial agreements of the specific local context."[43] This context-transcendent power is linked to the potential capacity of validity claims to disrupt and subvert the prevailing agreement in definitions and judgements; however, it is too vague and undetermined to be useful in providing standards that would permit the critical assessment of actual processes of argumentation or of actual definitions or judgements.

According to the second interpretation I proposed, truth claims and moral-validity claims may possess a special context-transcendent power by virtue of their unavoidable reference to discursively achieved universal validity (in a double sense of "universal"). Although I have deferred detailed discussion of this until chapter 5, I have hinted that Habermas may not be able to maintain this for all truth claims and that the category of moral claims for which he can assert it comprises no more than a small proportion of the class of moral claims. However, to the extent that moral claims do make reference to an idea of discursively achieved universal validity, this idea provides a standard for the critique of norms and principles that betray the promise to embody universal interests.

The third sense of context-transcendence that I proposed focuses on the critical evaluation of actual *processes* of argumentation; at the same time, it is restricted to criticism of the dishonesty and the injustice of practices of argumentation and can say nothing about the truth or the justice of validity claims themselves. Nonetheless, as we shall see in more detail in chapter 5, this is the area where the concept of communicative rationality has the greatest critical thrust. It should be noted that here, as in almost all of these cases,[44] the context-transcendent power of validity claims increases in the context of postconventional modes of (everyday) communicative action and decreases in the context of conventional modes.

The second sense in which communicative rationality is nondefeatist is that it has a utopian content; this is the idea of an "undamaged subjectivity and intersubjectivity" that would allow individuals to reach understanding with one another without any coercion and would permit the development of individual identities at harmony with their inner selves.

The notions of undamaged subjectivity and intersubjectivity suggest the possibility of symmetrical relationships of free mutual recognition.[45] Habermas also expresses the utopian content of the idea of communicative rationality in terms of "the rationalization of the lifeworld." We can see how he arrives at this if we recall his identification of three structural components in the symbolic reproduction of the lifeworld—cultural traditions, social integration, and the development of individual identities[46]—and apply to each of these the notion of reaching understanding through the open and critical evaluation of validity claims. This yields the idea of a society in which (a) there is permanent revision of traditional interpretations and practices, no element of which is regarded as being exempt from criticism, (b) all legitimate orders are dependent on discursive procedures for establishing and justifying norms, (c) the identities of individual subjects are self-regulated through processes of critical reflection and, to a high degree, detached from concrete cultural contexts.[47]

We must guard against the following common misinterpretations of the utopian content implicit in the idea of communicative rationality: that the ideas of undamaged subjectivity and intersubjectivity (a) describe the concrete shape of exemplary forms of life or paradigmatic individual life histories (as opposed to merely specifying the structural characteristics of possible forms of life and life histories), (b) suggest the possibility of either a perfectly harmonious or a perfectly transparent form of life (or individual identity) and, connected with this, (c) deny and suppress difference in favor of unity and consensus, or (d) imply a utopian vision that is the necessary or natural outcome of the developmental dynamics of modern societies.[48]

By now it should be clear why (a) is a misinterpretation: Communicative rationality, with its utopian idea of the rationalization of the lifeworld, does not tell us what we should believe or how we should live our lives; it merely attempts to specify formally what it means to deal with validity claims rationally, to establish legitimate norms and normative orders, and to develop a personal identity that is autonomous and individuated in a postconventional sense.

With regard to (b) and (c): In the face of the postmodernist suspicion of harmony, regularity, unity, and transparency, Habermas insists on the dialectical relationship between unity and singularity, on the one hand, and, on the other, difference and otherness.[49] He contends that "the transitory unity that comes about in the poriferous and broken intersubjectivity of a linguistically mediated consensus not only permits, but promotes and accelerates the pluralization of life forms and the individualization of lifestyles."[50]

Habermas points out that the more discourse (presumably in the broader sense of postconventional argumentation) there is in a given community or society, the more contradiction and difference there will be. The more consensus is achieved though processes of postconventional argumentation, the greater the amount of dissensus with which one can live without feeling threatened. I take it that this is because participation in postconventional modes of communicative action requires that participants be guided by the necessary presupposition that no argument they put forward is immune in principle to critical evaluation in discussion; this amounts to an awareness that what is here and now held to be justified (be it an opinion, a way of behaving, or a lifestyle) may always be called into question by new arguments at some future date. This awareness of the possibility that others may be right and that one may be wrong contributes to a tolerance of different or deviant opinions, ways of behaving, and lifestyles and thus increases the amount of dissensus with which one can comfortably live.

In addition, Habermas's insistence that the notion of communicative rationality does not suppress difference must be understood in terms of his distinction between moral questions and ethical questions.[51] As we have seen, Habermas distinguishes between moral questions in the strict sense and what he calls "evaluative questions of the good life." Whereas the former are defined by their internal connection with the idea of discursively reached universal agreement (in a double sense of "universal"), the latter are by definition not universalizable, since they are concerned with the self-realization of specific individuals and groups and are thus always bound to specific, local contexts. For this reason, Habermas's emphasis on reaching agreement (*Einverständnis*) is not incompatible with an acknowledgement of irreducible difference between individual subjects with regard to their individual life choices. Even though Habermas asserts that participants in moral argumentation aim to reach agreement on the universal validity of a given moral norm or principle, the agreement they aim for is not agreement as to the validity of individual life choices; it is at a high level of abstraction, and it leaves plenty of room for difference of opinion as to what counts as a good way of living one's life and how one should best go about achieving this. Moreover, although Habermas does also connect discussions on ethical questions with the idea of agreement, the agreement aimed for is not recognition of the universal validity of ethical judgements (that is, their validity *for everyone*) but, at most, merely acknowledgement of the rightness of particular life choices within the context of the specific life histories of individuals and groups.[52]

Here it could be argued that even this kind of connection with the idea of agreement is too much, to the extent that it implies the transparency (in principle) of rational reflection and, correspondingly, a problematic model of subjectivity. Habermas certainly asserts such a connection between ethical deliberation and agreement to the extent that he regards the assumption that, in a given case, understanding (*Verständigung*) could be reached about anything and everything as a necessary presupposition of participation in argumentation—as a strong idealization implicit in communicative action. This holds for

ethical discussions just as much as for moral ones. Habermas insists
that the *fiction* of the transparency of communication is built into the
structures of everyday communicative practice.[53] As we know, the
idea of a necessary presupposition expresses the intuition that participants in a given process of validity-oriented discussion must unavoidably suppose that certain conditions are fulfilled if they are to be able
to describe themselves, without self-contradiction, as participating in
discussion. In this case, what they must unavoidably suppose is that
agreement is in principle possible with regard to the validity of the
matters at hand. Otherwise there would be no point in entering into
discussion at all. As we have seen, strong idealizations such as these
allow us to criticize actual processes of discussion on the basis of the
tension between what is necessarily supposed by the participants and
what actually happens in a given discussion. If we consider the idealizing supposition that agreement is in principle possible about the matters of validity under discussion from this point of view, we can see
that it allows us to criticize participants in discussion only on the basis
of their motivation or attitude and not on the basis of a failure to
reach agreement. The idealization of the transparency of communication permits criticism of participants' lack of *willingness* to reach
agreement, but it is not based on an assumption that agreement is in
fact possible; this is why Habermas describes it as a fiction.[54] For this
reason, the idea of agreement as a necessary presupposition of participation in discussion should not be interpreted as the thesis that
agreement about everything and anything is possible. At the same
time, it does suggest that agreement is *desirable*. It could be argued
that this suggestion is problematic in (at least) certain contexts of
deliberation, to the extent that it relies on a view of transparent
subjectivity that has been undermined by twentieth-century psychoanalysis.[55] One of the fundamental insights put forward by post-
Freudian psychoanalysis is that there is an unavoidable gap between
linguistically interpreted subjectivity and subjectivity—between what
I interpret myself to be and what I *am*. In the case of ethical deliberation, the self claims validity for the ethical rightness of her actions and
judgements within the context of her particular life history.[56] What
would it mean for the self to suppose that, if her actions and judgements were right, everyone[57] would have to agree that they were
right? This can only mean that the self supposes that others would

agree with her actions and choices if only they knew everything about her and about her life history—in other words, if complete transparency were possible. Furthermore, one of the criteria relevant in the assessment of such claims to ethical validity is whether or not the actions and judgements in question are authentic expressions of the self's "inner nature."[58] But since "inner nature" is available only as *interpreted* inner nature, we are once again faced with the gap between linguistically mediated knowledge of subjectivity and subjectivity. We can agree that a given action or judgement is an authentic expression of "inner nature" only if we ignore this gap. If we take it seriously and give up the idea of transparent subjectivity, the idea of agreement on the validity of ethical claims is rendered meaningless, at least to the extent that ethical claims are concerned with interpretations of "inner nature."[59]

One way of weakening Habermas's connection between questions of (ethical) validity and agreement might be to replace the idea of a necessary orientation toward agreement with regard to the validity of claims with the idea of an orientation toward recognition of participants in their capacity as rationally accountable agents.[60] It could be argued that, in at least some kinds of validity-oriented discussion, what participants seek is not agreement on specific questions of validity but recognition of their autonomy as rationally accountable agents.[61] Following this line of thought, one could argue that the recognition sought by participants in at least some kinds of ethical discussion (but also in certain kinds of moral discussion) is not recognition of the rightness of moral choices or of individual life choices (and hence not agreement with what is said or done) but rather recognition of the individual subject's willingness to accept responsibility for these. This amounts to recognition of the other as a rationally accountable agent,[62] and does not necessarily imply agreement with the other as regards the moral rightness of a particular way of acting or of the specific choices the other makes in the conduct of his life.[63]

As further testimony to support the claim that his notion of action oriented toward understanding does not prioritize harmony and unity at the cost of difference and otherness, Habermas points out that the increasing reflexivity of communicative action goes hand in hand with the increasing autonomy and individuation of personal identities.[64] For Habermas, autonomy is moral autonomy, and it is directly linked to participation in processes of practical discourse.[65] I have argued elsewhere that Habermas's notion of autonomy is based on a model of transparent subjectivity[66]; I suspect that it could be shown that it equally rests on an idea of harmonious subjectivity (subjectivity at one with itself). Nonetheless, Habermas's conception of (moral) autonomy *includes* the idea that each individual is the sole author of her validity claims and, at least in what I have called post-traditional societies, accepts responsibility to defend them in (postconventional) processes of argumentation. This provides a basis for a notion of autonomy as rational accountability. On my view, Habermas's conception of autonomy is problematic only when it goes beyond this.[67] The notion of autonomy as rational accountability does indeed promote individual responsibility and individual difference, for in postconventional modes of communicative action the speaker undertakes to provide (if necessary) reasons that are, in the final instance, the products of her own reflections and are not simply taken over from the prevailing contexts of validity, thus underscoring her uniqueness and irreplaceability.

By "individuation" Habermas means the process whereby the individual subject comes to see herself as unique and irreplaceable and as the main author of her self-realization. Thus, as we have just seen, in postconventional modes of communicative action the act of raising a validity claim is also an act of individuation. It could also be argued that the conception of individual identity underlying this model implies that individual subjects will also be seen, and see themselves, as the answerable authors of their actions in *other* areas of social life— for instance, in the dimension of self-realization. To this extent also, Habermas is right in saying that the idea of action oriented toward understanding—at least in its various postconventional modes—supports a conception of the identity of the individual subject as unique and distinct from the identities of other subjects.[68] Nonetheless, despite my suggestion that we can sever the connection between some kinds of validity-oriented discussion and agreement and can replace recognition of the rightness of claims with the recognition of rational accountability, I must admit that this goes against the grain of Habermas's enterprise. As it stands, Habermas's account of rationality remains intimately bound up with the idea of consensus. Although I believe that these bonds can be loosened (and even severed in certain cases), there is little evidence that Habermas shares this view.

Finally (against the suggestion in point d above), the idea of the rationalization of the lifeworld is no more than the *promise* of undamaged structures of intersubjectivity and subjectivity; all postconventional modes of communicative action point toward the possibility of realizing this promise, but it remains abstract to the extent that it is not embodied in actual historical social institutions and practices. The notion of communicative rationality cannot itself say anything about how or when or if this will happen. Habermas insists on a distinction between the logic and the dynamics of development—that is, between the possible unfolding of potentials inherent in historical and social processes and what actually has happened or will happen.[69] The concept of communicative rationality is concerned only with the former. To this extent, Habermas distances himself from the notion of a natural or necessary dynamics of history which is pushing us inexorably toward the utopian vision of undamaged subjectivity and intersubjectivity. Indeed, he is careful to remind us that the increasingly sophisticated belief systems of modernity have been accompanied by ever more subtle forms of domination and control—that as, historically, more and more spheres have been subjected to argumentative validation, new forms of repression have emerged in response. As I shall discuss in more detail in chapter 5, Habermas sees the uncoupling of the subsystems of functional rationality that (historically but not necessarily) have colonized the communicatively structured spheres of the lifeworld as the ironic result of the increasing rationalization of the lifeworld. The concept of communicative rationality can, at most, provide standards for the critique of the effects of colonization. It cannot tell us anything about its own *fate* in the face of functional rationalization.

3

Speech Acts and Validity Claims

At the center of both Habermas's theory of communicative action and his account of communicative rationality is the thesis that speech acts—as the smallest unit of communication—raise various kinds of validity claim. In this chapter and the next I shall take a closer look at this thesis. As we know, Habermas maintains that analysis of the formal features of everyday processes of meaning and understanding will confirm his assertion of a connection between language and various dimensions of validity. Detailed examination of his formal pragmatic reconstructions of everyday language use is therefore necessary in order to assess the plausibility of this assertion.

What is the importance of Habermas's formal pragmatic analyses within the context of his theory as a whole? Here we should remember that Habermas's first concern is the development of a critical theory of society and that his attempt to work out a theory of communicative rationality is primarily of importance in this context. The question of the importance to his theory as a whole of his theory of validity claims and his theory of meaning is a complex one, and an adequate answer would take us beyond the scope of the present discussion; nonetheless, I think that it is possible to identify three main theses that Habermas must substantiate if his theory of communicative action (and his account of communicative rationality, which depends on the latter) is to be successful.

It is of crucial importance to Habermas's theory of communicative action that he show that communicative action is a mechanism of social (lifeworld) integration and reproduction in the domains of cultural reproduction, social integration, and socialization. It is of crucial importance to his theory of communicative rationality that he demonstrate a connection between everyday language and argumentation. It is of crucial importance to his attempt to work out a nonlogocentric, multi-dimensional conception of reason that he show that everyday language makes reference to a number of dimensions of validity in which rational argument is possible. In order to achieve these aims, Habermas must show, in particular, three things: that everyday communication is connected with validity claims that demand "Yes" or "No" responses, that these claims are of a number of different types, and that with every speech act the speaker raises three validity claims simultaneously. If Habermas cannot show the first, he cannot account for the binding force of speech acts, and his notion of communicative action as a mechanism of social integration runs into difficulty; furthermore, his concept of communicative rationality as a situated (and thus postmetaphysical) conception of reason collapses, for this is supposed to express the rational potential *already operative* in everyday processes of communication. (Communicative rationality would lose its seat within existing historical and socio-cultural practices.) If he cannot show the second, his multi-dimensional conception of rationality loses its basis, for it rests on the thesis that speech acts in everyday communicative action can be connected with a number of different kinds of validity claim and on the thesis that all these kinds of claim are susceptible to rational evaluation and justification in (in particular, postconventional modes of) argumentation. If he cannot show the third, his thesis that communicative action is a mechanism of social (lifeworld) reproduction in the domains of cultural reproduction, social integration, and socialization is undermined, for this thesis depends on his ability to demonstrate that communicative action has three functional aspects, corresponding to three functions of language represented by the three structural components of speech acts.

As a result, Habermas's formal pragmatic investigations into the workings of everyday language must provide evidence in support of all three of these concerns. They must show that it is the defining characteristic of speech acts that they raise validity claims, that these claims are of a number of different types, and that with every speech act the speaker raises three validity claims simultaneously. In support of the first concern, Habermas has to show, to begin with, that the communicative use of language is the primary mode of language use, on which other modes (for instance the indirect and instrumental modes) are parasitic.[1] He then has to show that there is an internal connection between communicatively used speech acts and validity claims; here he argues that to understand a speech act is to understand the claim it raises. Since that argument is a statement about the meaning of speech acts, it will be necessary (see chapter 4) to take a closer look at Habermas's account of meaning and understanding. In support of the second concern, Habermas argues that he must show that the various claims raised in everyday communicative action correspond to three distinct types, providing a basis for the classification of speech acts. I shall consider the details of this argument in sections 1–6 of the present chapter. In support of the third concern, Habermas argues that he must demonstrate that three dimensions of validity are represented in *every* speech act. I shall examine this thesis in section 7.

Although the present chapter is primarily concerned with Habermas's theory of validity claims, and his theory of meaning will be discussed in detail in the next chapter, it may be useful to indicate briefly where Habermas is situated in relation to other approaches to meaning and understanding. In order not to distract from my main concern in the present chapter, I do this here only in a very general and cursory way. I shall have more to say about Habermas's attempt to overcome the difficulties that he believes beset other approaches to meaning in chapter 4. However, even there, my discussion of this issue will be limited. It is certainly worth drawing attention to where Habermas's speech-act theory of meaning stands with regard to other approaches to meaning; however, for the purposes of our present inquiry any detailed discussion of Habermas's interpretations of the various approaches to meaning he criticizes would be a distraction. Habermas has freely admitted that his interpretations are always selective, and his interpretations of approaches to meaning theory are arguably no less so than his interpretations of other sociological theories. Habermas offers no more than one possible reading of each of the social theorists he deals with (Marx, Weber, Mead, Durkheim, Parsons, et al.), and the same could be said of the approaches to meaning theory that he discusses much more superficially. The selectivity of Habermas's interpretations may be justified on the basis of their contribution to his guiding intention of showing that an inde-structible moment of communicative rationality is anchored in every-day processes of linguistic activity. Since my main concern in the present context is whether Habermas can in fact do this, I accept un-critically his criticisms of other theorists and approaches. In conse-quence, I examine his theory of meaning and his theory of validity claims purely on their own merits, asking whether these accounts can show what they set out to show.[2] For this reason, even in the next chapter I will situate Habermas's account of meaning with regard to other approaches to meaning purely with a view to gaining better access to it.

Given Habermas's concern with mechanisms of societal integra-tion,[3] we should not be surprised that he focuses on the *coordinating power* of language. For this reason, his formal pragmatic examinations of everyday language take as a starting point the structure of linguis-tic expressions rather than the speaker's intentions. Habermas con-tends that the latter cannot account for the binding and bonding power of utterances (speech acts).[4] However, Habermas criticizes in-tentionalist approaches to meaning not just for their failure to explain the coordinating power of speech acts but also because he holds that the account of meaning they provide is unsatisfactory.[5]

Habermas argues that the communication-theoretic approach ex-pounded by the German psychologist Karl Bühler in the 1930s sug-gests a fruitful line of inquiry for investigations into language as a mechanism of social coordination. He also maintains that Bühler's or-ganon model of language, although it needs to be modified in certain ways, provides a basis for a more adequate account of meaning and understanding that any of the contemporary analytic approaches to meaning as they stand.[6]

In a work published in 1934,[7] Bühler puts forward a schema of language functions that places the linguistic expression in relation to the speaker, the world, and the hearer. He starts from the semiotic model of a linguistic sign used by a speaker with the aim of coming to an understanding with a hearer about objects and states of affairs. The linguistic sign functions simultaneously as *symbol* (by virtue of its being correlated with objects and states of affairs), as *symptom* (by vir-tue of its dependence on the sender whose subjectivity it expresses), and as *signal* (by virtue of its appeal to the hearer, whose internal or external behavior it steers).

Habermas attempts to release Bühler's schema from its origins in a particular psychology of language and, by expanding the semiotic approach, to develop it to give a broader interpretation of each of the three functions mentioned by Bühler.[8] At the same time, he tries to retain what he regards as Bühler's basic insight: that language is a medium that fulfils three mutually irreducible but internally connected functions. Bühler draws attention to the fact that linguistic expressions that are used communicatively (as opposed to strategically) function (a) to give expression to the speaker's intentions or experiences, (b) to represent states of affairs (or something in the world that confronts the speaker), and (c) to enter into a relationship with a hearer. Habermas, following Bühler, claims that these three functions cannot be reduced to any single one.[9] Thus, the three aspects involved in uttering a linguistic expression are the following: I (the speaker)/come to an understanding with a hearer/about something in the world. Habermas identifies these three aspects as the three structural components of speech acts: the propositional, the illocutionary, and the expressive.[10] The propositional component is constructed by means of a sentence with propositional content.[11] The illocutionary component consists in an illocutionary act carried out with the aid of a performative sentence.[12] The expressive component remains implicit in the normal form but can always be expanded into an expressive sentence.[13] Habermas interprets Bühler's thesis as the thesis that every communicatively (as opposed to strategically) used linguistic expression makes reference to each of these three aspects simultaneously. As a result, he believes that a nonreductive theory of meaning must take account of the relationship among what is *intended* with a linguistic expression, what is *said* with a linguistic expression, and how the linguistic expression is *used* in a speech act. Linguistic meaning cannot be reduced to any one of these aspects.[14] It is on this basis that Habermas criticizes three competing contemporary theories of meaning. He criticizes intentionalist semantics (as expounded by Grice and Bennett), formal semantics (from Frege through the early Wittgenstein to Dummett), and use theories of meaning (such as that expounded by the later Wittgenstein) for being reductive or one-sided. Intentionalist semantics prioritizes the speaker's intention, formal semantics prioritizes the truth content of what is said, and the use theories of meaning deriving from the later Wittgenstein prioritize the interactive relationship brought about by speech acts. Each of these accounts of meaning stylizes as "meaning" just one of the three aspects that constitute linguistic meaning.

From within the analytic tradition of meaning theory, Habermas sees speech-act theory as introduced by J. L. Austin as representing a paradigm change.[15] The speech-act theories of Austin and Searle[16] can be described as an important step forward within the philosophy of language to the extent that they attempt to bridge the gap between formal semantics and use-oriented theories of meaning. Although there are significant differences in approach between Austin and Searle, what they have in common is an emphasis on the fact that the speaker, in *saying* something, *does* something. Austin's and Searle's accounts of meaning recognize both the dimension of saying something (on which formal semantics focuses) and the dimension of doing something (on which use-oriented theories concentrate). Although Habermas acknowledges speech-act theory as a decisive step forward, he maintains that the very different theories of Austin and Searle suffer from a common weakness: They fail to recognize that speech acts can be connected with dimensions of validity that are distinct from, but on an equal footing with, the dimension of propositional truth. Habermas argues that the early Austin remains fixated on the dimension of propositional truth, conceiving only those speech acts that thematize the propositional content of what is said as raising validity claims. The later Austin recognizes that other modes of language use—promises, warning, etc., which do not in the first instance thematize a given propositional content but which serve to establish an interpersonal relationship—are also connected with validity claims; but this leads him ultimately to blur the differences between the various kinds of validity claim, and he ends up with a set of unordered families of speech acts.[17] Searle's theory is equally problematic, on Habermas's view. His attempts to sharpen Austin's classification ultimately lead him to a one-sided emphasis on the cognitive and instrumental relations to the world at the expense of other relations to the world and corresponding language functions. In attempting to provide an ontological grounding for the five different types of speech act that he identifies, Searle ultimately subsumes the multiplicity of illocutionary modes to one universal validity claim: that of propositional truth. "Searle," writes Habermas,

takes the step to a *theoretically motivated typology of speech acts* by giving an ontological characterization of the illocutionary aims and the propositional attitudes that a speaker pursues or adopts when he performs assertive (or constative), directive, commissive, declarative and expressive speech acts. In doing so he draws upon the familiar model that defines the world as the totality of states of affairs, sets up the speaker/actor outside of this world, and allows for precisely two linguistically mediated relations between actor and world: the cognitive relation of ascertaining facts and the interventionist relation of realizing a goal of action.[18]

Owing to what he perceives as the weaknesses of the respective theories of Austin and Searle, Habermas argues that the methods and insights of speech-act theory must be connected up with Bühler's theory of language functions. Habermas sees this as a radicalization of the paradigm change in the philosophy of language introduced by Austin.[19] Habermas's radicalization of speech-act theory entails above all two interconnected steps: (a) the generalization of the concept of validity beyond the truth of propositions and (b) the identification of validity conditions not just on the semantic level of sentences but on the pragmatic level of utterances.[20] In chapter 4 I describe this as Habermas's attempt to overcome the three "abstractions" of contemporary theories of meaning: a cognitivist abstraction (to be overcome by step a above) and a semanticist and an objectivistic abstraction (to be overcome by step b above). Of particular note in the present chapter are the modifications of speech-act theory necessary if other modes of language use on an equal footing with the assertoric mode are recognized. Habermas has to establish validity claims and world-relations for the expressive and interactive functions of language which he argues are neglected by (in particular, the early) Austin and Searle.

Habermas attempts (i) to take account of the three functions of language use identified by Bühler while (ii) drawing on the insight of speech-act theory that the speaker, in making use of a linguistic expression, both does something and says something. The result is a model of linguistic communication that emphasizes both that the speaker does something in using a linguistic expression and that what is said is connected with a conception of validity that is not restricted to the truth of propositions but allows for modes of validity in the expressive and interactive dimensions as well. What does the speaker do in performing a speech act? Habermas's answer to this goes beyond the answers given by Austin and Searle to the extent that he emphasizes the coordinating power deriving from the rational basis of what the speaker does and to the extent that he allows for this rational basis to extend beyond propositional truth to encompass dimensions of moral-practical and expressive truth.

What the speaker does in performing a speech act is enter into a relationship of obligation with the hearer.[21] This relationship is based on the speaker's undertaking to support what she says with reasons. Habermas conceptualizes this in terms of a validity *claim* raised by the speaker. The speaker claims that what she says is true or right and offers to provide reasons to support the claim she raises if the hearer argues that it is necessary. This is Habermas's distinctive interpretation of the illocutionary force of an utterance.[22] The illocutionary force of an utterance is not simply the aspect of its meaning that is or might be conveyed by a performative prefix (Austin); it is, rather, a *coordinating power*. This can be traced back to the speaker's assumption of responsibility to show that what she says is justified, for this brings about an intersubjective relationship bound by reciprocal obligations. Habermas describes it as a "warranty" (*Gewähr*) provided by the speaker to the effect that she could redeem her claim to the validity of what is said if that were necessary. When Habermas refers to illocutionary force, therefore, he is thinking in terms of this warranty. For Habermas, the illocutionary force is a *binding* force (in the twin senses of *bonding* and *compelling*.[23] It comes about, ironically, through the fact that participants can say "No" to speech acts. The critical character of this saying "No"—the fact that it must be capable of being backed up by reasons—distinguishes it from a reaction based solely on caprice. Habermas frequently draws attention to the ironic fact that assent implies double negation: (i.e., that the negation of the invalidity of the claim is affirmed).[24]

As we have seen, Habermas conceptualizes the double characteristic of speech acts first identified by Austin in terms of raising a validity claim. Not surprisingly, therefore, a theory of validity claims plays an important part in his account of meaning and understanding. In keeping with his desire to avoid what he sees as the logocentric bias of speech-act theory (its privileging of the representational function), Habermas makes productive use of Bühler's insights and identifies three kinds of claim that can be raised by a speaker while at the same time contending that every speech act makes reference to these three validity claims simultaneously. In turn, the claims raised by the speaker provide the basis for a classification of speech acts.

Habermas allows the possibility of three validity claims: a claim to propositional truth,[25] a claim to normative rightness, and a claim to truthfulness (*Wahrhaftigkeit*).[26] These correspond to the three structural components of speech acts: the propositional, the illocutionary, and the expressive.[27] The three validity claims represent three fundamental illocutionary modes and form the basis for distinguishing three corresponding categories of speech act: the constative, the regulative, and the expressive.

Every speech act can be shown to raise precisely one claim *in the first instance* (or "directly"), and this claim determines its illocutionary mode and its speech-act category. In addition to this "direct" claim, each speech act raises two other claims "indirectly." Habermas expresses this intuition as the thesis that the speaker, with every speech act, raises three validity claims simultaneously.

How do we know which kind of "direct" validity claim has been raised with a particular utterance? On a number of occasions, Habermas gives us a useful hint as to how to determine this. The key to deciding what kind of a ("direct") validity claim has been raised, and therefore what kind of a speech act we are dealing with, is to ask ourselves from what point of view the speech act as a whole could be negated.[28] Habermas distinguishes three points of view from which negation of the utterance is possible.

The hearer can reject *what is said.* This is an instance of disagreement regarding the *truth claim* raised with the proposition that has been asserted. The hearer challenges the speaker's attempt to establish an interpersonal relationship on grounds pertaining to the matter at hand. We can imagine a hearer demanding: "What reasons do you have for saying *that?*" Habermas identifies a speech act that calls for this mode of response as a "constative" speech act (i.e., one that raises a claim to propositional truth).

A second possibility is that the hearer challenges the speaker's *right to say what she says to the hearer(s)* in the particular context. This is an instance of disagreement regarding the legitimacy of the normative context in which the utterance is expressed. The hearer challenges the speaker's attempt to establish an interpersonal relationship on grounds pertaining to the speaker's entitlement to raise that particular claim to that particular hearer in that particular context. We can imagine a hearer demanding: "What reasons do *you* have for saying that to *me* just now?" A speech act that calls for this mode of response is identified by Habermas as a "regulative" speech act (one that raises a claim to normative rightness).

The final possibility is that the hearer questions the speaker's *truthfulness* in saying what she says. This is an instance of suspicion regarding the subjective truthfulness of the speaker. The hearer challenges the speaker's attempt to establish an interpersonal relationship on grounds pertaining to the subjectivity of the speaker; more precisely, the hearer challenges the speaker's truthfulness. We can imagine a hearer demanding: "What reasons do you have for expecting me to believe you *mean* that". Habermas identifies a speech act that calls for this mode of response as an "expressive" speech act (one that raises a claim to subjective truthfulness).

The foregoing provides us with some practical guidelines as to how we should determine what kind of validity claim a speaker is raising with a particular utterance (that is to say, its "illocutionary mode"). At the same time, although it is a useful rule of thumb, it is at least potentially confusing. When Habermas tells us that we can identify the illocutionary mode of an utterance by asking ourselves from which point of view we would challenge it if necessary, he is, of course, attributing to the speaker a primary intention in saying what she says, and he is assuming that the hearer recognizes this. Therefore, the fact that the hearer challenges the utterance from the point of view of the speaker's truthfulness is not sufficient grounds for classifying the utterance as an expressive speech act. If the speaker says "It is raining outside" and the hearer accuses her of lying (thus challenging the speaker's truthfulness), the fact that the hearer responds in this way does not, of course, mean that this expression is to be viewed as an expressive speech act. To argue this would be to see the hearer's response as the *sole* determining factor in deciding illocutionary mode— a clearly absurd position. The fact that any given speech act can be contested from more than one point of view supports Habermas's claim that every speech act raises three validity claims simultaneously. However, as we have seen, Habermas distinguishes between "direct" and "indirect" claims. Every speech act raises just one claim "directly" and raises two "indirect" claims. We can also say that each speech act raises just one claim *in the first instance* and two others only in a *secondary* way. This is the source of our confusion in the present context: Only the "direct" claims count when it comes to determining illocutionary mode. Speech acts can be classified according to the point of view from which the speech act as a whole can be negated *in the first instance*.

It is important not to misunderstand the contention that it is necessary to attribute to the speaker a primary intention in saying what she says. The assertion that we have to be able to identify the speaker's primary intention in performing a speech act has relevance for the question of how we can identify different types of validity claim and classify speech acts. It is not to be confused with the position that understanding utterances is *purely* a matter of understanding the speaker's intention (in whatever complex form).[29] As I have already indicated, Habermas insists that the aspect of intention is only one of three aspects involved in understanding utterances. Although Habermas acknowledges the role of the speaker's intention, his position is not an intentionalist one. He explains what it means to understand an utterance not in terms of the speaker's intention—for this is only one of the aspects involved—but in terms of understanding the *claim* that the speaker raises with her utterance.

Habermas's suggestion that we classify speech acts according to the point of view from which they can be negated in the first instance has the advantage that it relativizes the importance of grammatical factors: In attempting to decide to which class of speech act a given utterance belongs, we need not pay too much attention to the grammatical form of the utterance (for example, the occurrence or nonoccurrence in the utterance of a particular performative verb). It is not the presence or absence of a particular performative verb that determines illocutionary mode; rather, it is which claim has been raised with the utterance. In actual cases of communication, this must be identified by a given hearer on the basis of that hearer's grasp of the situation in question (and, in the case of confusion or misunderstanding, through clarification with the speaker). Habermas himself acknowledges that the presence of a particular performative verb in a given utterance is of limited importance to its classification as one of the three types of speech act. This is evident in his recognition that speech acts of different modes can be performed with the same performative verb. He acknowledges that the performative verbs "to warn" and "to advise" can be used to predict or to make a moral appeal, which is to say that they can be part either of the cognitive use of language (in constative speech acts) or of the interactive use of language (in regulative speech acts).[30] By the same token we might say that the occurrence in an utterance of the verb "to promise" does not mean that such an utterance must be taken as an act of promising. Conversely, and obviously, the speaker does not have to say "I (hereby) promise" in order to make a promise, or "I (hereby) assert" in order to make an assertion, or "I (hereby) avow" in order to make an avowal. To be sure, it does appear to be a feature of regulative speech acts—and only regulative speech acts—that in cases of unwillingness to accept the speech-act offer the actual utterance of the relevant performative verb reinforces the original act of promising, requesting, etc. The actual utterance of the words "I *beg* you," or "This is a *request*," or "That's a *promise*" functions to confirm or convince the hearer of the speaker's truthfulness. There is no apparent parallel here with constative speech acts. However, despite his recognition[31] that it is difficult to achieve any clear-cut classification of performative verbs in terms of the three main illocutionary modes, Habermas holds onto the idea that certain verbs are "prototypes" of specific modes of utterance: verbs of asserting and stating of constative speech acts, verbs of promising and requesting of regulative speech acts, and verbs of avowing of expressive speech acts. I take this to mean that he maintains an internal connection between *acts* of asserting and stating and constative speech acts, between *acts* of promising and requesting and regulative speech acts, and between *acts* of avowing and expressive speech acts. As we shall see, this intuition is a correct one.

2

As we know, Habermas defines a constative speech act as one that raises a propositional truth claim. He tends to associate truth claims with utterances that contain, or could plausibly be expanded to contain, performative verbs such as "assert," "claim," "inform," and "predict." At the same time, he restricts the category of assertions and claims, and hence of truth claims in general, to claims to empirical or theoretical truth. Presumably, his reasons for doing so are connected with his theory of truth (theoretical discourse). As we saw in chapter 2, Habermas argues that it is a distinguishing feature of claims to propositional truth and of claims to moral validity that they make reference to a sense of universal validity (in a double sense of "universal"). *Only* these kinds of claim are connected with the "strong idealization" that everyone would agree that they are valid, if at all, for everyone. This is intended as a (partial) explication of the meaning of claims to propositional truth and of claims to moral validity, and it is convincing as far as it goes. Certainly, it is difficult to challenge the assertion that at least some kinds of truth claim make implicit reference to an idea of universal validity in a double sense of "universal"; empirical and theoretical truth claims seem clearly to fall into this category.[32] This is presumably the main reason why Habermas restricts his category of truth claims (and hence of constative speech acts) to claims to theoretical and empirical truth.[33] However, while I agree that such claims share certain features that distinguish them from other kinds of validity claim, it seems to me that Habermas's restriction of the class of constative utterances to utterances that raise truth claims of this type is not productive. For one thing, it results in a problematic characterization of moral validity claims as claims to normative rightness (and thereby as regulative speech acts). For another, it results in the neglect of the wide variety of claims that are connected with everyday communicative action. As it stands, Habermas's theory of validity claims fails, in particular, to do justice to the aesthetic validity claims raised in everyday language use or to the disclosing and articulating functions of everyday language. (I have more to say about this in sections 5 and 6.)

3

Habermas describes moral validity claims as claims to normative rightness (which, as we know, are the defining feature of regulative speech acts). However, he is able to include claims of this kind in the class of regulative speech acts only by systematically confusing two quite distinct types of validity claim: normative validity claims and claims to normative rightness.

Whereas utterances that raise normative validity claims thematize the validity of what is said, claims to normative rightness are raised implicitly with every utterance and concern the rightness of the speaker's speech act as an action in a specific context of interaction. Moral validity claims, in contrast, display close affinities with constative utterances to the extent that the speaker claims validity for what she says—one need only think of assertions such as "Everyone is entitled to a free education" or "Homosexuality is wrong." As I have indicated,[34] Habermas defines moral validity claims as claims that are connected with the idealizing supposition that, in a practical (moral) discourse, everyone would agree to their universal validity. In order for this kind of universal validity (in a double sense of "universal") to be achieved, such claims must, by definition, be detached from the particular interests of particular individuals and from particular contexts of action. As a result, moral validity claims are always *context-unspecific*.[35] Since a claim to normative rightness is a claim to the rightness of a particular speech act *in a particular context*, this suggests at least one compelling reason for distinguishing such claims from moral validity claims. The latter bear far closer resemblance to claims to propositional truth, although clearly they are not identical to empirical and theoretical truth claims. (The constitutive role played by the idea of a discursively achieved agreement in defining moral but not empirical truth claims marks one obvious point of distinction.[36])

Of course, some normative validity claims *are* situation-specific: for instance, those raised with acts of warning or advising. Moreover, such claims often also have a clear moral content: for example, "You ought to take better care of your children."[37] In fact, acts of warning and advising do not fit into either the category of regulative utterances or the category of constative utterances in a straightforward way. However, since acts of warning and advising are paradigm examples neither of regulative speech acts nor of constative speech acts, only an exceedingly rigid proposal for classifying speech acts would be disturbed by this.

Since Habermas classifies moral validity claims as regulative speech acts and confusingly describes them as claims to normative rightness, it is worth taking a closer look at the category of regulative speech acts and the claim to normative rightness they raise in order to clarify the distinguishing features of these.

In his essay "What Is Universal Pragmatics?"[38] Habermas distinguishes what he calls the cognitive use of language from the interactive use of language. He describes the difference as one of focus. In the cognitive use of language, with the help of constative speech acts, the thematic emphasis is on the propositional content of the utterance. In the interactive use of language, with the help of regulative speech acts, the thematic emphasis is on the relationship that the utterance establishes between speaker and hearer; in such speech acts the propositional content is only *mentioned*. What is the nature of this "certain kind of relationship" which is established between speaker and hearer with the help of regulative speech acts? The first "Intermediate Reflection" in *The Theory of Communicative Action* makes clear that it is a relationship of *obligation*. But what is the nature of this obligation?

As we shall see,[39] Habermas tells us that in order to understand a speech act we have to know both the "conditions of satisfaction" and the "conditions of validation." In the case of regulative speech acts, part of what is entailed by knowing the conditions of satisfaction is knowing that acceptance of the speech-act offer will involve the speaker and/or the hearer in certain obligations. Agreement with or acceptance of a regulative speech act gives rise to an obligation *to act in a certain way*. In the cases of commands and directives, this obligation is principally for the addressee; in the cases of promises and announcements, it is principally for the speaker; in the cases of agreements and contracts, it is symmetrical for the two parties; in the cases of advice and warnings, it is for both parties, but asymmetrically. Habermas makes frequent references to the obligations "for the sequel of action" that arise from the acceptance of regulative speech acts.[40] He contrasts this kind of obligation with the "validity related obligations" or "speech act immanent obligations" that characterize all three categories of speech act.[41] The "validity related obligations" referred to here are the (rational) obligations which Habermas sees as the source of the binding force of speech acts. Habermas argues that every speech act serves to establish an interpersonal relationship on two levels. On the one hand, the speaker enters into a *moral* relationship with the hearer to the extent that the speaker undertakes to vouch for the normative rightness (appropriateness) of the speech context in question. (This is what Habermas means by an "indirect claim to normative rightness.")[42] However, the binding force of the speech act derives not from this but from the speaker's *warranty* to defend the claim raised with good reasons, if necessary. Habermas describes the interpersonal relationship established on *this* level as a validity-related (which I take to mean rational) obligation: The speaker is obliged to support her claim with reasons if necessary, and the hearer is obliged to accept a claim unless she has good reasons not to do so. The penalty for failure is the charge not of immorality but of irrationality.[43]

The important point in the present context is that the obligations that arise for the sequel of action from the acceptance of regulative speech acts are not (primarily) rational obligations; they are (primarily) moral ones. Although Habermas does not make this distinction explicitly, it is possible to distinguish analytically between the obligations that are connected with the *validity claim* raised with constative utterances and those that are connected with the *interpersonal* relationship established with every utterance. Whereas the former can be characterized as rational obligations, the latter kind of obligation is always a moral one.

In regulative speech acts the speaker does not in the first instance claim validity for what she says; as Habermas puts it, the thematic emphasis is not on the propositional content of the utterance. Thus, we might say that the main point about regulative speech acts is not that they raise a validity claim; it is that they are constitutive of a certain kind of intersubjective relationship. This relationship is one of obligation—more precisely, one of moral obligation. This, as we saw, may be incumbent on the speaker, or on the hearer, or on both, either symmetrically or asymmetrically, and will take a different form depending on the precise nature of the speech act in question. That it has a more or less weak moral sense can be seen if we ask ourselves what happens if we fail to act in the way prescribed by the satisfaction conditions of the speech act (that is, if we fail to keep a promise, or fail to carry out a request to which we have agreed, or disregard an invitation that we have accepted). In each of these instances, the success of the speech act commits us to a certain way of acting: If I accept a promise, I am committed to keeping it; if I agree to a request, I am committed to carrying it out; if I accept an invitation, I am committed to turning up. If I fail to do any of these things, I am morally obliged to give an account of myself—I must explain, excuse, or justify my behavior or else accept the blame.

In a regulative speech act, the *act* of promising constitutes the moral obligation to keep the promise. The obligation is not present until the act is *performed*. The obligation in question is a moral one, to the extent that failing to keep a promise or to carry out a request to which one has agreed impairs the interpersonal relationship that has been constituted by the act of promising or requesting. Habermas recognizes that regulative speech acts give rise to an obligation to act in a certain way, and distinguishes this kind of obligation from the validity-related (rational) obligation to which all speech acts give rise. However, it could be argued that he does not pay sufficient attention to the fact that the *act* itself *constitutes* this obligation. Certainly, his focus is not on this normative aspect of regulative speech acts; rather it is on a different normative aspect: the fact that the speaker, with every regulative speech act, raises a claim to normative rightness that has a special importance for its meaning. What Habermas wants to maintain is that understanding the claim to normative rightness raised with every regulative speech act is a constitutive part of understanding that speech act. Quite apart from the question of whether Habermas's intuition here is correct, the idea that regulative speech acts are *defined* by claims to normative rightness may be misleading. I see two sources of potential confusion here. Firstly, it may obscure the fact that regulative speech acts, at least paradigmatically, are *constitutive* of a moral relationship—this, surely, is their defining feature. Secondly, it may lead us to suppose, wrongly, that all normative validity claims are regulative speech acts—I have already suggested that moral validity claims, to the extent that they thematize the validity of what is said, might be classified as constative speech acts. However, if we guard against these possible confusions (and the latter is one to which Habermas himself falls prey), it may in a sense be correct to say that regulative speech acts raise claims to normative rightness. Whether this is the case is a question for Habermas's theory of meaning.

Habermas's intuition is that a speaker, with every act of promising or requesting, raises a claim to the normative rightness of that act in a given context. This claim is not an "indirect" one but is constitutive of the meaning of the speech act. Habermas argues that to understand a given promise, request, or invitation we have to know what kind of reasons the speaker could provide to convince a hearer that the speaker's act is normatively right in the given context. Habermas's thesis is that we would not understand the meaning of a given promise, request, or invitation if we were not able to reconstruct possible reasons in support of the speaker's claim to the normative rightness of the act in question. If Habermas's argument in this regard is correct, then he is correct to maintain that acts of promising, requesting, and inviting, although they do not "raise claims" in the strict sense (to the extent that they do not thematize a given propositional content), are in fact internally connected with a claim to normative rightness. All of this remains to be shown; however, it suggests, at least, that we should be wary of dismissing Habermas's thesis out of hand. At the same time, we should bear in mind that claims to normative rightness may be of many different kinds: various kinds of validity can be claimed or denied.

It is useful to make a distinction between the *normative* presuppositions that have to be satisfied before agreement can be reached between speaker and hearer and the *existential* presuppositions of the speech act. A regulative speech act can fail if either of these sets of presuppositions is not satisfied; however, we speak of the *refusal* of a request or the *rejection* of an invitation only if we believe that the normative presuppositions of the action are not satisfied. For instance, your request that I fetch you a glass of whiskey might fail because there is no whiskey in the house (the existential presupposition is not satisfied). I do not refuse your request; I simply am not in a position to satisfy it. Strictly speaking, the refusal of a request is always on normative grounds: I can refuse your request only if I have moral (or related normative) reasons for turning it down. Thus, a refusal of a request always has a weak moral sense.

We must be careful not to interpret the idea of a claim to normative rightness too narrowly. We should bear in mind that there are different kinds of norms. There are norms in the sense of regulations, there are norms in the sense of prevailing conventions, there are norms of rational behaviour, and there is the broad spectrum of moral norms. Thus, for example, in the case of requests, we can distinguish various ways in which a request may be refused. For instance, if a stranger sitting beside me in an airplane asks me to stop smoking and I reply that I shall not do so until requested by someone in authority (for example, the stewardess), I suggest that the stranger's action in requesting me to do something is normatively invalid in the sense that it is not authorized. In contrast, one might refuse an invitation to take part in a bank robbery because the activity in question is morally reprehensible. Another example: I might respond to a street beggar's request for some money on the grounds that begging is not permitted (i.e. authorized) on the streets of Dublin or, equally, on the grounds that begging is morally wrong.

Although many kinds of claims to normative rightness are conceivable, all of these must be distinguished from *normative validity claims*. We have already seen that moral validity claims are normative validity claims but not claims to normative rightness, for the latter are always context-bound and the former are typically abstracted from the context in which the speech act is performed. Equally, in the normal case, speech acts that raise claims to normative validity are not regulative speech acts; the act of asserting a normative validity claim is not normally constitutive of a moral relationship, and this, as we know, is one of the defining features of regulative speech acts.

The category of normative validity claims does not just include moral claims, although these are paradigmatic. It also extends across prudential claims ("Look before you leap"), evaluative claims ("The 1991 Beaujolais is a better vintage than the 1992 one"), religious claims ("Honor the Lord thy God"), grammatical claims ("In the German language, the verb goes to the end of the sentence after the conjunction *weil*"), rules of etiquette ("Men should stand up when a lady enters the room"), etc. All of these claims assert *general* validity for a particular point of view or way of acting, as opposed to asserting the validity of a particular action in a particular context. Nor is the act of asserting any of these claims constitutive of a relationship of moral obligation. To this extent, nonmoral normative validity claims, too, seem to bear a closer resemblence to propositional truth claims than to claims to normative rightness, and they fit more easily into constative than regulative speech acts.

Acts of warning and advising complicate the issue. To the extent that they are situated normative validity claims, they cut across the distinction between claims to normative rightness and propositional truth claims and that between regulative and constative speech acts.[44] On the one hand, acts of warning and advising raise a claim for the normative rightness of a given act in a given context not "indirectly" but by their very meaning; this connects them with paradigmatic regulative speech acts such as promises or requests. On the other hand, they are not constitutive of a *moral* relationship as are acts of promising and requesting.

The main point of connection between acts of warning and advising and acts of promising and requesting is their possible internal link with a claim to normative rightness.[45] Habermas would argue that understanding a warning or a piece of advice, like understanding a promise, is bound up with knowing possible reasons for the speaker's entitlement to offer it. Claims to normative rightness are not just offered "indirectly" with acts of warning and advising; it can be argued that they play a special meaning-constitutive role.

The main point of divergence between acts of warning and advising and paradigmatic regulative speech acts, and their main point of convergence with constative speech acts, is that the act itself is constitutive of only a rational obligation (and not of a moral obligation) to act in a certain way.[46] If I accept the truth of an assertion (for instance, some empirical or theoretical truth claim), I stand accused of inconsistency or illogicality if I act in a way that undermines its validity. In the same way, if I accept the rightness of a warning or a piece of advice, I stand accused of inconsistency if I act in a way that is incompatible with it. In both cases I stand accused of irrationality. Of course, this holds good only so long as I continue to agree that the assertion is true or that the warning or piece of advice is valid. I may always have good reasons (for instance, new relevant information) for changing my mind. I am not even rationally obliged to act in a way consistent with my professed beliefs of two hours before if I have good reasons for changing my mind (for instance, if in the meantime I have had access to new information or have gained a new perspective on the matter). Nonetheless, exercising caution, we may say that the acceptance of the truth of an assertion or of the rightness of a piece of advice imposes a rational obligation to act in a certain way.

That the obligation is in the first instance a rational and not a moral one is clear in the case of most assertions. If I accept that excessive exposure to the sun causes skin cancer, then I may be accused of irrationality if I spend my holidays on a beach in the sun but I cannot (in the first instance) be accused of immorality; [47] similarly, if I agree that refined sugar is bad for human beings but persist in eating large quantities of chocolate, I may be accused of irrationality but not of immorality (at least not in the first instance). As a general rule, I have no *moral* obligation to act rationally. [48] Warnings with a strong moral content or pieces of moral advice may look as though they give rise to a moral rather than a rational obligation, but this in fact is not the case. Even moral advice is not *constitutive of* a moral obligation; instead it refers to an *already existing* moral obligation. If we imagine a situation in which the addressee accepts the moral validity of a piece of advice ("You ought not to avoid paying your fare on the bus"), we can see that the moral obligation to follow this piece of advice results from the moral validity of the underlying norm or principle ("Fare evasion is dishonest") and not from the *act of advising*. This is what links pieces of advice (warnings, etc.) with normative validity claims. At the same time, the moral obligation also depends on the addressee's accepting the validity of the advice *as addressed to her in that particular situation;* that is, it depends on her acceptance of the claim to normative rightness raised with the speech act. This is what links pieces of advice (warnings, etc.) with regulative speech acts.

From the foregoing it appears that Habermas's correlation of the class of constative speech acts with propositional truth claims and the class of regulative speech acts with claims to normative rightness holds only if we allow that propositional truth claims include normative validity claims. This is hardly the traditional way of understanding propositional truth—but does that matter? Alternatively, we may want to say that constative speech acts simply raise truth claims, where the notion of a truth claim is no longer restricted to empirical or theoretical truth but is expanded to include claims to moral, legal, evaluative, aesthetic, ethical, grammatical, and other kinds of truth. Or we may prefer to say that constative speech acts are acts that *raise validity claims* in the sense that they thematize the validity of the content of the assertion, allowing that many different types of validity are possible. Whatever formulation we decide to opt for, the result is an expanded category of constative speech acts. [49] It should be noted, however, that what is being proposed is *not* that there are no significant differences between (e.g.) claims to theoretical and empirical truth and moral claims, legal claims, evaluative claims, aesthetic claims, etc. *All* of these claims can be distinguished from one another on the basis of the modes of justification appropriate to them. The proposal to subsume them under one general class of speech act by no means implies that they are all the same. Already a number of possible differences have been indicated: I have drawn attention to Habermas's assertions that moral claims make reference to an idea of discursively achieved universal validity in a double sense of "universal," that claims to empirical and theoretical truth make reference to the idea of universal agreement (in a double sense of "universal") but not necessarily to the idea of a discursively achieved universal consensus, and that neither evaluative nor ethical nor aesthetic claims make reference to the idea of universal agreement (in a double sense of "universal") at all.[50]

4

The suggestion that we extend the class of constative speech acts beyond that which Habermas proposes has implications for the third category of speech act he identifies: the class of expressive speech acts. If we take a look at the class of expressive utterances, as defined by Habermas, it is hard to find compelling reasons for splitting them off from the general category of speech acts that thematize the validity of what is said—and, therefore, from the now expanded class of constative utterances.[51]

Habermas defines expressive speech acts as those that raise claims to truthfulness. Expressive speech acts raise claims to the subjective truthfulness of the speaker. More precisely, they raise what Habermas describes as a "direct" claim to truthfulness. (Once again, we must distinguish this from the indirect claim to truthfulness that Habermas attributes to all utterances.) With the notion of a direct claim to truthfulness, Habermas wants to draw attention to the fact that certain utterances *disclose* an inner experience. Consequently, the paradigms of this kind of speech act are first-person sentences in which the speaker's wishes, intentions, or feelings are revealed.[52] Habermas includes in this category utterances that make use of linguistic expressions such as "I long for . . . ," "I wish that . . . ," and "I must confess that . . . ," but also first person experiental sentences such as "I am afraid of . . . " and "I am in pain."

Habermas's point in describing expressive utterances as raising claims to truthfulness is that speech acts that disclose inner experience can be validated only by reference to the speaker's subjective truthfulness. You have no way of verifying the expressive claim that I am longing for a glass of milk except by testing my truthfulness, which involves looking at the consistency of my actions in order to see if I really mean what I say. In the case of such speech acts, if the speaker is truthful, the utterance will be valid. If we bear in mind that this holds only for those speech acts that in the first instance disclose inner nature (as opposed, e.g., to reporting on it or using it as a basis of commitment),[53] then there seems to be no good reason to disagree with Habermas on this count.

The mode of justification appropriate to expressive validity claims marks them off clearly from empirical truth claims. They clearly constitute a distinct type of validity claim. But is this sufficient reason to create a third speech-act category? The case for this would be stronger if the class of constative speech acts could be restricted straightforwardly to claims to theoretical and empirical truth. But if the category of constative speech acts—the category of speech acts that thematize the validity of what is said—is expanded to include a wide variety of kinds of normative validity claim, then there seems to be no compelling reason for setting up a third category of speech act to accommodate claims to truthfulness. The utterance "I am in pain" may be described as raising an expressive validity claim to the extent that it discloses an inner experience, but it also claims validity for what is said. The fact that the validity of what is said can be determined only by reference to the subjective truthfulness of the speaker is not a compelling reason for excluding this kind of utterance from the class of constative speech acts, for the inclusion of normative validity claims in this category already implies that the validity claims raised with constative speech acts may require very diferent kinds of justification. The only possible grounds for distinguishing utterances that raise expressive validity claims from the expanded class of constative utterances is that the former raise a claim *in a particular way*. They do not simply assert; they *disclose*. However, for reasons that will become clearer in the following, I do not think that this constitutes a sufficient reason for creating a third class of speech act. I have already suggested that Habermas's theory of validity claims as it stands is too restrictive to the extent that it cannot plausibly account for normative validity claims without illicitly equating them with claims to normative rightness; we shall now see that, in addition, it cannot accommodate evaluative validity claims, that it has an uneasy relationship with aesthetic claims, and that it ignores the disclosing and articulating functions of everyday language use. The solution is relatively simple, however. If we expand the category of constative speech acts to include a wide variety of kinds of validity claim, distinguishable by virtue of the mode of justification appropriate to them and united by their connection with utterances that thematize the validity of what is said, it is easy to find room for aesthetic and evaluative validity claims as well as for other kinds of claim currently neglected by Habermas. This would mean, however, that not only do constative utterances raise many different kinds of validity claim, they also frequently raise them in many different ways. If this is the case, then it is even harder to find reasons for creating a third category of speech act to accommodate expressive validity claims.[54]

5

As it stands, Habermas's theory of validity claims has an uneasy relationship with aesthetic validity claims, acknowledges but can find no room for evaluative validity claims, and ignores certain kinds of claim connected with the disclosing and articulating functions of language.

Habermas seems to recognize that evaluative utterances satisfy the central presupposition of rationality: They can be contested on the basis of reasons that are open to intersubjective assessment. Thus, claims such as "I enjoy the rich river-smell of mud" are acknowledged to raise criticizable validity claims.[55] At the same time, evaluative claims do not fit easily into any of the three categories of speech act that Habermas's schema allows; sometimes Habermas associates them with expressive validity claims. But evaluative claims can be clearly distinguished from expressive claims to the extent that they are not justified primarily through reference to the speaker's subjective truthfulness: A speaker may be perfectly truthful yet *wrong* to claim that mud has a rich river-smell or that this smell is enjoyable. Equally, they are clearly distinct from empirical or theoretical truth claims. Because they do not fit easily into any of the three categories of speech act defined by Habermas, he is forced to conclude that they raise "no clear-cut validity claim."[56]

Similarly, the articulating, world-creating, and disclosing modes of language use pose difficulties for Habermas's theory of validity claims in its current form. Habermas has now admitted that he has failed to do justice to these functions.[57]

Furthermore, Habermas has an uneasy relationship with aesthetic validity claims and has not yet accounted for them convincingly. Although at one stage Habermas failed to distinguish adequately between expressive and aesthetic validity claims, correlating both with the dimension of subjective truthfulness, he now recognizes that aesthetic works raise validity claims that are distinct from claims to truthfulness. This acknowledgement is problematic, however, to the extent that it is accompanied by the suggestion that aesthetic validity claims do not belong to the sphere of everyday communicative action. Habermas's present position with regard to aesthetic validity claims appears to be as follows:

The fact that we can dispute the reasons for evaluating a work of art . . . is . . . an unmistakable indication for a validity claim inherent in works of art.[58]

Drawing on an essay by Albrecht Wellmer,[59] Habermas argues that the aesthetic validity or unity that we attribute to a work of art refers to its singularly illuminating power to open our eyes to what is seemingly familiar—to its power to disclose anew an apparently familiar reality. However, this validity claim stands for a potential for "truth" that can be released only in the whole complexity of life experience; therefore, this "truth potential" may not be correlated with (or even identified with) any one of the three validity claims constitutive for communicative action. Habermas's solution to the problem raised by the question of the truth of art is thus to split off the validity claim(s) peculiar to art from the sphere of communicative action. The truth claim raised by aesthetic works is seen as categorially distinct from the kinds of truth claim raised with constative utterances in everyday communicative praxis. The truth potential of art is a potential for *disclosing* truth and to this extent must be experienced before its validity can be assessed. Moreover, aesthetic experience has moral, cognitive, and expressive dimensions: It transforms relations between the self and *all three* worlds; it reaches into our cognitive interpretations, into our normative expectations, and into our subjective preferences and transforms the totality in which these are related to each other.

In earlier works Habermas tended to refer to the third dimension of validity implicit in everyday language use as the dimension of aesthetic-expressive validity.[60] On this model, art is conceived as an expression of the self and its validity is assessed on the basis of whether it authentically expresses internal nature. Although it is extremely dubious as an account of aesthetic validity, the advantage of this conception was that it appeared to allow for a dimension of aesthetic validity *within* everyday communicative action. Habermas's present position, in contrast, acknowledges the distinctive features of aesthetic validity claims at the cost of denying them a place within everyday communicative action.

Indeed, Habermas is forced to split off aesthetic validity claims from the sphere of everyday communicative action by his restrictive speech-act classificatory schema (in particular, his narrow conception of a constative speech act) and by his overly narrow conception of communicative *action*.

Habermas defines action as "coping with situations."[61] The term "action" is restricted to attempts to resolve difficulties or to solve problems.[62] Of course, in emphasizing the teleological aspect of communicative action, he wants to draw attention to the fact that it, like strategic action in this respect at least, results in the realization of specific purposes and goals.[63] The purpose of communicative action is the coordination of *plans* of action.[64] Habermas frequently refers to the "pressure to reach a decision" (*Entscheidungsdruck*), a permanent external constraint on communicative action.

This narrow conception of action results in a problematic connection between those modes of language use that are oriented toward understanding (*Verständigung*) and the coordination of action plans via the intersubjective recognition of criticizable validity claims. Other modes of language use that serve purposes other than the coordination of action plans are thus excluded from the sphere of language oriented toward understanding.[65] The articulating, world-disclosing, and world-creating dimensions of linguistic activity fall into this category. Although Habermas recognizes that he has tended to treat these dimensions of language usage as the poor relations of the representational, illocutionary, and intentional functions,[66] his basic conceptual framework prevents him from redressing the balance. The result is a foreshortened conception of communicative action and, in consequence, also of communicative rationality as the rational potential implicit in this.

Even if Habermas is justified in emphasizing the teleological aspect of communicative action, this does not mean that he may legitimately restrict the notion of a *speech act* to actions oriented toward problems and goals. The conception of action contained within the notion of a speech act is not necessarily the same as that on which the notion of communicative action relies. The suggestion that all speech acts are directed toward the realization of specific purposes and goals implies a very restricted conception of linguistic activity. Doesn't unstructured conversation, for instance, often rely on an exchange of speech acts in some less restricted sense of action? Habermas seems to regard this as a "special case."[67] The closest Habermas comes to admitting that not all speech acts are oriented toward achieving specific goals and solving specific problems is when, in the context of a discussion of *Verstehen* in the social sciences, he tells us:

. . . speaking and acting are not the same. Those immediately involved in the communicative praxis of everyday life are pursuing aims of *action;* their participation in cooperative processes of interpretation serves to establish a consensus on the basis of which they can coordinate their plans of action and achieve their aims. [68]

However, once again he seems to see the social scientist's detachment from contexts of action (in *his* sense of action) as a special case.[69] If the aesthetic, world-articulating, and world-disclosing modes of language use, too, are to be regarded as special cases, this amounts to a considerable impoverishment of the notion of communicative action. All in all, Habermas's acknowledgement of the distinctive features of aesthetic claims and his recent acknowledgement of the world-disclosing and world-articulating functions of language seems to have been bought at the price of their exclusion from the sphere of everyday communicative action. Indeed, it would seem that, strictly, speech acts do not raise these kinds of claim at all, for speech acts are by definition acts that raise claims and that, by virtue of being embedded in contexts of communicative action, are oriented toward understanding.

This is made clear in Habermas's discussion of the speech acts of literary discourse. The speech acts of literary discourse are detached from everyday contexts of action. As a result they have no illocutionary force (which for Habermas refers to the binding and bonding effect that results from the recognition of validity claims). In literary discourse,

> The neutralization of the binding/bonding power frees the illocutionary acts (now robbed of their power) from the pressure to reach a decision which obtains in everyday communicative praxis; it removes them from the sphere of normal speech and reduces their role to that of the playful creation of new worlds—or rather, to a pure demonstration of the world-disclosing power of innovative linguistic expressions. [70]

The implication here seems to be that those speech acts that function primarily to create, disclose, or articulate do not, by virtue of this very fact, fulfil functions of reaching understanding.[71]

It is not clear to me that anything of crucial importance to Habermas's theory depends on a restricted conception of action as that which coordinates plans of action with a view to realizing specific goals and achieving specific aims. This is undoubtedly a subcategory of human action, but not necessarily its primary form. As applied to speech acts, it seems unnecessarily narrow. An alternative way of defining action might be the following, suggested by J. B. Thompson: "an event which can be described as something that someone (or group) does, and not simply as something that happens to someone or group."[72]

A broader conception of action, such as that proposed by Thompson, would have the advantage of conceptually making room within the sphere of communicative action for modes of language use that in the first instance function not to coordinate plans of action but to articulate and disclose. Admittedly, it could be argued that Habermas does not *need* to do this, since those modes of language use that function to disclose and articulate are not part of *everyday* language use; they belong to the esoteric spheres of literature and formal aesthetic discourse. This objection loses its force, however, if it can be shown that everyday processes of communication also rely on articulating and disclosing modes of language use.

6

We have seen above that one of the main reasons Habermas offers for his categorial distinction of the validity claims raised by works of art from those constitutive for communicative action is that the former stand for a *"potential* for truth" that can be released only in the whole complexity of life experience. The validity claims raised by aesthetic works refer to a potential for *disclosing* truth. Furthermore, this potential for truth has cognitive, moral, and expressive dimensions; it transforms relations between the self and *all three worlds.* In short, the successful work of art opens a perspective on some aspect of our human or personal situation that has to be experienced before its validity can be assessed. Three points are particularly relevant here:

• Works of art are connected with validity claims. If we wished to speak generally of the validity claim raised (implicitly) by aesthetic works, we might characterize it as a claim to the validity of a perspective.

• This claim is not "raised" in the strict sense. Although the claims raised by works of art can be described as claims to the extent that they may be reformulated in the grammatical form of an assertion, something is always lost in the reformulation. This is what is meant by saying that works of art *disclose* a perspective. Moreover, validity is claimed not just for the perspective but for the way in which it is disclosed. This means that works of art claim validity in two respects: for the perspective opened and for *the way in which it is opened.*

• The validity claims connected with works of art must be justified in the first instance through reference to the subjective experience of those affected and cannot be justified directly through reference to facts or theories. Here it is important to note that although aesthetic claims have to be experienced before they can be justified, this does not mean that the subjective experience of the addressee is the *only* kind of reason that counts in the process of justification or, indeed, that it carries more weight than other kinds of reason.

Are the claims raised by works of art really so different from claims raised in everyday modes of language use? Can we point to everyday modes of language use that disclose a perspective, thereby raising a claim that has to be experienced before it can be justified? In concluding this section, I will draw attention to the work of three theorists who (indirectly) suggest that the speech acts of everyday communicative practice raise claims similar to those raised by works of art, and in a similar way.

Mary L. Pratt introduces a new category of speech act into the speech-act theory of Austin, Searle, and Grice.[73] She makes the case for "verbal displaying" as a type of speech act frequently encountered not just in literary discourse but also in everyday processes of communication. Pratt is here referring to utterances or sequences of utterances the purpose of which is not a maximally effective exchange of information in the Gricean sense. In what she calls "acts of verbal displaying," the speaker aims ultimately at an agreement with the hearer(s) with respect to the proffered interpretation of an event of state of affairs. I would prefer to characterize the speaker's aim as agreement with the hearer(s) regarding the validity of a perspective opened on some aspect of the speaker's (or the speaker's and the hearer's) personal situation, or on the human situation. Pratt defines such acts as acts that raise a claim to "tellability"; that is, the speaker raises a claim that what she has to say is "worth listening to" (or, indeed, that what she has to show is "worth looking at"). This is a claim, and as such it gives rise to mutual obligations which Pratt explicates, but it is not a *validity* claim. The validity claim raised is the claim to the validity of the interpretation of experience that the speaker offers (better: to the validity of the perspective opened on experience)— that is, to the validity of the speaker's assignment of meaning and value.

Drawing on William Labov's work and on Labov's idea of "natural narratives" as examples of "aesthetically structured discourse which is not, by anyone's definition, literature,"[74] Pratt provides several examples of speech acts of this kind. For instance, the remark "Bill went to the bank today" might well fall into this category: "Suppose Bill is a miser, notoriously mistrustful of banks, and known to keep his money at home stuffed in an old sock. In this case, the information that Bill actually went to the bank today is downright spectacular and can be volunteered for that reason alone. It is news. It can be displayed."[75] But acts of verbal displaying do not have to be news, and need not be particularly spectacular. They do not even have to be true; anecdotes, apocryphal tales, and jokes, are all acts of verbal displaying in which it is entirely appropriate for the question of fictivity to remain undecided. What they have in common is that they disclose a perspective, implicitly claiming validity not just for this perspective but for the way in which it is disclosed. Most good jokes are good not just because of the interpretation of the world they offer but also because of *the way in which they are told.* Furthermore, because what is offered is an interpretation of some aspect of human experience, it is clear that the hearer will have to relate it to his own experience as part of the process of evaluating the success of the joke.

Charles Taylor also draws attention to ways in which everyday language functions to articulate and disclose.[76] One way it does this is by means of acts of *formulating.* Taylor remarks on the fact that often the very act of formulating something brings about an awareness of something of which the speaker had been only vaguely or implicitly aware. Of course, it can also have a similar effect on the hearer(s). When I am formulating something, it often happens that I bring something to better and fuller consciousness. In saying something, I can surprise my hearer but I can also surprise myself. Thus, formulating is an important dimension of everyday language activity. In this dimension language often functions to open up reality: It leads to my seeing something that I had not seen up to now, or to my seeing something in a new way. It can also, of course, have this effect on others. In such instances, therefore, acts of formulating fall into the category of speech acts that function to disclose (in the sense of opening up a perspective on reality).

Martin Seel's explication of the meaning of (nonliterary) metaphorical utterances lends further support to the thesis that everyday language also functions to articulate and disclose reality.[77] Moreover, his account suggests that these modes of language use can be conceptualized in terms of validity claims. Seel's analysis is motivated by the question of the meaning of nonliterary metaphorical utterences. His answer is that metaphorical utterances of this kind function—in a special way—to articulate, and raise a claim for, the appropriateness of the perspective they open on the subject matter at hand; as the idea of "opening a perspective" suggests, a metaphorical utterance does not thematize the object of speech *directly* but rather gives voice to it as the background of which it speaks. To "agree with a metaphor" (i.e., to find it convincing or successful) is to accept as appropriate the understanding of a situation (perspective) that it articulates, in the way in which it articulates it.

Pratt, Taylor, and Seel each draw attention to one particular way in which everyday language functions to disclose and articulate (in the sense of opening up a perspective on some aspect of a situation or on some aspect of reality). Pratt focuses on acts of verbal displaying, Taylor on acts of formulating, and Seel on the metaphorical use of everyday language. Moreover, although none of the three is specifically concerned with meaning and validity, their analyses suggest that "tellable utterances," acts of formulating, and everyday metaphorical utterances can be described in connection with validity claims; that these acts and utterances do not so much raise a claim as disclose a perspective; and that this perspective must be experienced before it can be evaluated.[78]

According to Habermas's theory of validity claims as it stands, utterances that disclose a perspective on experience, while raising claims both for the validity of the perspective and for the way they disclose it, would have to be excluded from the class of communicative actions for at least two reasons.[79]

First, these utterances do not fit into any of the three categories of speech act as Habermas defines them. They are clearly not claims to empirical or theoretical truth, they are certainly not always claims to normative rightness, and it is difficult to see how they could qualify for inclusion in the class of claims to truthfulness.[80] I have already drawn attention to Habermas's ambivalence concerning the status of aesthetic utterances; even if we were to include claims raised with articulating and disclosing modes of language use within the general category of aesthetic claims, it would not help us very much, for these too are denied a connection with action oriented toward understanding. However, the expansion of Habermas's notion of a constative speech that I proposed above is useful here. I proposed that we include all utterances that raise a claim to the validity of *what is said* in the broad category of constative utterances. Correspondingly, this becomes an umbrella category. Within it we can identify many different types of validity claim, to be distinguished on the basis of the mode of validation appropriate in each case. Even within one subgroup of the class of constative utterances (for example, normative validity claims), we can distinguish many different kinds of claim, requiring correspondingly different modes of validation. If the validation of truth claims in this broader sense can take many different forms, the point that experience plays a distinctive role in the validation of aesthetic claims or of claims to the validity of a perspective cannot constitute a serious objection to their inclusion within the broad class of constative utterances.

Second, claims to the validity of a perspective are not communicative *actions* as defined by Habermas. I have suggested that Habermas's conception of (communicative) action is overly narrow to the extent that it is defined as coping with situations in the sense of overcoming obstacles and solving problems. But it is not clear that anything crucial to his program of formal pragmatics, or indeed to his project of a theory of communicative action, depends on the retention of a conception of action defined in this way. If we replace it with a broader conception of action, such as that suggested by Thompson,[81] there are no longer any conceptual reasons why acts of disclosing and articulating should not be regarded as actions.

The discussion so far has cast some doubt on Habermas's attempt to distinguish within everyday communicative action precisely three types of validity claim and to correlate these with precisely three classes of speech act. One reason why Habermas may be anxious to correlate propositional truth claims with constative speech acts, normative validity claims with regulative speech acts, and claims to subjective truthfulness with expressive speech acts is in order to show that everyday language makes reference to three distinct types of validity claim corresponding to the three dimensions of validity opened up with the decentering of the modern consciousness. But from this chapter it is apparent that everyday language use cannot be divided up quite so neatly. Nonetheless, if we bear in mind that one of the main aims of Habermas's formal pragmatic investigations is to redress the logocentric balance of traditional philosophy by showing that rational action and rational practices of justification are possible in more than just one dimension of human experience, nothing so far has undermined this endeavor. The suggestion that everyday language use makes reference to not three but *many* different kinds of validity claim simply means that his proposed three-dimensional notion of reason will have to be understood in a more multi-dimensional way.

Habermas's conception of communicative rationality can only profit from this.

7

Up to now I have concentrated on Habermas's attempt to distinguish three categories of speech act, each in terms of a particular validity claim. Although I have mentioned his thesis that the speaker, with every speech act, raises three claims simultaneously, Habermas's argument for this has not yet received sufficient attention. It is time to look at it more closely.

Habermas argues that *every* communicative utterance *simultaneously* raises a claim to truth, a claim to normative rightness, and a claim to truthfulness.[82] As we have seen, he accompanies this with the qualification that every speech act raises one validity claim *in the first instance,* or "directly," and two others *in a secondary way,* or "indirectly." Habermas also expresses this as the thesis that every speech act can be contested (that is, rejected as invalid) from three distinct points of view.[83] Although these are presented as merely two different ways of formulating the same thesis, the two claims are not equivalent. That is, it is possible to accept that every speech act can be contested from precisely three points of view while rejecting the stronger thesis that every speech act simultaneously raises three validity claims. Habermas's "stronger" argument must be seen in the broader context of his theory of communicative action. It can be reconstructed as the claim that the *illocutionary success* of the speech act depends on the reaching of agreement (*Einverständnis*) with regard to all three validity claims.[84]

Habermas's position here seems to be as follows: In order for successful communication to take place, we must either presuppose the validity of the one direct and two indirect claims raised or else challenge the offending claims. The speaker's implicit warranty (*Gewähr*) that she will, if challenged, redeem the claim presumably applies to all three claims raised. Thus, if a speaker claims that it is raining, and the hearer can clearly see that it is raining, moreover judges the speaker to be truthful, but happens to find the remark "inappropriate" (perhaps they are both at a Quaker prayer meeting), then the speech act will be unsuccessful on Habermas's terms. In the model case, the hearer will give voice to reservations and the speaker will provide reasons for why she believed the speech act to be normatively in order (that is, the speaker and the hearer will engage in argumentation, of however rudimentary a form). Depending on whether or not the hearer finds the speaker's reasons ultimately convincing, the communicative exchange will be successful or unsuccessful. The illocutionary act remains unsuccessful so long as the hearer is unconvinced by any one of the three claims raised by the utterance.

With every speech act, the speaker raises one direct and two indirect validity claims simultaneously. With a constative speech act the speaker raises a direct claim to truth and indirect claims to normative rightness and truthfulness. If a speaker says "it is raining outside," she (on Habermas's definition) clearly raises a truth claim; at the same time, however, she indirectly raises a claim to the normative rightness of the speech action (that it is "appropriate in the given context") and also a claim that she is truthful in saying that it is raining.

Similarly, with a regulative speech act the speaker raises a direct claim to normative rightness and indirect claims to truth and truthfulness. Since it is difficult to see how many regulative or expressive speech acts raise indirect truth claims, Habermas suggests a modification: The indirect claim to truth may also be regarded as a claim to the validity of certain existential presuppositions.[85] Thus, for example, if a professor in a classroom says to a student "Please fetch me a glass of water," Habermas sees this as a regulative speech act that, as such, raises a direct claim to normative rightness.[86] The student might contest the professor's *right* to make this request (i.e., may contest the (direct) claim to normative rightness); but the student might also challenge the truth of the existential presuppositions (e.g., by arguing that the nearest water tap is too far away) or the speaker's sincerity (e.g., by arguing that the professor's main concern is not to quench his thirst but to humiliate the student).[87]

With an expressive speech act the speaker raises a direct claim that she is truthful and indirect claims to truth and normative rightness. An utterance such as "I am afraid" is an expressive speech act according to Habermas's classificatory procedure. It thus raises a direct claim to the truthfulness of the speaker and two indirect claims. The indirect claim to normative rightness is the implicit claim that this utterance is appropriate in the context in question. (It might be inappropriate if uttered by the Queen of England during her Christmas speech—although, of course, it is always possible to question the grounds on which such judgements of "appropriateness" are made.) Once again, the sense of an indirect claim to truth is better captured by the idea that certain existential presuppositions have to be satisfied. The success of the speech act "I am afraid" depends on the existential presupposition that the speaker is a person who is capable of experiencing fear.[88]

The notion of an indirect claim to truthfulness may be misleading to the extent that it seems to imply that we must mean what we say. But there are a number of senses in which we can mean what we say, and only *one* of these is relevant to illocutionary success. The illocutionary success of a speech act depends on the speaker's meaning what she says only in the sense that she must not be acting strategically; the speaker's motivation must be a genuinely communicative one in that she must be genuinely oriented toward reaching understanding. In many cases the genuineness of the speaker's communicative offer will coincide with the speaker's truthfulness; however, a speaker can, without contradiction, have a genuinely communicative intention and not tell the truth; jokes are a good example of this, but it also holds for many kinds of acts of "verbal displaying." As Pratt points out, we usually *expect* elaboration, embellishment, and exaggeration in such cases. At the same time, this does not mean that we suspend the requirement that the speaker should have a genuinely communicative motivation in the case of acts of verbal displaying; the illocutionary success of a joke or anecdote is certainly impaired if the hearer believes that the speaker is telling it primarily in order to ridicule or embarrass him.

Furthermore, the indirect claim to truthfulness might be more convincingly characterized as an *idealizing supposition* of communicative action.[89] In actual cases of everyday language use, an unambiguous orientation toward reaching understanding is more the exception than the rule. Habermas recognizes this; he points out that the claim to truthfulness can be redeemed "more or less" and that how much truthfulness is required depends on the context.[90] Moreover, not only is it often difficult to determine whether the motives of others are completely straightforward; at times even I myself may be unable to decide whether my communicative offer is genuinely oriented toward understanding or whether I also have some ulterior (strategic) motive. The point of the idea of an indirect claim to truthfulness seems to be this: As participants in everyday communicative action, we must, if we are to coherently describe ourselves as such, presuppose that we and the people we are dealing with are genuinely oriented toward understanding. This presupposition must be *sufficiently* satisfied in every specific instance if communication is to be successful—but what counts as sufficient will vary from case to case.

The suggested universality of the claim to normative rightness has been criticized most vehemently. Not only has it been denounced as clearly implausible[91]; it has been seen by some as an insidious attempt to anchor the moral "ought" so deeply in universal linguistic structures that the question of its possible rational meaning would become redundant.[92] It seems to me, however, that Habermas's thesis is surprisingly convincing. I think it can be shown that the claim to normative rightness is a universal maxim of successful communication, and furthermore that this claim has a weak moral sense. The moral "ought" does in fact appear to be rooted in the structures of human communication. Since morality is concerned with relationships between persons that are based on recognition as opposed to manipulation, and since relationships of this kind are characteristic of communicative action, this conclusion should be no cause for surprise. However, the question of the *implications* of such a conclusion remains open.

The thesis of the universality of the claim to normative rightness requires that one of the conditions of successful communication be that the utterance in question is accepted by the hearer as appropriate or right in the particular context. That is, the hearer must ultimately accept the speaker's right to say what she says in the particular situation. This is not the same as requiring that the hearer accept the *relevance* of the speaker's utterance. The rules of relevance are *internal* to a particular kind of discourse—more accurately, to a specific kind of discourse situation. What counts as relevant and what as irrelevant is governed both by conventions internal to the kind of discourse in question and by the concerns of those participating in a given discourse situation. In general, the rules of relevance (though always flexible in principle) are fixed most rigidly in discourse situations in which the individuals involved are concerned with the exchange of information—although, of course, information can be exchanged in many different kinds of ways. One reason for the apparent plausibility of Grice's conversational maxim "Be Relevant!"[93] is that Grice defines conversation in terms of a maximally effective exchange of information. Were participants in conversation always concerned with the effective exchange of information, the need to be relevant would certainly be more important. However, conversation is in fact usually not concerned with this—conversations seldom have *any* well-defined goals. It is precisely because the concerns of the participants in a conversation are usually ill-defined or nonspecific that a contribution to a conversation can rarely be dismissed as "irrelevant."

There are no concrete rules of relevance prior to an actual discourse situation, although we can conceive of types of discourse in which the concerns of the participants are such that what counts as relevant will be narrowly and rigidly defined. Even in contexts of this type, however, the rules of relevance are never hard and fast. An utterance is always only relevant or irrelevant within a given discourse situation; relevance is not an attribute of the utterance itself. To this extent, Pratt's formulation is misleading when she claims that "tellable utterances" are usually relevant simply because they are tellable.[94] But utterances are never *in themselves* relevant or irrelevant. Pratt's real point presumably is that anecdotes or jokes appear to be exempt from the rules of relevance and are tolerated in even the most inflexible discourse situations. But even this way of putting things may be misleading. Though it is correct to say that a joke or an anecdote cannot easily be dismissed as irrelevant, the act of telling a joke or relating an anecdote is not always tolerated; the ground on which it can be criticized, however, is not irrelevance but inappropriateness. This brings us back to Habermas's idea of an indirect claim to normative rightness.

We can contrast relevance with the idea of appropriateness connected with Habermas's notion of a claim to normative rightness. The idea of appropriateness at issue here must be understood in terms of the speaker's attempt to establish an interpersonal relationship with the hearer(s) by means of a speech act. The speaker (in a sense) claims the right (entitlement) to establish the interpersonal relationship in question. The hearer who challenges the appropriateness of an utterance calls this right into question. The speaker's right can be challenged on many grounds. An utterance may be inappropriate because the normative presuppositions (such as the presupposition of authority) have not been fulfilled. A hearer might challenge a fellow airline passenger's request to stop smoking on the ground that only the stewardess has the authority to stop him. Or I might refuse a beggar's request for money on the ground that I disapprove of begging, or on the ground that it is forbidden by the prevailing laws. But there are other ways in which an utterance can be inappropriate. Habermas tells us that a disclosure can be offensive, a report can be out of place, and a confession can be awkward.[95] I might continue: A piece of information can be a breach of confidence, a joke can be in bad taste, sarcasm can be destructive, and a question may be inopportune. It seems that what is common to the charge of inappropriateness in all these cases is the feeling of damaged intersubjectivity. A speaker who is irrelevant violates the rules internal to a certain discourse situation (as determined by the concerns of those participating), and a speaker who is inappropriate damages or impairs her relationship with the hearer(s). To this extent, whereas irrelevance is a mistake, inappropriateness is a moral transgression.[96] The moral weight we attach to the charge of inappropriateness will, of course, vary with the circumstances, but nonetheless the charge of inappropriateness always has a (more or less weak) moral sense. Furthermore, although there are contexts in which it makes no sense to speak of irrelevance and in which any kind of utterance must count as relevant (for example, certain kinds of meandering conversations), there are no contexts in which it is meaningless to speak of inappropriateness. The objection to a risqué joke in the middle of a funeral service is not that it is irrelevant but that it is inappropriate. Since every utterance can be seen as an attempt by a speaker to establish an interpersonal relationship with a hearer or hearers, and since the claim to normative rightness refers to the rightness of this attempt, every utterance can be challenged from this point of view. Every utterance is potentially inappropriate. Habermas's claim is that only speech acts that are regarded as appropriate by the hearer are successful. If what I say is true, and if it is clear that I am sincere in saying it but it is seen as being out of place in the context in question, then the achievement of understanding (*Verständigung*) with my hearer(s) will be at worst impossible and at best flawed.

From the foregoing it would appear than Habermas's claim that with every speech act a speaker raises three validity claims simultaneously has some plausibility—at least if we do not take the idea of "raising a claim" too literally. For, rather than saying that the speaker *raises* three validity claims simultaneously, it would seem more accurate to say that the success of each speech act depends on a number of presuppositions, of which we can distinguish three distinct kinds.[97] In view of the fact that it is somewhat misleading,[98] it is worth considering why Habermas is so insistent that the speaker raises three *claims*. On the basis of the discussion so far it is possible to identify at least three (interconnected) reasons for this insistence: Habermas argues for this point in order

• to show that communicative action is a mechanism of social (lifeworld) integration and reproduction in the domains of cultural reproduction, social integration, and socialization,

• to reinforce the idea of a multi-dimensional (nonlogocentric) conception of reason, and

• to provide a basis for the idea of the formal unity of reason as the interpenetration of dimensions of validity.

What is not clear, however, is whether anything of crucial importance to any of these concerns depends on the formulation that the speaker *raises three claims*. The first purpose will have been adequately served if Habermas can demonstrate that every speech act fulfils three functions: the thematization of a propositional content, the entering into a mutually binding and bonding relationship with others, and the expression of the speaker's subjectivity.[99] The second and the third will have been given support if Habermas can show that the speaker, with every speech act, simultaneously makes reference to three dimensions of validity in which rational reflection is possible.

The discussion in this chapter has lent support to the thesis that every speech act has three components. Accordingly, to the extent that every speech act has a propositional, an illocutionary, and an expressive component, it fulfils three functions simultaneously: It thematizes a given propositional content, it establishes a mutually binding and bonding relationship with the hearer, and it expresses the speaker's subjectivity. Of course, as we have seen, speech acts usually specialize in just one of these functions; regulative speech acts specialize in establishing a mutually binding and bonding intersubjective relationship, speech acts that raise expressive validity claims specialize in expressing the speaker's subjectivity, and the many kinds of validity claim that are raised with constative speech acts specialize in thematizing a given propositional content. Since speech acts in everyday communicative practice appear to fulfil these three functions, Habermas appears to have some basis for his thesis that communicative action fulfils functions of cultural reproduction, social integration, and socialization.

The thesis that the speaker, with every speech act, raises three validity claims simultaneously also has implications for the notion of a postmetaphysical conception of reason as, on the one hand, split up into various nonhierarchical dimensions and, on the other hand, based on a formal unity. At the same time, nothing depends on the demonstration that the speaker raises precisely three claims or on the formulation that the speaker "raises (a number of) claims" simultaneously. With regard to the former, it is sufficient to show that speakers in everyday communicative action raise various kinds of validity claim, all of which are susceptible to rational evaluation in argumentation; with regard to the latter, it is sufficient to show that it is a presupposition of successful participation in everyday communicative action that the speaker has learned to adopt a reflective self-relation in three dimensions.

Habermas uses the idea of "transitions between worlds" in connection with his tentative proposal of a formal notion of the unity of reason as part of his attempt to work out a postmetaphysical conception of reason.[100] In the second volume of *The Theory of Communicative Action*, Habermas provides an interesting note on how a child learns what it means to raise a criticizable validity claim.[101] He tells us that the child learns to conduct an inner monologue in which he preempts the hearer's objections by querying the validity of his utterance on three levels of validity. We can characterize this as the ability to take up three different kinds of relation to the world[102] or as the ability to adopt a reflective self-relation that has three aspects. The growing child learns to take up a relation to the world of facts, states of affairs, and disputable propositions, to the social world of normatively regulated intersubjective relationships, and to the inner world of subjective nature. In learning to conceive of himself as a self, he learns to take up a relation to himself as the accountable author of contestable validity claims, as the accountable author of his own actions, and as an individuated affective subject and responsible subject of his life history. This implies that the child, in learning what it is to raise a criticizable validity claim, learns how to consider the validity of a speech act under three mutually irreducible aspects simultaneously. This ability to switch perspectives from one dimension of validity to another (to "move between worlds") is thus part of what Habermas calls "the performative attitude" necessarily adopted by participants in communicative action.[103] Accordingly, the thesis that with every speech act the speaker raises three validity claims simultaneously amounts to the thesis that the capacity to "move between worlds" is built into everyday communicative action. Habermas sees this as the formal-pragmatic underpinning of the idea of the formal unity of reason.

As we saw in chapter 2, Habermas argues that the differentiation of reason into three separate moments—identified by Max Weber, among others, as one of the defining characteristics of the modern age—is irreversible; at the same time, he believes that the separated moments of reason must once again communicate with one another: The productive insights gained in one dimension must be brought into play in discussions in the other two dimensions, while the distinctive logic of each validity dimension must be respected. The differentiation of the three validity dimensions is most developed on the level of specialized and formalized argumentation, in the spheres of science, law and morality, and aesthetic discourse, respectively. Consequently, the need for a productive interpentration of the spheres is most urgent here. The problem, as we have seen, is one of justification. No metadiscourse is available that might show that participants in argumentation in one sphere of validity *ought* to bring to bear arguments from other spheres, or *when* they should do so, or *which* point of view is desirable in the given context.[104]

Habermas tells us that the kind of judgement that is required here[105] is "linked with the performative attitude of the participant in communicative action and is thus anchored in practices that are prior to argumentation."[106] This makes sense if we recall that the performative attitude adopted by participants in everyday communicative action refers (in part) to the ability to consider every utterance under three aspects of validity simultaneously. Analysis of everyday communicative action thus suggests that the ability to switch perspectives (to move from one validity dimension to another) is a presupposition of competent participation in such action. This should not be misinterpreted as some kind of justification for the normative requirement that participants in specialized and formalized argumentation should draw on arguments from the various validity spheres. The kind of judgement that is required by participants in such forms of argumentation (in order to give substance to the notion of the formal unity of reason) relies on this kind of ability but it goes beyond it. The ability to move between validity dimensions does not imply possession of the kind of judgement necessary here. Nonetheless, the latter presupposes the former. To this extent, Habermas's thesis that with every speech act the speaker raises three validity claims simultaneously is a useful first step in the explication of a formally conceived idea of the unity of reason.[107] We should also note here that what is at issue is the speaker's ability to consider the validity of an utterance under three distinct aspects. Nothing crucial to Habermas's project seems to turn on the characterization of this as the ability to raise three claims simultaneously.

The thesis that with every speech act the speaker raises three validity claims simultaneously thus plays a role in Habermas's attempt to work out a distinctively modern idea of the unity of reason, although nothing crucial to this depends on the terminology of "raising a claim." However, Habermas appears to have a further reason for asserting this thesis; he hints at this further reason by referring to his thesis as that of the universality of the three validity claims.[108] Here, his choice of the language of validity *claims* seems more important.

Through showing that the claims to truth, normative rightness, and truthfulness are universal, in the sense of *present in* (connected with) every speech act, Habermas believes, it is possible to distinguish three universal and categorially distinct validity claims, corresponding to three dimensions of rationality. This conclusion appears to be important to his attempt to redress the logocentric bias of traditional conceptions of reason, and it relies on two arguments. The first is the thesis that the communicative mode of language use can be further divided up into precisely three illocutionary modes (or classes of speech act), each of which is distinguished by its characteristic connection with one of three possible validity claims; these claims thereby receive a special status. (We looked at his attempt to show this in sections 1–6 of the present chapter.) This first argument is presumably reinforced by a second one: the thesis that with every speech act the speaker raises three validity claims simultaneously. The second argument reinforces the first to the extent that the three claims raised correspond exactly to those that define the three fundamental illocutionary modes.

The discussion in sections 1–6 of this chapter undermined the first part of Habermas's argument by casting doubt on his thesis that we can distinguish three categories of speech act, each of which "specializes" in just one of three supposedly fundamental validity claims. It seems that participants in everyday communicative action raise not just three but many different kinds of validity claim. However, I argued that this conclusion need not be a cause for concern, for it in no way undermines Habermas's endeavor to redress the logocentric bias of traditional conceptions of reason; indeed, it seems to point toward a genuinely multi-dimensional as opposed to merely three-dimensional conception of reason. If this is so, we can conclude that nothing depends on the formulation of Habermas's further thesis as the thesis that with every speech act the speaker raises three kinds of claim simultaneously. I have already suggested that the idea that the speaker *raises three claims* may be misleading and that it seems more accurate to say that every speech act makes reference to three aspects of validity, or that every speech act relies on three kinds of presupposition. In view of the fact that the idea of raising precisely three validity claims does not appear to play a crucial role in the broader context of Habermas's theory, there do not appear to be strong reasons for retaining this somewhat misleading terminology.

4

A Pragmatic Theory of Meaning: From Comprehension to Consensus

1

The thesis that speech acts, as the smallest unit of everyday communication, raise different types of intersubjectively criticizable validity claims plays an important part in Habermas's theory of communicative action and in his attempt to work out a conception of communicative rationality that depends on his theory.

In chapter 3 I looked at Habermas's argument that three distinct dimensions of validity are represented in the speech acts performed in everyday communicative action from the point of view of his account of social (lifeworld) reproduction and within the context of his attempt to put forward a postmetaphysical conception of reason. In the present chapter I consider Habermas's pragmatic theory of meaning, which revolves around the assertion that to understand an utterance is to understand the claim it raises. Although this theory is important in its own right as an account of meaning, its main function must be seen within the broader context of Habermas's project as a whole. Within this context, the theory represents an attempt to demonstrate an internal connection between everyday language use and argumentation; this is the point of Habermas's thesis that understanding is internally connected with reaching understanding (*Verständigung*). I will suggest that we should interpret this as the thesis that the very comprehension of a linguistic utterance is connected with the evaluation of reasons in argumentation (which is, by definition, oriented toward reaching agreement (*Einverständnis*), according to Habermas). In the following it is useful to bear in mind that Habermas's pragmatic theory of meaning is guided by this intention.

Habermas tells us that "we understand an utterance when we know what makes it acceptable."[1] He elaborates: "In distant analogy to the basic assumption of truth-conditional semantics, I now want to explain understanding an utterance as knowledge of the conditions under which a hearer may accept it."[2] Habermas has confirmed that his undertaking should be seen as a development of truth-conditional semantics,[3]—more precise, as a *generalization* of Michael Dummett's suggested explanation of the meaning of the assertoric sentences employed in constative speech acts (that is, as a conception expanded to include the sentences employed in other modes of language use).[4] The comparison with truth-conditional or assertibility-conditional semantics may be misleading, however. Habermas's *intersubjectivist*[5] or *formal-pragmatic* approach to meaning theory is better understood as an attempt to combine the insights of truth-conditional (and assertibility-conditional) semantics and use-oriented theories of meaning in a productive and nonproblematic way.

Habermas argues that neither semantic nor use-oriented approaches to the problem of meaning are adequate as they stand. As we shall see, he claims that semantic approaches are guilty of various "abstractions," while use-oriented theories lose sight of the connection between meaning and a sense of validity that goes beyond the conventional validity of a given form of life. Although Habermas comes down clearly in favor of a pragmatic approach to meaning, he wishes to hold on to the connection between meaning and "truth" (in the sense of a context-transcendent concept of validity) that he discerns at the heart of semantic theories. It is this connection that Habermas has in mind when he speaks of the inherent rationality of the linguistic medium, and it is this connection that I believe explains why he formulates his pragmatic or intersubjectivist theory of meaning "in distant analogy" to the idea that we understand a sentence when we know its truth conditions. It will be helpful to bear in mind that this is the insight of truth-conditional semantics that Habermas wants to integrate within his pragmatic account of meaning.

Habermas wants to overcome the limitations of use-oriented theories of meaning by showing that understanding is connected with reaching understanding through the evaluation of validity claims in argumentation. To this extent, my discussion of his account of meaning will also throw light on his frequently repeated assertion that "*Verständigung* is the inherent telos of human speech."[6] The assertion of a link between understanding and the evaluation of validity claims in argumentation within the context of a pragmatic account of meaning makes good what Habermas believes to be the main weakness besetting existing pragmatic theories: their reduction of validity to the conventional validity of a given form of life. However, the assertion that understanding is connected with intersubjective processes of evaluation not only adds a new dimension to pragmatic accounts of meaning; it also reveals the inherently pragmatic dimensions of understanding. As we shall see, Habermas argues that the "validation conditions" which a speaker has to be able to reconstruct in order to understand an utterance are tied to pragmatic contexts of interpretation and discussion. Habermas's assertion that understanding is inextricably bound with *Verständigung* may thus allow him to retain what he sees as the valid insight of truth-conditional semantics while radically undermining the very notion of a semantic theory of meaning.

I have suggested that Habermas's pragmatic account of meaning is best understood as an attempt to combine the insights of truth-conditional (and assertibility-conditional) semantics and use-oriented theories of meaning in a productive but nonproblematic way. More specifically, he wishes to develop a pragmatic account of meaning that avoids what he sees as the main weakness of pragmatic acccounts: the tendency to reduce validity to the conventional validity of given forms of life. He thus aims at developing a pragmatic account that holds on to an idea of validity that potentially transcends all accepted agreements in definitions and judgements. The idea that we understand an utterance when we know what makes it acceptable is intended as an attempt to make room for some notion of context-transcendent validity ("truth") within a pragmatic framework. The points of convergence and divergence between Habermas's pragmatic approach and traditional semantic approaches are instructive, so I start by taking a closer look at Habermas's critique of the semantic approach to meaning.

Habermas argues that traditional semantic approaches to meaning (from Frege to Davidson) have been guilty of three "abstractions"[7]: a "semanticist" one, a "cognitivist" one, and an "objectivist" one. The semanticist abstraction is the belief that the analysis of linguistic meaning can confine itself to the analysis of *sentences,* abstracting from the pragmatic rules that affect the use of sentences. The cognitivist abstraction is the belief that all meaning can be led back to the propositional content of utterances, thus indirectly reducing meaning to the meaning of *assertoric* sentences. The objectivist abstraction has to do with the semanticist conception that truth conditions are what make a sentence true, abstracting from the *knowledge* of truth conditions that can be be ascribed to a hearer or to a speaker. These three abstractions, taken together, considerably restrict the scope of semantic theories. As Habermas points out, Davidson himself lists the categories of sentences that cannot be explained by means of his theory.[8] What is needed, in Habermas's opinion, is a theory of meaning that overcomes all three limitations while holding on to the idea of an internal connection between meaning and validity in a context-transcendent sense. Although use-oriented theories of meaning draw attention to utterances as the smallest unit of communication (thus overcoming the semanticist abstraction), and although they overcome the cognitivist abstraction to the extent that they draw attention to the multiplicity of meaningful modes of language use, they do not so much overcome the third abstraction as dispense with the idea of validation conditions completely. Use-oriented theories of meaning have been responsible for drawing attention to the entire spectrum of linguistic activity. They have emphasized that language functions not only to assert and describe but also, in equal measure and equally importantly, to command, request, promise, advise, tell jokes, wish, confess, disclose, and so on. Moreover, they have insisted, correctly, that meaning is always relative to the institutions and conventions of a social practice—to the "agreement in definitions and judgements" of a prevailing "form of life."[9] However, in doing so, they have tended to dispense with the idea of an internal connection between meaning and a sense of validity that cannot be reduced to that of any given context. And, as I have already said, this is the connection that Habermas sets out to retain.

Habermas seems to regard the need to overcome the "cognitivist abstraction," understood as the prioritizing of the assertoric function, as intuitively evident. He points out that, as participants in communication, we know that we use language to fulfil various kinds of very different functions, and that it is not intuitively clear why one should accord priority to the assertoric aspect. As far as the cognitivist abstraction goes, the burden of proof is on the "cognitivist," who has to convince us that our intuitions are mistaken.[10]

The necessity of overcoming the objectivist abstraction is also regarded as evident by Habermas. He argues that the need to replace a conception of meaning in terms of truth conditions with one in terms of *knowing* the conditions under which a speaker is entitled to assert it as true is obvious if we aspire to explain the meaning of a wide range of sentences and if we recognize that in a large class of cases the truth conditions are not available. Michael Dummett is praised for having recognized this.[11] The traditional belief of theories of meaning that truth conditions can be specified semantically rests on the unrealistic assumption that for every sentence, or at least for every assertoric sentence, procedures are available for effectively deciding when the truth conditions are satisfied. As Habermas puts it, "this assumption rests implicitly on an empiricist theory of knowledge that takes the simple predicative sentences of an observor language to be basic."[12]

From within the semanticist tradition, Dummett has seen this most clearly. He suggests replacing the idea that the meaning of a sentence can be specified in terms of its truth conditions with an orientation toward the question of what it is for a speaker or a hearer to *know* the conditions under which the truth conditions would be satisifed. Habermas refers to this as the "epistemic turn" in truth-conditional semantics. However, although Habermas applauds Dummett for making a move in the right direction, he feels that he does not turn far enough, for not only does Dummett continue to fall prey to the "semanticist" and "cognitivist" abstractions; he also fails to fully overcome the "objectivist" abstraction. As I see it, Habermas's critique of Dummett is twofold. On the one hand, he criticizes Dummett's fixation on assertoric truth; on the other, he criticizes his "monological" interpretation of the "conditions of justification" that a speaker has to know in order to understand an utterance.[13] Accordingly, although Habermas's idea of acceptability conditions can be seen as analogous to Dummett's idea of assertibility conditions, it represents a modification of Dummett's conception on two important counts.

First, the notion of "acceptability" rather than "assertibility" is an attempt to make room within a semantic framework for the dimensions of subjective truthfulness and normative rightness. For Habermas, not only constative speech acts but also regulative and expressive ones must be understood in terms of their validation conditions. This modification helps to overcome the "cognitivist" abstraction.

Second, the notion of "acceptability" replaces "assertibility" in order to combat the idea that the conditions of justification of (even assertoric) sentences can be known or "recognized" as true independently of discussion with others. Habermas insists that the conditions of validation cannot be produced according to a procedure that can be applied monologically, but only through a procedure of discursive justification.[14] The crucial twist that Habermas gives to the notion of knowing the conditions of justification (Dummett) is that these conditions have to be understood in a dialogical and fallibilistic way.[15] This step takes us beyond the "objectivist" abstraction and also beyond the "semanticist" abstraction to the extent that it compels us to recognize that understanding is inescapably tied to pragmatic contexts of intersubjective evaluation. If successful, Habermas's dialogical-fallibilistic interpretation of what it is to know the conditions of justification itself amounts to a change in the level of analysis; it forces us to move from a semantic level to a pragmatic one.[16]

The idea that we understand an utterance when we know what makes it acceptable, by taking account of nonassertoric modes of communication and by its dialogical-fallibilistic interpretation of the conditions of justification, sets out to overcome the three "abstractions" of traditional semantic approaches to meaning while holding on to a sense of validity that potentially transcends all spatio-temporal contexts. Since I have already dealt with the first count on which Habermas wants to modify Dummett's idea of "assertibility-conditions" (in chapter 3), I shall now turn to a closer examination of the second count. This will require a detailed discussion of the notion of "acceptablity conditions."

2

The notion of "acceptability conditions" is central to Habermas's pragmatic account of meaning, but it is not immediately clear from Habermas's writings how exactly we are to interpret it. Thus, for example, although in *The Theory of Communicative Action* Habermas introduces his thesis that "we understand an utterance when we know what makes it acceptable" as a modification of the basic assumption of truth-conditional semantics,[17] the situation is complicated by the fact that he proceeds to refer to acceptability conditions in "the narrower sense,"[18] thus implying a distinction between a broader and a narrower sense of acceptability conditions without at any stage giving us a clear idea of what the former would look like.

If we, like Habermas, focus on the notion of acceptability conditions "in the narrower sense," we learn that, in this sense, the idea of acceptability conditions refers to "those *essential conditions* under which . . . (a hearer) . . . could be motivated by a speaker to take an affirmative position."[19] More precisely, we are told that these "essential conditions" refer to the "illocutionary role which S, in the standard case, expresses with the help of a performative clause."[20] A speaker can *rationally motivate* a hearer to accept a speech act offer because she—on the basis of an internal connection between the *validity* of an action (or of the norm underlying it), the *claim* that the conditions for its validity are satisfied, and the *redemption* of the validity claim—issues a warranty to produce, if challenged, convincing reasons that resist the hearer's criticism of the validity claim.[21] The essential conditions which a hearer has to know in order to understand an utterance thus appear to be the conditions that would make it valid, where validity is a *claim* and is tied to the speaker's undertaking the responsibility to provide convincing reasons.

These acceptability conditions break down further into two components, most clearly distinguishable in the case of regulative speech acts such as requests or promises. To know what makes an utterance acceptable is to know (a) its conditions of satisfaction (its *Erfüllungsbedingungen*) and (b) its conditions of validation (its *Gültigkeitsbedingungen*).

Habermas tells us that a hearer, in order to understand a request such as "you are requested to stop smoking," has to know (a) the conditions under which an address could bring about the desired state (not smoking) and (b) the conditions under which a speaker could have convincing reasons for regarding a request with that particular content as valid (in the sense of normatively justified).[22]

In the case of regulative speech acts, the conditions of satisfaction (a) refer to obligations to act in a certain way which, as we have seen, result from the act of promising or requesting itself. These, as we know, may be incumbent on either the speaker or the hearer or on both, either symmetrically or asymmetrically.[23] Thus, as part of what it is to understand a promise such as "I shall call on you tomorrow," the hearer has to know that the speaker has committed herself to calling on the hearer tomorrow and that his acceptance of the promise commits him to being at home.[24] Equally, as part of what it is to understand a request such as "please stop smoking," the hearer has to know that acceptance of the request commits him to not smoking.

The conditions of validation (b) refer to the validity claim raised for the normative rightness of the act in question. Thus, to understand a promise "I shall call on you tomorrow" the hearer also has to know the kind of reasons that the speaker could produce to support her entitlement or competency to make that promise if the normative grounds on which her promise rests were to be challenged.[25] Similarly, to understand the request "Please stop smoking" the hearer also has to know the kind of reasons the speaker could produce in support of her entitlement to make that request.

The distinction between conditions of satisfaction and conditions of validation is not quite so clear-cut in the case of constative and expressive utterances. Habermas tells us that in order to understand a prediction such as "I can predict to you that the vacation will be spoiled by rain" the hearer has to know (a) the conditions that would make the prediction true and (b) the conditions under which S could have convincing reasons for holding a statement with the content in question to be true.[26] In order to understand a disclosure such as "I confess to you that I find your actions loathsome," the hearer has to know (a) the conditions under which a person could experience loathing for the person addressed and (b) the conditions under which S says what he means and thereby accepts responsibility for the consistency of his further behavior with this confession.[27]

Habermas distinguishes between validity-related obligations and obligations for the continuation of the interaction.[28] All speech acts give rise to validity-related obligations to the extent that every speech act gives rise to an obligation for the speaker to support the validity claim raised with the relevant kind of reasons, if necessary, and to an obligation for the hearer to accept the validity of the claim unless he can provide good reasons for rejecting it. To know what it would mean to fulfil these obligations is to know the "validation conditions." As we shall see, to know the validation conditions is to know the kind of reasons that a speaker could provide in support of the claim raised with a given utterance.

Whereas all speech acts give rise to validity-related obligations, only regulative speech acts give rise to a (moral) obligation to act in a certain way.[29] Since the obligations for the continuation of the interaction are part of the meaning of regulative speech acts, understanding the meaning of such speech acts requires knowledge of what it would mean to fulfil these obligations—that is, knowledge of the "satisfaction conditions." However, as we have seen, neither constative nor expressive speech acts give rise to the same kind of obligation to act in a certain way.[30] For this reason, knowledge of what it would mean to fulfil these obligations is not part of what it is to understand such speech acts. What then might the "conditions of satisfaction" be?

The examples given by Habermas are not very useful; in each case, the knowledge required is either presupposed by knowledge of the validation conditions or indistinguishable from it. Habermas tells us that to know the satisfaction conditions of constative and expressive utterances is to "understand the propositional content."[31] But how are we to make sense of this as a kind of knowledge distinct from knowing the validation conditions? We have seen that Habermas applauds Dummett for replacing the idea of truth conditions with that of assertibility conditions on the ground that knowledge of the truth conditions is readily available for only a small class of assertoric utterances (such as simple empirical utterances, of which the prediction "The vacation will be spoiled by rain" is an example). Indeed, one of the reasons that Habermas appeared to regard a conception of understanding as "knowing the satisfaction conditions" as problematic was that satisfaction (truth) conditions are available for only a small class of assertoric utterances. In view of this, it is very difficult to make sense of his assertion that knowledge of *both* satisfaction conditions and validation conditions is necessary in the cases of constative and expressive utterances. To be sure, for simple predictions such as "The vacation will be spoiled by rain" it is possible to identify truth conditions that are distinct from the conditions under which the speaker would be entitled to claim validity for her assertion. However, in this instance (in contrast to what appeared to be the case for regulative speech acts), to know the assertibility conditions presupposes knowledge of the truth conditions. The reverse also holds: to know the truth conditions is to know the assertibility conditions—I would not know how to test the truth of the statement "It is raining outside" if I did not also know the kind of convincing reasons that a speaker could provide in support of such a claim. Moreover, and more importantly, simple predictions represent no more than a small subgroup within the wider category of assertions for which validity is claimed and for which truth conditions are often not available. It seems to me, therefore, that for constative and expressive utterances the only plausible way of interpreting Habermas's requirement that the hearer possess knowledge distinct from knowledge of the validation conditions is as the idea that the hearer must have a general knowledge of linguistic meanings before he can know the conditions of validation for a given utterance.[32] That is, in order to know the conditions under which the speaker could have convincing reasons for holding a statement with the content "Your vacation is going to be spoiled by rain" to be true, the hearer has to know what a vacation is, what rain is, what counts as raining, what it means for a vacation to be spoiled, and so forth. Similarly, in the case of an avowal such as "I find your actions loathsome" the hearer has to know the conditions of validation (i.e., the conditions under which the speaker could produce convincing reasons in support of her claim that she means what she says); before he can know these, however, he has to know what it means to experience loathing for someone.

The foregoing suggests that the notion of conditions of satisfaction, as a distinct component of the conditions of acceptability that a speaker has to know in order to understand an utterance, makes sense as a general rule only in the case of regulative speech acts. In contrast, in the case of constative and expressive speech acts—with a few exceptions[33]—to understand an utterance is simply to know its validation conditions. But what precisely is meant by "knowing the validation conditions"?

The discussion so far has led to the conclusion that a hearer, in order to understand a given (constative or expressive) utterance, has to know the conditions under which a speaker could have convincing reasons for holding that statement (prediction, assertion, disclosure) to be valid. How are we to understand Habermas's intuition here? When Habermas speaks of the "conditions of validation" of an utterance, or simply of its "acceptability conditions," he means "objective conditions of validation (*Gültigkeit*) which are not to be taken directly from the semantic content of the linguistic expression used, but only as mediated by the epistemic claim that the speaker, in the performance of his illocutionary act, raises for the validity (*Gültigkeit*) of his utterance."[34] He goes on to say that the validity claim raised with an utterance rests on "a potential of reasons" with which it can be redeemed, if necessary.[35] What are the implications of the fact that the validation conditions are not specified semantically but are, rather, to be taken from the epistemic *claim* that the speaker raises with her utterance, and what is involved in knowing a *potential* of reasons?

As we know, Habermas takes issue with (a) Dummett's focus on *assertoric* sentences, neglecting the regulative and expressive modes of language use and with (b) Dummett's *"monological"* interpretation of the assertibility conditions that the hearer must know in order to understand an utterance. With regard to the former, Habermas, as I have mentioned, *generalizes* the notion of assertibility conditions or conditions of justification to that of acceptability conditions or conditions of validation. With regard to the latter, Habermas attempts to take Dummett's "epistemic turn" even further by connecting these validation conditions with an intersubjective concept of justification through argumentation (*begründen*). It is the second of the proposed modifications that has to be clarified now. To what extent does Dummett's "epistemic turn" represent an advance over the "objectivism" of earlier semantic accounts of meaning, and why does Habermas think that he does not turn far enough? Habermas applauds Dummett for shifting the emphasis from "knowing the truth conditions" (of an assertoric sentence) to the speaker's *entitlement* to claim truth for what she says. He then draws out the implications of this move within semantic theories of meaning in two interdependent ways: He shows how this entitlement must be understood as a *claim* to entitlement, and he asserts a connection between entitlement and intersubjective assessment. With regard to the latter thesis, we can further distinguish two arguments in Habermas's writings: the argument that the validity of claims cannot be decided independently of discussion with others and the argument that no claims are, in principle, immune to critical evaluation in argumentation.

In order to understand an utterance, the hearer must be able to attribute to the speaker reasons with the aid of which the speaker could defend the claim if challenged. The hearer must be able to attribute to the speaker "a potential of reasons"—that is, the hearer has to know *the kind of reasons* the speaker could bring to bear in support of the claims raised. According to Habermas, we understand an (assertoric) sentence when we "know *the kind of reasons* a speaker would have to provide in order to convince a hearer that he is entitled to raise a truth claim for the sentence in question." [36]

There are at least two ways to interpret Habermas's emphasis on knowing the kind of reasons that a speaker might provide in support of her entitlement to claim truth for a given proposition. On the one hand, one could take this to mean that what counts as a good reason is itself determinable only in processes of argumentation. On the other hand, one could take it to mean that what counts as a good reason is never immune, in principle, to critical evaluation in argumentation. Both of these interpretations can be found in Habermas's writings, the first more clearly than the second. In the following I suggest that the first (and stronger) argument implies a position that is not tenable without qualification; I then show how the second argument can also be used to assert a connection between understanding and *Verständigung*, thereby drawing attention to the pragmatic dimensions of understanding.

The first interpretation makes more sense of Habermas's accusation that Dummett's approach is "monological" and is supported by passages such as the one in which Habermas, in connection with Dummett's "epistemic turn," points out that "a speaker might still produce such grounds [the reasons in support of her entitlement to raise a given truth claim —MC] according to a procedure that can be applied monologically; then even an explanation of truth conditions in terms of justifying a truth claim would not make it necessary to move from the semantic level of sentences to the pragmatic level of using sentences communicatively." [37] In this instance, Habermas is clearly referring to the *production* of reasons in support of an entitlement to raise a validity claim and suggesting that such reasons cannot be produced independently of discussion with others. In a more recent essay, Habermas tells us that we understand the meaning of the term "justify" (*begründen*) when we know what we must do to redeem discursively a contested validity claim. By "discursively" he means "in argumentation," "with the help of reasons."[38] He tells us that "we understand the expression "justify" (*begründen*) when we know the rules of the argumentation game within which validity claims can be redeemed discursively."[39] Here, too, Habermas appears to assert an internal connection between validity and agreement reached through critical evaluation in argumentation. The problem with this position is that it cannot be maintained for all validity claims; it appears to suggest an internal connection between validity and justification in argumentation that does not hold without qualification. Habermas himself now acknowledges that such a connection cannot be maintained for a significant category of truth claims; in the case of some kinds of truth claim, at least, there appears to be no internal connection between the validity of reasons that support the claim and agreement reached in argumentation.[40] On the other hand, there are a number of kinds of validity claim for which there does appear to be an internal connection between validity and agreement reached in discourse. Moral claims are one example, and an internal connection between truth and argumentation could possibly also be asserted for certain kinds of theoretical claims. Since Dummett's theory of meaning is not concerned with the multiple types of claim that, according to Habermas, characterize everyday linguistic practice, it is not surprising that his notion of assertibility conditions fails to take account of the (possible) internal connection between validity and argumentation in (for example) the case of moral validity claims. To this extent, if we interpret Habermas's objection to Dummett along these lines, we should recognize that his objection can be directed less against Dummett's theory of truth than against Dummett's focus on theoretical and empirical truth at the expense of other dimensions of validity.

In that Habermas cannot assert without qualification that validity is inherently dialogical, the second interpretation of his objection to Dummett's "monological" approach seems more promising.[41] Understood in this way, Habermas's position is that what counts as a good reason is always in principle subject to critical evaluation by others in dialogue. On this reading, his criticism of Dummett's "monological" approach to the question of assertibility conditions is that Dummett is not sufficiently fallibilist.

Although Dummett has given up the basic idea of verificationism in favor of a falsificationist theory of meaning, Habermas argues that "it would be more consistent to avoid both verificationism and falsificationism and to interpret the discursive redemption of validity claims fallibilistically.[42]" Dummett's "falsificationism" sees an assertion as "a kind of a gamble that the speaker will not be proved wrong"; Habermas argues that this conception relies on an inverted verificationism to the extent that the speaker's entitlement to assert a given proposition, if it can not be falsified, is verified by default.[43] Habermas, in contrast, puts forward a fallibilist interpretation of the process of justifying validity claims; by this he means that no proof is ever conclusive, for no proof is ever in principle immune to challenge through new evidence or insight; one could also say that no justification of a given claim to validity is ever in principle immune to critical reevaluation (on the basis of new evidence or insight); a fallibilist theory thus recognizes a connection between justification and critical evaluation of which falsificationism fails to take account.

However, this is misleading if it suggests that what divides Habermas and Dummett is the latter's belief in the possibility of a *conclusive* demonstration of falsity; this is unfair to Dummett, and it obscures the real nature of Habermas's objection to Dummett's falsificationism. Habermas objects to Dummett's disregard for the—in his view—ineradicable connection between validity and argumentation. To this extent, it is not so much Habermas's fallibilist approach to truth that distinguishes him from Dummett as his *dialogical* interpretation of fallibilism.

Habermas asserts a connection between the justification of validity claims and the critical evaluation of reasons in argumentation; he emphasizes, in addition, that argumentation is essentially open. He explains: " . . . it belongs to the grammatical role of the expression "to justify" (*begründen*) that we cannot once and for all place reasons, or kinds of reasons, in a hierarchy in which "final" reasons would stand at the top."[44]

On Habermas's fallibilist understanding of the notion of justification, all actual agreements reached as to the validity of a claim are always in principle subject to revision in the light of new relevant arguments. Any actual consensus (*Einverständnis*), no matter how closely the conditions under which it is reached satisfy the "strong idealizations" implicit in argumentation,[45] is never proof against the challenge of new evidence and insights. As Habermas sees it, although we aspire to truth, all we ever have at any given moment is a more or less well-grounded agreement. Whereas "truth," for Habermas, always has a moment of "unconditionality" that transcends all spatio-temporal contexts, justification (in the sense of a well-grounded agreement (*Einverständnis*)) is always conditional.[46] Moreover, since for Habermas what counts as new evidence or insight can be explored only in and through argumentation, fallibilism for him has an inescapable dialogical dimension; even if the methods employed to call into question a hitherto accepted viewpoint or fact are not in themselves discursive, arguments that make use of the new empirical data are necessary before these viewpoints or facts can finally be replaced by new ways of seeing things. For the latter reason, a genuinely fallibilist approach to the problem of truth (or, more generally, validity) implies, for Habermas, a connection between validity and argumentation. However, in order to avoid confusion, we should note that this relationship is not necessarily a *constitutive* one. In a significant number of cases the validity of truth claims is not constituted by agreement reached in argumentation (empirical truth claims are a good example of this); at the same time, the validity of all truth claims is inextricably bound to argumentation in the sense that even a claim for which there appears to be conclusive evidence is never in principle proof against reassessment through argumentative evaluation.[47]

This dialogical-fallibilist perspective should not be misunderstood as the thesis that any given claim can be called into question at any given time; it merely asserts that we can never know when new evidence may cast doubt on what now appear to be true or established facts. It is certainly compatible with the recognition that, at the level of everyday communication, there is a sense in which certain utterances *require* agreement. Recall Wittgenstein's famous point that, without a foundation of institutionalized public norms, shared by a group and constituting a "form of life," language and even thought would be impossible.[48] Hilary Putnam, drawing attention to the institutionalized nature of the implicit norms to which we appeal in ordinary perceptual judgements, says that statements such as "I am standing on the floor" *require* agreement in the appropriate circumstances.[49] While it is important to keep Putnam's Wittgensteinian point that everyday language operates against a background of shared agreement in definitions and judgements in mind, this background consensus is not, of course, proof against change; rather, it is inherently open to revision in the light of new habits of perception (which can have various causes), although, as should also be clear, it cannot change all at once.

As we saw in chapters 1 and 2, a dialogical-fallibilist perspective is not built into the structures of communicative action *as such;* it is only a part of the process of raising validity claims in postconventional modes of communicative action. I described these as forms of communicative action that are guided by the idealizing supposition that no argument is in principle immune to critical evaluation in argumentation. Whereas modern societies are characterized by a decentering of consciousness which makes a reflective relation to the world (and hence communicative action) possible, postconventional forms of communicative action are characteristic of only certain sorts of modern society. For this reason, Habermas's explication of what it is to understand the concept of justification (*begründen*), his dialogical-fallibilist interpretation of acceptability conditions, and, in consequence, his pragmatic account of meaning as a whole have to be placed within the context of those communicative practices in modern societies in which action oriented toward understanding is guided by the strong idealization that no argument is in principle exempt from critical evaluation in argumentation.

A terminological clarification that may be useful at this point has to do with the distinction between *Verständigung* and *Einverständnis*. Whereas the concept of *Verständigung* cannot easily be pinned down to a single English equivalent, stretching as it does from comprehension to consensus, *Einverständnis* translates fairly easily (at least in the context of Habermas's writings) as "a well-grounded agreement"— that is, one that has been reached in, or tested in, a process of genuine argumentation (discourse). Although *Verständigung* too can be used in this sense (i.e., to refer to a "well-grounded agreement"), the concept of *Verständigung* suggests less the *state of having reached* agreement than the *process of reaching* agreement.[50] Although, as we have seen, Habermas uses *Verständigung* to refer to both the agreement reached[51] and the process of reaching it, I find it useful to distinguish terminologically the two aspects. It seems to me less confusing to reserve *Einverständnis* for the idea of a genuine (discursively reached) consensus and *Verständigung* for the idea of a process of intersubjective critical evaluation that (according to Habermas) has, by definition, such a genuine consensus as its implicit aim. As we saw in chapter 2, Habermas insists that the very idea of intersubjective critical evaluation (serious discussion with others with regard to the validity of a claim) makes sense only if we posit agreement as its, at least implicit, goal. He suggests that we cannot imagine seriously entering into discussion with others with regard to the validity of some claim (viewpoint, norm, regulation, etc.) if we do not simultaneously imagine that we and the other participants have agreement as our goal. He dismisses as absurd the notion that participants in genuine argumentation (that is, argumentation in which we have reason to believe that their motivations are genuinely communicative) could aim at disagreement.[52] For this reason, *Verständigung* and *Einverständnis* are intimately connected. At the same time, since (for many reasons) actually achieving *Einverständnis* turns out to be the exception rather than the rule in everyday communicative practice, we can help to avoid unnecessary misunderstandings (and hence criticisms) of Habermas's perceived disregard for the disharmonies and disagreements of modern social life by emphasizing that his concept of *Verständigung* by no means implies that agreement will in fact be reached. Thus, Habermas's thesis that *Verständigung* is the inherent telos of human speech, although it asserts a connection between understanding and intersubjective evaluation through discussion with others (discussion which Habermas claims has, by definition, agreement as its implicit aim), by no means implies that an *ability* to reach agreement on matters of disputed validity is built into everyday communicative practice. While Habermas does not at any point claim to discern a potential for actually reaching agreement in the communicative practice of modern social life, the fact that the German term *Verständigung* has the double sense of a process of reaching agreement and an agreement reached is sometimes confusing, at least for English-speaking readers. Perhaps we can avoid some of this confusion if we use only *Einverständnis* to refer to the state of having reached agreement or consensus. Admittedly, this way of interpreting the notion of *Verständigung* shifts the emphasis somewhat, for Habermas himself tends to focus on the idea that an orientation toward consensus (*Einverständnis*) is anchored in the structures of communication: " . . . it can already be seen from the conditions for understanding linguistic expressions that the speech acts which are carried out with their help are oriented toward *Verständigung*, that is, towards a rationally motivated agreement as to what is said. One would fail to grasp what it means to understand an utterance if one did not recognize that it is supposed to serve the purpose of bringing about an agreement (*Einverständnis*)."[53]

However, I have suggested that formulations of this kind are not so much wrong as possibly misleading. Habermas's position, as we have seen, can be interpreted as the position that the notion of a rationally motivated agreement is an idealizing supposition of all argumentation; this does not imply that agreement is possible in practice. On the other hand, the discussion so far has suggested that, in the case of the passage cited above, at least two qualifications would be necessary: that Habermas's thesis holds (if at all) only for those validity claims for which justification is inherently discursive, and that the idea of a rationally motivated agreement is an idealizing supposition of only *some* forms of argumentation.

I have suggested two possible interpretations of Habermas's criticism of Dummett and, in connection with this, two ways in which understanding may be linked to critical evaluation in argumentation in postconventional forms of communicative action. In the first case, Habermas asserts an *internal* connection between validity and argumentation that is not tenable without qualification. However, it may be maintained for *some* kinds of validity claims. In such cases, the validity of reasons is itself a pragmatic question that has to be tested in intersubjective contexts of argumentation. With regard to these kinds of validity claims only, knowing the grounds on which a speaker is entitled to claim validity for what is said means knowing the kind of reasons that would count as *possible* reasons in support of a given claim; the question of which reasons are actually good or convincing reasons is a pragmatic one, and has to be tested in actual processes of argumentation. Claims of this kind make sense of Habermas's observation that an account of understanding formulated in terms of knowing the acceptability conditions points to the holistic nature of natural languages.[54] Most importantly, such claims lend strong support to his thesis that a dialogical interpretation of what it is to know the validation conditions compels us to move from the level of semantic analysis to a pragmatic level.[55] If the validity of reasons can be shown to be internally linked with argumentation that is essentially open-ended, then Dummett's "epistemic turn" is given an additional pragmatic swirl. However, it is not clear how this interpretation of validation conditions can be maintained for *all* validity claims.

The second kind of asserted connection between validity and argumentation holds for all validity claims (within postconventional contexts of communicative action) but has the disadvantage that it is weaker; the asserted connection is not an internal one but rather links the notion of validity to intersubjective processes of critical evaluation from the outside (or, as we might say, "externally"). It relies on a dialogical-fallibilist interpretation of validity whereby the validity of claims is never immune in principle to critical scrutiny in processes of argumentation. Thus, although it asserts a connection between validity and pragmatic contexts of critical evaluation, it cannot show that understanding itself is inescapably pragmatic. Nonetheless, it acts as an important complement to the first thesis; indeed, since this does not hold for all validity claims, it is important in its own right in that it draws attention to the way in which understanding is connected with intersubjective contexts of critical evaluation in postconventional forms of communicative action, even though the concept of a valid reason is not always internally linked to argumentation.

The idea that the validity of reasons is connected (internally or "externally") to pragmatic contexts of argumentation is, in Habermas's writings, linked up with another thesis that, if successful, would reinforce the idea that understanding is inescapably pragmatic. Habermas not only argues that the validity of reasons is tied (be it internally or "externally") to intersubjective contexts of argumentative evaluation (*Verständigung*); he also attempts to show that "knowing the validation conditions" itself requires evaluation. Habermas's apparently stronger—and much-disputed—claim[56] is that to regard something as a (potentially) valid reason is to "take up position" with regard to its validity. If reconstructing (possible) reasons is an integral part of understanding utterances, then Habermas's stronger thesis is that to reconstruct reasons is to evaluate their validity. This would constitute a further sense in which understanding is tied to reaching understanding (*Verständigung*).

Habermas's basic idea seems to be the following: The reasons that a hearer attributes to a speaker in order to understand the claim(s) raised with a given utterance are merely potential reasons and thus are themselves validity claims.[57] A validity claim is something inherently intersubjective; it is a demand for recognition. To raise a claim is always to call for a response. This demand for recognition will be satisfied only if the person to whom it is addressed meets it "frontally" (i.e., responds by taking its challenge seriously). To do so, the addressee must embark on a process of critical evaluation, weighing the validity of the claim and demanding reasons from the speaker if its validity is questionable. A hearer who is not in a position to actually ask the speaker for reasons must reconstruct such reasons and attribute them to the speaker. All this amounts to a more or less rudimentary "argumentation game"—and, as we have seen, Habermas maintains that the very notion of argumentation is internally connected with the idea of reaching agreement. Furthermore, as we have also seen, Habermas maintains that anyone who persistently refuses to enter into argumentation can do so only at the risk of suicide or schizophrenia, for to do so is to opt out of the lifeworld.[58] Habermas is not, of course, saying that the hearer always in fact responds to the challenge issued by validity claims. There are many reasons why we, in given instances, are not able or willing to pick up the challenge issued with a given validity claim.[59] Nonetheless, he is putting forward the thesis that the very process of reconstructing reasons involves critical evaluation and that, as a result, understanding itself demands an evaluative reaction from the hearer. If we can provide neither reasons as to why we accept the validity of the claim in question nor reasons as to why we do not accept it (nor, presumably, reasons as to why no conclusion as to the validity of the claim is possible in the circumstances), then there are good grounds for saying that we have not understood the claim. Habermas tells us on a number of occasions that if a hearer does not take up a "Yes" or a "No" position on the validity of a claim, but leaves it to one side as not yet decided, this is equivalent to conceding lack of understanding.[60] Thomas McCarthy is just one of the commentators who disagree with Habermas on this count.[61] McCarthy argues that, even if we accept that we cannot understand reasons as reasons without relying on our own competence to judge validity, cogency, or soundness, it does not follow that we have to actually or implicitly "take a position" on reasons in order to understand them. McCarthy points out that interpreters raised in pluralistic cultures and schooled in cultural and historical differences are quite capable of understanding symbolic expressions without taking a position on their validity; moreover, not only is an objectivating, hypothetical attitude in which judgement is simply bracketed a structural possibility, it is sometimes even desirable. Against this Habermas replies that: "such an abstention is also a rationally motivated position, as much as a 'yes' or a 'no,' and in no way relieves us of the necessity of taking a position. Abstention in this context does not really signify a true declaration of neutrality, but only signals that we are putting off problems for the time being and wish to suspend our interpretative efforts."[62]

In another response to his critics, Habermas illustrates his case with three examples: the justification of metamathematical positions in the dispute between intuitionists and formalists; the reasons for the superiority of Newtonian over Aristotelian physics; and explanations for what, from the point of view of a lecturer, appears to be an unmotivated outburst of laughter from the audience.[63] Habermas's point appears to be that in each of these cases—even in the third and seemingly least plausible one—one cannot claim to have understood the claims in question if one cannot argue either in support of them or against them (or, we might add, if one cannot show why no conclusion as to their validity is possible in the given context). Habermas contends that both Wittgenstein and Gadamer are right in this regard—Wittgenstein because he believes that we understand an utterance only insofar as we share the pre-understandings of the language game in question and can be said to agree in a common form of life, Gadamer insofar as he maintains that we understand an utterance only to the extent that we reach agreement (*sich verständigen*) with regard to a common object. According to Habermas, Wittgenstein is right with respect to the background lifeworld and Gadamer is right with respect to that which is said.[64] To be sure, we should be careful how we understand Gadamer's idea of "reaching agreement" (*sich verständigen*); the capacity in question here can refer either to the ability to reach agreement or to the process of argumentation with regard to a claim. The discussion so far has suggested that not the ability to reach agreement but the ability to enter into discussion is required by the notion of understanding (at least for some kinds of validity claim).

Perhaps some of the criticism directed against Habermas's thesis that reconstructing reasons itself requires us to take a position can be deflected if we recognize, first, that it holds (if at all) only for those validity claims the justification of which is internally connected with argumentation and, second, that the idea of "taking a position" (like that of justification) can have a weaker and a stronger sense. In its stronger sense it implies that a final position as to the validity of a claim is possible. On such an interpretation, I understand a claim if I know conclusively why it is valid or invalid. In its weaker, dialogical-fallibilist sense it implies the ability *to argue for* why a claim is valid or invalid. In view of Habermas's current dialogical-fallibilist interpretation of validity, the second interpretation seems to make more sense. On this interpretation, understanding a claim involves the ability to argue for its validity or its lack of validity (or for why no conclusion is possible in the circumstances).

So far, I have been concerned with interpreting Habermas's thesis that we understand an utterance when we know what makes it acceptable. I have argued that, at least in the cases of most constative and expressive utterances, this amounts to the thesis that we understand an utterance when we know the validation conditions. To know the validation conditions is to be able to reconstruct the kind of reasons that would entitle the speaker to raise the validity claim raised with a given utterance.

There are at least two ways in which this knowledge is connected with the ability to enter into critical discussion with others with regard to the validity of the claim. First, there are certain kinds of validity claim for which validity is internally connected with agreement reached in argumentation and for which to reconstruct reasons is to reconstruct *possible* reasons, the validity of which is not available independently of argumentation; furthermore, in such cases, reconstructing reasons involves taking up a position with regard to their validity, interpreted as an ability to argue why they are valid or invalid. For these kinds of claim, the following formulation appears to hold:

We would not understand the meaning of a linguistic expression if we did not know how to make use of it in order to enter into discussion/reach

A Pragmatic Theory of Meaning

agreement with someone (*sich verständigen*) with regard to the validity of something.[65]

However, although Habermas appears to believe that this account of understanding is applicable to all validity claims, the above discussion has suggested the need for qualification. It holds, if at all, only for those claims for which justification (*begründen*) is internally linked to argumentation. Second, at least in postconventional forms of communicative action, understanding validity claims that do not fall into this category is also tied to intersubjective contexts of critical evaluation to the extent that "validity" is interpreted in a dialogical-fallibilist way; however, as we saw, here the connection is not an internal one but an "external" one.

3

Up to now, in discussing the notion of acceptability conditions, I have concentrated on constative and expressive utterances. I have done so on the basis of my argument that, for most constative utterances and all expressive utterances, knowing the acceptability conditions of (and hence understanding) a given utterance amounts to no more than knowing its validation conditions. As I have argued, only in a small number of cases (for instance, simple observational sentences such as "It is raining outside") does it make any sense to speak of satisfaction conditions, in the sense of empirically specifiable truth conditions; moreover, to know these is always also to know the validation conditions (and to know the validation conditions is always also to know the satisfaction conditions). This raises the question of whether it makes sense in such cases to speak of two distinct sets of conditions that a hearer must know in order to understand the utterance in question. In contrast, in the case of regulative utterances such as promises and requests, it does seem possible to identify two distinct sets of conditions that a hearer has to know. To know the satisfaction conditions of "Pass me the butter" is to know that acceptance of such a request obliges the hearer to pass the butter, but to know this does not necessarily imply that he knows the validation conditions (that is, the kind of convincing reasons that the speaker could provide in support of her claim that she is entitled to, or competent to, pass the hearer the butter if he were to challenge her request).

This suggests a disanalogy between understanding constative and expressive utterances, on the one hand, and regulative utterances, on the other. The disanalogy has to do with the (moral) obligations for the sequel of action that are constituted by the act itself only in the case of regulative speech acts.

A further distinctive feature of regulative speech acts is that their validation conditions always refer back to the normative presuppositions of the situation in which they are uttered. As we have seen, Habermas takes account of this distinctive feature by connecting regulative speech acts with a direct claim to normative rightness. (Recall his thesis that regulative speech acts are internally connected with a claim that the act in question is normatively right in the situation in question.)

Although we have seen that there is a sense in which every speech act raises a claim to normative rightness, we can see that this kind of claim assumes a special significance in the case of regulative speech acts. In order to clarify this special significance, it is helpful to return to Habermas's distinction between illocutionary success "in the narrower sense" and illocutionary success "in the broader sense."[66.] Illocutionary success in the narrower sense refers to understanding; in this sense, a speech act is successful when the hearer understands what the speaker says. In the broader sense, it refers to the hearer's acceptance of the speech-act offer; in this sense, a speech act is successful if agreement is reached between the speaker and the hearer with regard to all three of the validity claims raised. In the case of constative speech acts, the "indirect" claim to normative rightness raised with every speech act has implications for the success of that speech act in the broader sense of illocutionary success; however, it is not relevant to its success in the narrower sense—that is, to the attempt to understand its propositional content (which, as we have seen, is to know its "validation conditions"). For example, if a guest at a wedding stands up after the ceremony and says to those assembled "(I predict that) X and Y (the bridal couple) will be divorced by this time next year," we understand what the utterance says (its propositional content) if we are able to reconstruct possible reasons as to why this prediction is valid or invalid. Knowing the validation conditions of the "direct" claim raised by the utterance ("that the couple will be divorced by this time next year") does not, however, require us to know anything about the speaker's claim to normative rightness. In other words, to understand what the speaker says we do not have to be able to reconstruct possible reasons which the speaker could provide in order to claim that her utterance was appropriate in the circumstances. We can understand the propositional content of the prediction without knowing anything about its appropriateness. At the same time, the success of the speech act (in the broader sense) requires that the hearer(s) accept the speech act as normatively right in the circumstances. Here the idea of agreement seems to extend to all three claims raised with a given speech act: a speaker can achieve illocutionary success in the broader sense only if (to take the example of a constative speech act) the hearer accepts not only the validity of what is said but also that the speech act is appropriate in the given circumstances and that the speaker means what she says. But, as Habermas himself recognizes, illocutionary success in this sense goes beyond mere comprehension of the propositional content. Understanding what a constative speech act says (knowing its validation conditions) does not require us to know anything, or to have any opinion about, the "indirect" claims raised with the utterance.[67]

In contrast, Habermas argues that to know the validation conditions of a regulative utterance is to understand the claim to normative rightness that it raises. However, Habermas's account of understanding regulative utterances has not gone undisputed. Habermas argues against critics such as Ernst Tugendhat and Rolf Zimmermann that an orientation toward validity claims is part of the pragmatic conditions of linguistic understanding.[68] Tugendhat disputes this, arguing that if a child beggar in Lima says, "Give me a *sol*", I can understand this request completely without knowing anything about the normative structure of the situation.[69] Zimmermann's objection is in the same vein. He believes that I can, for example, "completely understand semantically the request to stop smoking without any further knowledge of why the person speaking to me has an interest in my compliance with the request."[70]

Against this, Habermas insists that: "knowledge of the conditions of satisfaction, which are taken from the propositional content of a request, is not sufficient in order to understand its illocutionary meaning, that is, the specific imperative character of the request. . . . Rather, the hearer has to understand the normative context which authorizes the speaker to make his demand and which legitimizes the expectation that the adressee has reasons to carry out the action demanded by him."[71] In other words, to understand *what a regulative speech act says*, we have to understand the speaker's claim that it is normatively right in the particular context. For this reason, knowledge of the conditions of satisfaction has to be complemented by knowledge of the conditions of validation. To know the conditions of validation is to know *the kind of reasons* that would entitle the speaker to regard a given imperative as valid (*gültig*), that is, normatively justified. It is worth recalling that, in certain forms of communicative action and in the case of certain kinds of validity claim, the validity of these reasons is internally connected with critical evaluation in argumentation; in such cases, to know the validation conditions is to know how to enter into discussion with someone with regard to the validity of these reasons. In the case of Tugendhat's example, to know the kind of reasons that would entitle the speaker to claim validity for her utterance might be to know that children are allowed to beg from strangers in the streets of Lima,[72] but it might also be to know that children are allowed to beg in the streets of many cities, or to know that for some people begging is a holy and thus morally permissible act. More generally, it is to know how to enter into discussion with someone with regard to the normative validity of the act of begging in the streets of Lima. I take Habermas's thesis to be that we could not claim to understand the utterance if we could not attribute to the speaker reasons that might support her entitlement to perform that utterance in the given context. Tugendhat would have to show, against Habermas, that it would be possible for Tugendhat, in Lima, to understand the child beggar's request, while at the same time being unable to attribute to the child reasons with which she could defend the rightness of the request in the given situation. Zimmermann would have to show, against Habermas, that he could understand a given request to stop smoking without being able to attribute to the speaker reasons with which she could defend the normative rightness of the request in the given situation. In this instance I am in agreement with Habermas, who finds Tugendhat's and Zimmermann's positions "counterintuitive."[73] In view of the fact that we end up disputing intuitions, the debate is unlikely to end here.

A Pragmatic Theory of Meaning

4

I have suggested in the foregoing that we can understand what a constative speech act [74] says without having any opinion about the normative structure of the situation in which it is performed. This is not to say that understanding a constative speech act does not require any knowledge of the context of interaction in which it is uttered. To understand an utterance is to understand it as an utterance in a situation. Habermas's account of what it is to understand a constative (and expressive) utterance tends to underplay this aspect of understanding utterances. This is connected with his focus on utterances "in the standard form" performed "under standard conditions." While this is a perfectly legitimate methodological restriction, an important fact about understanding utterances tends to slip from view in Habermas's analyses as a result of it: that utterances are embedded in specific contexts of interaction, so that to understand an utterance is to understand it as an utterance-in-a-situation. Habermas does in fact acknowledge this in a number of ways; for instance, his attribution to constative and expressive speech acts of an "indirect claim to normative rightness" could be interpreted as evidence of such an acknowledgement, even though these indirect claims are relevant, not to understanding the speech act, but to illocutionary success in the broader sense. His recognition that linguistic expressions change their meaning as they are used in different contexts also points to an awareness of the importance of the context of interaction for an account of understanding utterances. [75] Further evidence of an acknowledgement that utterances should be understood as utterances-in-situations is the fact that Habermas draws attention to the role played by background knowledge in understanding speech acts. He points out that speech acts are always understood against a background of various kinds of implicit knowledge; at the same time, it is difficult to avoid the impression that this is not so much an integral part of his theory of meaning as it is an afterthought. This impression is reinforced by Habermas's emphasis on the fact that speech acts are self-interpreting, by his confusing formulation of "the standard case," and by his reference to "grammatical well-formedness" as a condition of understanding utterances. In the final pages of this chapter I will draw attention to Habermas's tendency to overemphasize the context-independence and to underplay the context-dependence of speech acts while showing that he ultimately remains true to the spirit of his pragmatic approach to meaning by acknowledging that utterances should be conceived as utterances-in-a-situation.

An utterance is a *situated* linguistic expression. To understand an utterance is generally to understand it as an speech act in a particular context of interaction. A pragmatic theory of meaning that professes to focus on the meaning of utterances as opposed to sentences has to take account of this. Such a theory must recognize the role played by the context of interaction in understanding utterances and accommodate it within its framework.

Although Habermas's account of meaning clearly focuses on the use of linguistic expressions in utterances, for methodological reasons it restricts itself to the "standard form" of utterances and to the use of such utterances "under standard conditions."

An explicit speech act satisfies the standard form in its surface structure if it is made up of an illocutionary component and a propositional (or locutionary) component. The illocutionary component refers to what I do in saying something; the propositional component is what I say. The illocutionary component consists in an illocutionary act carried out with the aid of a performative sentence. This sentence is formed in the present indicative, affirmative, and has as its logical subject the first person and as its logical (direct) object the second person; the predicate, constructed with the help of a performative expression, permits in general the particle 'hereby'. The performative component needs to be complemented by a propositional component, constructed by means of a sentence with propositional content. The standard form of most constative and many regulative utterances can thus be expressed as, "I . . . (hereby) you that . . . ," although regulative utterances can also have the form "You are (hereby) . . . to. . . ."[76] Habermas further restricts his analyses to propositionally undifferentiated and institutionally unbound speech acts.[77]

The fact that every speech act both establishes an interpersonal relationship and says something means it has a "double structure."[78] Although we can distinguish analytically between the illocutionary and the locutionary component, analysis of the meaning of what is said in a given utterance cannot be separated from analysis of the act of saying it. Only through its performance in a given context of interaction is an abstract sentence transformed into a meaningful utterance. This suggests that any account of meaning that takes utterances or speech acts as the smallest units of linguistic communication and thus as the starting point of its investigations has to recognize that utterances are utterances in specific situations. However, Habermas restricts his formal pragmatic investigations to speech acts carried out under "standard conditions."[79] He excludes those explicit speech acts in standard form that appear in contexts that produce shifts in meaning. According to Habermas, this is the case where the pragmatic meaning of a context-dependent speech act diverges from the meaning of the sentences used in it.[80] For this reason, Habermas restricts his inquiries to explicit speech acts in the standard form in which "the literal meaning of the sentences uttered coincides with what the speaker means with his speech act."[81]

Habermas recognizes that formal pragmatic approaches to meaning are open to the charge that, by focusing on isolated and highly idealized speech acts, they remain hopelessly removed from the complexity of everyday linguistic activity. Nonetheless, he defends the need for formal pragmatic in addition to empirical pragmatic investigations. Although he acknowledges the wealth of existing empirical pragmatic contributions in linguistics, sociology, anthropology, psychology, and other spheres, he argues that only formal pragmatics has at its disposal the conceptual instruments that are necessary if the rational bases of linguistic communication are to be discerned amidst the confusing complexity of everyday linguistic activity.[82] Furthermore, he maintains that the gap between the "pure types" of speech act on which he focuses in his investigations and everyday communicative activity can be lessened by means of a controlled reversal of the strong idealizations on which he bases his conception of communicative action. By means of such a controlled reversal, his methodologically restricted focus on just three basic illocutionary modes could be dropped and the multiplicity of illocutionary forces could be acknowledged; his exclusive concentration on communicative actions might be given up, and the role of the background knowledge that acts as a resource for these actions could be recognized; analysis might be extended from the restricted focus on isolated speech acts to a consideration of sequences of speech acts (texts or conversations); nonstandard forms of speech act could be acknowledged; in addition to direct speech acts, indirect, figurative, and ambiguous utterances might be admitted; and not just explicit speech acts but also implicit and elliptically abbreviated ones might be allowed. Habermas mentions a number of other possible "controlled reversals" of his strong idealizations.[83]

For our present purposes it is important to note that Habermas's concentration on speech acts in the standard form is merely a methodological restriction for the purposes of avoiding unhelpful confusion and that Habermas recognizes that his focus on speech acts carried out under "standard conditions" is an abstraction and needs to be complemented by an account of the implicit knowledge that is the background against which communicative action takes place.[84] Despite these useful reminders, it seems to me that Habermas's notion of "the standard case" is at least potentially problematic. In characterizing "the standard case" as that in which the literal meaning of the sentences uttered coincides with what the speaker means with the speech act, Habermas appears to deny the important difference between the meaning of a sentence and the meaning of an utterance that makes use of that sentence. He implies that it makes sense to speak of the literal meaning of an *utterance*.[85] We know from Habermas's criticism of the "semanticist abstraction" that he rejects approaches to meaning that attempt to explain the meaning of an utterance purely in terms of the meaning of the sentence contained within it, where the meaning of the latter is determined independently of its *use* in actual situations. However, in suggesting that sentence meaning and utterance meaning coincide "in the standard case," Habermas himself comes close to succumbing to the semanticist abstraction. Even though (as we shall see) Habermas does acknowledge that the meaning of a sentence cannot be determined independently of its use in actual situations, in that he draws attention to the various kinds of implicit knowledge that both produce and complement communicative actions, the suggestion that sentence and utterance meaning may coincide "under standard conditions" is at best misleading and at worst gives rises to a false model of understanding utterances.

Habermas's tendency to underplay the context-dependence of speech acts is reflected in his formulation of "the standard case," but this is not the only instance of it. Another example is his reference to the "grammatical well-formedness" of an utterance as one of the conditions of understanding.[86]

Habermas implies on occasion that grammatical well-formedness is a condition that has to be satisfied before an utterance can be understood.[87] Thus, in *The Theory of Communicative Action* he describes the well-formedness of the expression used in an utteranace as a condition of understanding.[88] Habermas elaborates on this with an example to the effect that if a promise were to take the form "I promise you that I was in Hamburg yesterday" one of the conditions of grammatical well-formedness would be violated.[89] We should be wary of interpreting the idea of grammatical well-formedness as a *requirement* that has to be met before understanding is possible. We should distinguish here between the view that grammatiacal well-formedness is a condition of successful understanding and the view that it is a *presupposition* of communication.[90] If Habermas wishes to maintain the former position, then it seems to me that not only is this position too strong; it may also be indicative of his general lack of appreciation of the fact that an utterance is an utterance-in-a-situation.

Often a grasp of the situation in which a linguistic expression is uttered can compensate for deficiencies in the semantic or the syntactic structure of that linguistic expression. It is a normal experience in the everyday practice of communication that we understand an utterance even though the expression employed is not used in a grammatically correct way. The ability to understand the speaker's communicative intention even where the language used is unclear, ungrammatical, or even partly unknown is part of most people's general linguistic competence. Most importantly for our present purposes, it is intimately bound up with our ability to understand situations, a practical ability which we learn as part of our linguistic competence. On the basis of our understanding of the situation in which a speech act is performed, we are often able to deduce from this what the speaker intends to convey, even where the speaker expresses herself ungrammatically.[91]

Of course, some minimum of grammatical correctness is usually necessary if the hearer is to understand a given utterance, although no hard and fast rules are possible here. Not only will the degree to which a grasp of the speech situation helps to compensate for a lack of grammatical well-formedness vary according to the type of speech act in question; in addition, the practical ability to deduce meaning on the basis of an understanding of the situation can be possessed in varying degrees.[92]

Habermas's tendency to underplay the fact that to understand an utterance is to understand it as an utterance-in-a-situation may be connected with his emphasis on the self-interpreting character of linguistic utterances. He emphasizes that speech acts, in contrast to non-linguistic actions, are self-interpreting—at least in "the standard case."[93] To the extent that it can be expanded into an explicit speech act,[94] and is to be understood literally, the speech act "It is snowing in Germany at the moment" *itself* tells us that it is an assertion. The illocutionary component (the implicit "I assert that . . .") establishes the meaning of what is said as a kind of pragmatic commentary.[95] While this is undoubtedly an important characteristic feature of linguistic utterances, Habermas should equally acknowledge the various ways in which understanding utterances is context-dependent.

However, although I think that Habermas underplays the fact that utterances are utterances-in-situations, I do not think that his account of meaning as *a whole* denies this dimension of understanding. For this reason, his definition of the "standard case" in terms of a coincidence of sentence meaning and utterance meaning, and his interpretation of the idea of grammatical well-formedness as a condition of successful understanding, may be no more than unhappy formulations. In the remaining pages of this chapter, therefore, I draw attention to Habermas's acknowledgement of the role played by implicit knowledge in understanding utterances.

Although his concentration on speech acts used "under standard conditions" distracts attention from this aspect of understanding utterances, Habermas acknowledges the role played by various kinds of background knowledge in understanding utterances. From Husserl he borrows the term "unthematic knowledge" to refer to "the presuppositions that participants in a communicative process have to make in order that the speech act can take on a specific meaning in a specific situation and (hence) be capable of being valid or invalid."[96]

Habermas further distinguishes between (i) the universal pre-reflexive knowledge that is part of a speaker's linguistic competency and

(ii) the speaker's knowledge of the lifeworld. With (i) Habermas appears to have in mind the kind of pre-reflexive knowledge that makes possible the production of speech acts in the first place (for instance, the general generative knowledge that enables competent speakers to use sentences in utterances grammatically); he is also referring to knowledge of how to satisfy the general pragmatic presuppositions of communicative action (for example, the ability to orient oneself toward validity claims and to impute accountability to oneself and others; or the ability to identify objects and thus to produce connections between language and the world; or the ability to distinguish between perlocutionary and illocutionary goals, between the subjective, objective, and social worlds, and so on). All of this is implicit knowledge that can only be mastered intuitively and which requires a reflective process of rational reconstruction in order to be transformed from a "know-how" into a "know-that." Habermas's main interest is with (ii), however. This second sort of unthematic knowledge does not serve to produce communicative action; rather, it complements, accompanies, and provides the framework for such action. The background knowledge of the lifeworld is a concrete knowledge of both language and the world; remaining in the half-shadows of the pre-predicative and the pre-categorial, it provides the unproblematic ground for all forms of thematic knowledge.[97]

Within this category of background knowledge of the lifeworld, Habermas introduces a distinction between the background knowledge that is relatively close to the foreground and the background knowledge that remains in the shadows. With regard to the former, he further distinguishes (a) a situation-specific background knowledge and (b) a topic-dependent contextual knowledge.[98] What Habermas has in mind with (a) seems to be the normally implicit background information about persons and situations that is necessary to render an utterance intelligible in any given situation. In *After Virtue*, Alasdair MacIntyre suggests an example that illustrates this kind of knowledge[99]:

I am standing waiting for a bus and the young man standing next to me suddenly says: 'The name of the common wild duck is *Histrionicus, histrionicus, histrionicus.*' There is no problem as to the meaning of the sentence he uttered: the problem is, how to answer the question, what was he doing in uttering it?[100]

As MacIntyre recognizes, I can understand the meaning of the sentence uttered (that is, the propositional content of the utterance) and still find the utterance unintelligible. The utterance becomes intelligible as soon as I can place it in an intelligible context. MacIntyre points out that it would be possible to render the young man's utterance intelligible by finding for it a place in a particular narrative (for instance, by presuming that he had mistaken me for someone who yesterday had approached him in the library and asked "Do you by any chance know the Latin name of the common wild duck?"); or by presuming that he has just come back from a session with his psychotherapist, who has urged him to break down his inhibitions by talking to strangers; or by presuming him to be a spy waiting at a prearranged rendezvous and uttering the ill-chosen code sentence that will identify him to his contact. In each case, the utterance becomes intelligible by finding its place in a narrative.

This ability to place a given utterance in a narrative seems to be what Habermas has in mind when he refers to situation-specific background knowledge. Habermas himself illustrates the need for such knowledge with the following example: If he is chatting with an acquaintance he meets in a park in Frankfurt and mentions that it is snowing in California, his acquaintance will not query this assertion if he is aware, for instance, that Habermas has just returned from San Fransisco or, alternatively, that he works as a metereologist. Understanding the assertion presupposes possession of this kind of information about the speaker and about the speaker's life history.[101] Hearers possess such information most of the time and it remains in the background and unthematized.

With the notion of (b), "a topic-dependent contextual knowledge," Habermas attempts to take account of the fact that participants in conversation normally presuppose that they share certain assumptions concerning the validity of the topic they are discussing, as well as certain asssumptions concerning the contexts in which this topic is appropriate or inappropriate. As an example of this Habermas suggests the fact that if he introduces the topic of the lifeworld to an academic audience in Madrid or Paris it will spark off different questions and objections than it will if he introduces it to a similar audience in Berkeley. In every discussion, certain implicit assumptions pertaining to the topic are likely to remain unchallenged, whereas they might well be challenged in a different context of interaction.

Habermas identifies a "situation-specific background knowledge" and a "topic-dependent contextual knowledge" as two kinds of knowledge that, although part of the background knowledge against which communicative action operates, are relatively close to the foreground.[102] Although the assumptions on which they are based are not normally thematized by participants in everyday communication, they are relatively susceptible to problematization. This contrasts with a third kind of unthematic knowledge which, like the other two mentioned, accompanies and provides a framework for communicative action. Habermas refers to this third kind of knowledge simply as the "background knowledge of the lifeworld." This forms the stable bottom layer of unthematic knowledge in which the more readily problematized kinds of unthematic knowledge have their roots. While all forms of unthematic knowledge are forms of implicit and pre-reflexive knowledge, the "background knowledge of the lifeworld" is further characterized by (1) its unmediated certainty (it cannot be problematized and called into question at will), (2) its totalizing power (the lifeworld forms a totality with the intersubjectively shared speech situation as the center from which concentrically overlapping social spaces and vertically overlapping dimensions of time extend, and (3) its holistic character (its elements are interconnected and form an impenetrable "undergrowth").

With "the background knowledge of the lifeworld" Habermas seems to have in mind the background assumptions that competent language users regard as trivial and obvious. He draws on Searle's recognition that the truth conditions of the assertoric and imperative sentences employed in such simple assertions as "The cat is on the mat" and "Give me a hamburger" depend on implicit background assumptions such as gravity, in the case of the first assertion, and, in the case of the second, that the hamburger when it comes will not be a mile wide.[103] Habermas's point here is that this kind of background knowledge is much further in the background and hence less susceptible to problematization than the situation-specific and contextual knowledge that he mentions.

Habermas is correct to draw attention to the way in which the understanding of utterances depends on various kinds of unthematic background knowledge. At the same time, only some of this knowledge is specifically connected with the situation of interaction (although, as Habermas also points out, situations overlap and refer to other situations, and their boundaries are never clearly defined). Nonetheless, utterances are always utterances not just against the background of the lifeworld but also in situations. This fact about utterances merits attention in its own right. Although Habermas now [104] appears to acknowledge this dimension of the understanding of utterances explicitly, with his references to a situation-specific background knowledge and to a topic-dependent contextual knowledge, it seems to be tacked onto his account of meaning as an afterthought rather than to form an integral part of it. This impression is reinforced by Habermas's tendency to underplay the fact that utterances are utterances-in-situations as reflected in his formulation of "the standard case," by his reference to grammatical well-formedness as a condition of understanding, and by his emphasis on the self-interpreting character of speech acts. Nonetheless, as I have tried to make clear, as a whole Habermas's account of meaning does not deny the difference between sentence meaning and utterance meaning and thus, in the end, merits description as a pragmatic theory. More precisely (recall the discussion in the main part of this chapter), it merits description as a pragmatic theory that seeks to retain the idea of an connection between meaning and the critical evaluation of validity claims in intersubjective processes of reaching understanding (*Verständigung*). In the next chapter I shall return to the questions of the extent to which and the sense in which this amounts to a connection between meaning and a notion of validity that potentially transcends all local contexts, and of what the implications of this might be.

5

Communicative Rationality: Concluding Discussion

1

The concept of communicative rationality expresses the potential for rationality that is supposedly implicit in the everyday linguistic practices of modern societies. It is located in certain idealizations that guide communicative action in modern societies to the extent that everyday communication is connected with validity.

The thesis of a connection between language and validity is not new. It has long been acknowledged by philosophers of language as diverse as Frege and the later Wittgenstein. However, Habermas gives a distinctive interpretation to the connection between language and validity. Against the tradition of formal semantics from Frege to Dummett, he generalizes the notion of validity from that of the truth (or assertibility) of propositions to include the dimensions of moral-practical and aesthetic-expressive validity. Against the use-oriented approach to meaning of the later Wittgenstein, Habermas insists on a connection between language and a sense of validity that cannot be reduced to the conventional validity of a local form of life. Thus, on the one hand, he gives up a restricted focus on representational truth in favor of a theory of validity claims corresponding to different validity-based modes of using language; on the other hand, he asserts the *context-transcendent* power of validity claims, which results from their (internal or external) connection with the process of argumentative evaluation. Accordingly, the concept of communicative rationality is based on the connection between speech acts (as the smallest unit of everyday linguistic communication) and various kinds of validity claim (which in turn are connected with the idea of an argumentatively achieved agreement). In chapters 3 and 4 I found no reason to query the basic shape of such a notion of communicative rationality. Although in chapter 3 I suggested that certain modifications (in particular of Habermas's theory of validity claims and his proposed classification of speech acts) might render his account more plausible, the proposed amendments leave Habermas's conception fundamentally intact. Similarly, although in chapter 4 I argued that certain qualifications of Habermas's account of meaning (and, in connection with this, of his thesis that understanding is internally connected with *Verständigung*) were necessary, I found his basic intuition to be convincing. In those chapters I thus gave qualified support to Habermas's contention that an orientation toward *Verständigung* is built into the everyday linguistic practices of certain sorts of modern society. This final point is worth emphasizing: The connection between understanding and reaching understanding (*Verständigung*) was found to obtain only in certain sorts of linguistic practice; that is, understanding and *Verständigung* are linked only in those postconventional forms of communicative action in which the validity of certain kinds of validity claim is conceived as inherently discursive and in which there is a commitment to the open and critical evaluation of validity claims in argumentation.

While we should bear in mind the need for modification and qualification, in the foregoing discussion I have provided support for Habermas's endeavor "to construct a voice of reason that we cannot avoid using (whether we want to or not) in everyday communicative practice."[1] It is not yet clear, however, what this voice is able to say.

What are the implications of Habermas's conception of communicative rationality? Indeed, what is its point? We have seen that it is intended as a postmetaphysical yet nondefeatist conception of reason. But what is the point of such a conception? Habermas tells us that the task of reason in the modern world is to bring forms of unreason to reason.[2] Its task is to give voice to silent suffering.[3] This indicates that it has a part to play in Habermas's critical theory of society. In this concluding chapter I consider the part played by the concept of communicative rationality within the framework of Habermas's social theory. I sketched the basic outline of this in chapter 1. In order to consider the implications of the concept of communicative rationality from the point of view of Habermas's critical theory, a closer look at his account of the pathologies of modernity is necessary.

Although in chapter 1 I mentioned only one kind of pathology of modernity, Habermas in fact identifies two main kinds of pathological development in modern societies: the colonization of the lifeworld by mechanisms of functional (system) integration and the cultural impoverishment of the lifeworld.[4]

I shall begin the present discussion by taking a closer look at the colonization thesis—the one about which Habermas has more to say. As will be recalled, this thesis describes a conflict between two modes of societal integration: social and functional integration. Social (lifeworld) and functional (system) integration can be distinguished as modes of action coordination as follows: The primary mode of social (lifeworld) integration is communicative action, described by Habermas as action oriented toward understanding. As we know, influence (*Einflußnahme*) is also a mechanism of action coordination within the lifeworld; actions coordinated in this way are termed strategic by Habermas and are oriented toward success. Communicative action is the primary mode of action coordination in the lifeworld to the extent that it is necessary for reproductive processes in the lifeworld's three main domains: Neither cultural traditions nor group memberships nor the socialization of individuals could be reproduced purely by way of strategic action.[5] Nonetheless, both communicative action and strategic action are forms of social (lifeworld) coordination to the extent that they rely on a consciously acting agent. Action cannot take place unless the agent decides to initiate it—recall John Thompson's definition of action as something that someone (or some group) does and not something that simply happens to someone (or group).[6] This is not to deny that actions can result from conscious decisions to varying degrees. Nonetheless, for something to count as an action the agent must, at least in principle, be able to give an account of what she has done—and this means what the agent has decided to do. In contrast, functional (system) integration as a mechanism of societal coordination is neutral with regard to the intentions of the agent; in Habermas's words, it bypasses the consciousness of the agent.[7] It operates by way of the functional interconnection of action-consequences.[8] This is why the terms "system integration" and "functional integration" can be used interchangeably (as will become clearer, this accounts for why the second volume of *The Theory of Communicative Action* is subtitled *Lifeworld and System: A Critique of Functionalist Reason*). In contrast to social integration, which is directed toward the symbolic reproduction of the lifeworld, functional integration is directed toward the material reproduction of society, which is conceived as the maintenance of the system. Actions attain a functional value according to their contribution to this maintenance. System integration thus amounts to a non-normative regulation of individual decisions which extends beyond the agent's consciousness.[9] Corresponding to the distinction between social (lifeworld) and functional (system) integration, we can distinguish between the rationalization of the lifeworld and the rationalization of the system. The former, as we know, takes place in the three lifeworld dimensions of cultural reproduction, social integration, and socialization, and refers to the increasing detachment of interpretations (including self-interpretations) and practices from existing normative contexts and the increasing reliance of all justificatory procedures on open and critical argumentation; historically this has been accompanied by an increasing generalization of values and norms resulting in universal systems of law and morality (in addition, the rationalization of the lifeworld is characterized by an increasingly clear demarcation of strategic and communicative action).[10] The rationalization of the system,[11] in contrast, refers to a growth in complexity as well as a growth in capacity to take on "steering functions" (of material reproduction and administration) in society.

Habermas claims that rationalization processes in the dimension of system integration are necessary to the functioning of modern societies—that they are not in themselves problematic. They remain unproblematic to the extent that they interrelate in a balanced way; the path of development has to be a *nonselective* one. However, according to Habermas, the development of modern societies has not been balanced; it has been selective or one-sided. The rationalization processes of modern societies have led to a colonization of the lifeworld by the system,[12] which has given rise to deformations of the lifeworld. Habermas sees this development, ironically, as a by-product of the rationalization of the lifeworld. The rationalization of the lifeworld gives rise, paradoxically, both to its own subjugation and to a utopian perspective.[13]

The paradox of modernity, as Habermas conceives it, amounts to the following: With the development of modern societies, the life-world has become increasingly rationalized; that is, the actions, practices, and interpretations of its members have become increasingly detached from established normative contexts and increasingly reliant on action oriented toward understanding. As processes of action oriented toward understanding extend into ever more domains of social life, the medium of communicative action becomes overburdened. Communicative action can no longer cope with the burden of societal integration, for the more this depends on the interpretive capacities of agents the greater the input necessary to come to an agreement and the greater the possibility of misunderstanding or dissensus and ensuing breakdown of interaction.[14] As communicative action becomes overburdened as a mechanism of societal integration, pressure arises for the creation of relief mechanisms to ease the burden and reduce the risk of a breakdown. Habermas identifies two kinds of relief mechanism: one that "condenses" communicative action and one that replaces it.[15] The former refers to generalized forms of communication that do not replace reaching agreement in language but merely condense it (make it both denser and more abstract), and thus remain tied to lifeworld contexts. The latter refers to money and power, the "steering media"[16] that uncouple the coordination of action from reaching understanding altogether.[17] The mass media, as generalized forms of communication,[18] release communicative processes from the provincialism of local (spatio-temporally restricted) contexts and permit public spheres to emerge. Their ambivalence resides in the fact they both hierarchize and remove restrictions on the horizon of possible understanding (*Verständigung*); that is, on the one hand they make knowledge the perogative of specialists and thus remove it from everyday communicative practices; on the other, they are dependent on the opening up of a general public sphere; in consequence of these two characteristics, they have both an authoritarian and an emancipatory potential.[19] However, Habermas's main interest lies with the second kind of relief mechanism that he identifies. The overburdening of communicative action also gives rise to a transfer of action coordination from language to steering media which uncouple interaction from the context of the life-world. Habermas focuses on money and power, the steering media that make possible the differentiation out of subsystems of economic activity and administrative activity which are functionally independent of the lifeworld. These subsystems provide the basis for the functional regulation of action, that is, for functional interconnections of action that bypass the individual's capacity as a responsible agent and create their own norm-free social structures jutting out from the social world. As we know, this is what Habermas means by functional (system) integration. To be sure, as Habermas reminds us, the subsystems of money and power are norm-free only *in the final instance;* they remain linked with everyday communicative practice via basic institutions of civil or public law.[20]

The uncoupling of subsystems of economic and administrative activity from the lifeworld is not in itself problematic. From the mere fact that social and system integration have become largely uncoupled from each other we cannot infer the subjugation of the lifeworld by imperatives of system integration. The institutions that anchor the economic and adminstrative subsystems in the lifeworld could function as a channel either for the influence of the lifeworld on formally organized domains of action or for the influence of the system (mechanisms of system coordination[21]) on communicatively structured contexts of action. Habermas puts it this way: "In the one case, they function as an institutional framework that subjects system maintenance to the normative restrictions of the lifeworld, in the other, as a base that subordinates the lifeworld to the systemic constraints of material reproduction . . . ."[22]

Reference to the colonization of the lifeworld suggests that it is the latter possibility that has in fact come about. But why has this happened? Why have not "institutions of freedom"[23] developed that would protect communicatively structured areas in the private and the public spheres against the "reifying inner dynamics of the economic and administrative systems"?[24] Habermas's explanation of the causes of this phenomenon picks up his argument in *Legitimation Crisis* and is, in the final instance, a Marxian one.[25] In broad outline it runs as follows:

An explanation of the Marxian type points us in the direction of class domination based on economic power. The colonization of the lifeworld can ultimately be traced back to class conflict. One of the weaknesses of Marx's account of class conflict is his exclusive focus on the economy in accounting for the subsumption of the lifeworld under the system (that is, under mechanisms of system integration). Habermas draws our attention to the role played by the administrative system (e.g., the state and the bureaucracy) in this process. As he argued in *Legitimation Crisis*, the administrative system can defuse potential conflicts deriving from the economically based class system by a series of rewards and compensations. Equally, crisis tendencies in the administrative subsystem (e.g., political alienation) can be headed off by distribution of the benefits at the disposal of the welfare state. Here Habermas is putting forward a model of two subsystems that compensate for weaknesses in each other and which enter into interchange relations with both the private and the public spheres of the lifeworld. The market and the state intervene in the lifeworld in order to pacify potential conflict. They turn the citizen—the role played by the agent in the public sphere of the lifeworld—into a *client* of public bureaucracies and thereby neutralize possibilities for political participation that have been opened up by the rationalization of the lifeworld. They turn the employee into a *consumer* of what the market has to offer, thereby defusing class conflict. However, these strategies for avoiding economic disequilibrium are not without side effects. Habermas believes that the colonization of the lifeworld will reach a threshold where it is perceived as intolerable. He claims that new conflict potentials are gathering in each of the two channels through which compensations flow from the subsystems into the public and private spheres of the lifeworld, and he points to the emergence of new social movements as evidence of this.[26] When he points to the emergence of protest potentials along the lines of conflict one would expect if the thesis of the colonization of the lifeworld were correct, Habermas is thinking of the ecology movement, the feminist movement, experiments with "alternative" lifestyles, local autonomy groups, gay liberation, etc., which emerged in the 1970s and the 1980s in developed capitalist societies such as the Federal Republic of Germany and the United States of America. Habermas claims that it is characteristic of these new social movements that they are primarily concerned not with the compensations that the welfare state can provide but with defending and restoring endangered forms of life. The issues that occupy them have to do not with problems of distribution but with the quality of life, equal rights, individual self-realization, human rights, participation, and so on.[27] The correctness of this description and this diagnosis must be tested empirically. Some commentators have argued that Habermas's model provides the best available framework for an explanation of new social movements and of what is at stake in the struggles in which they engage.[28] Others have suggested that Habermas's perspective is an unjustifiable generalization of the special path of development within the Federal Republic of Germany (before unification).[29] It can be argued, for instance, that unemployment is very much a pathology of modern life but that it cannot be explained in terms of the conflict between the system and the lifeworld; furthermore, and connected with this, it can be argued that what Habermas describes as pathologies of modernity are problems and tendencies that are specific to societies in which there is continuous economic growth. In response to criticisms of this kind, Habermas has replied that the conflicts that arise in countries where there is not continuous economic growth are variations of traditional kinds of conflict.[30] Presumably, this means that they are not specifically modern pathologies at all. However, this response is hardly satisfactory, implying as it does that the thesis of the colonization of the lifeworld holds only for societies in which there is continuous economic growth. In view of the world's present economic climate, this would represent a considerable restriction. Moreover, it fails to take account of societies in which there is continuous economic growth but very high unemployment.[31] It would be unfair to nail Habermas on a response to a question in an interview, but it certainly appears that further clarification is necessary here.

Quite apart from whether Habermas is correct to discern protest potentials in contemporary societies and whether his perspective is too narrowly focused, one could ask why there should be *any* conflict. One could ask (as does Habermas himself) why, in the face of a more or less successful welfare-state compromise, any conflicts should be gathering in the lifeworld at all. Habermas suggests the following response:

Welfare-state mass democracy is an arrangement that renders innocuous the class antagonism that is still built into the economic system. However, the condition of its success is economic growth. Only when there is economic growth are the material resources for compensation available. At the same time, however, the internal dynamics of the economic system, bolstered by the state, gives rise to a progressive increase in the system's complexity. Not only is there an *extension* of formally organized domains of action; there is also an increase in their internal *density*.[32] This in turn implies increasing colonization— increasing penetration of the economic and administrative subsystems into the symbolically structured lifeworld. Habermas points to the phenomenon of the increasing juridification (*Verrechtlichung*) of the public dimension of social life in order to illustrate his colonization thesis.[33] One could also point to the increasing commodification of the private dimension of social life as further evidence of this.[34] In addition, Habermas argues that his colonization thesis offers a fruitful perspective for explaining structural changes in personality development (psychopathologies).[35] However, even if Habermas can show that the colonization of the lifeworld results in certain social pathologies, this does not in itself imply that they will be perceived as such by members of the lifeworld, or, over and above this, that they will give rise to protest. Habermas suggests that the new social movements are evidence of such conflict but admits that the answer to the question is ultimately an empirical one. He acknowledges that it remains an empirical question *to what extent* the need for integration in modern societies can be covered by the achievements of system integration.[36]

Despite acknowledging that it is an open question whether the tendencies toward monetarization and bureaucratization will ever reach a state in which the integrative functions of the lifeworld have been completely given over to the mechanisms of the system, Habermas continues to hope that this cannot happen. He claims that the spheres of social life that are integrated via mechanisms of communicative action *cannot* be integrated by system mechanisms.[37] They are *by their very nature* dependent for their reproduction on the medium of communicative action.[38] The spheres of the lifeworld that are dependent for their reproduction on action oriented toward understanding break down "in some way or other" when they are uncoupled from communicative action and subjected to mechanisms of system integration.[39] Habermas thus insists—albeit rather vaguely—that commercialization (commodification) and bureaucratization *must* give rise to pathologies.[40]

This does not mean that the causes of the pathologies must be perceived—a fact that Habermas recognizes. His optimism in pointing to the emergence of protest potentials is tempered by caution; he also draws attention to the fragmentation of consciousness, which has replaced ideological thought forms as a means of suppressing conflict in modern societies. This brings me to the second main type of pathological development that Habermas sees as characteristic of modern societies: the cultural impoverishment of the lifeworld.

As we know, Habermas takes over Max Weber's characterization of cultural modernity in terms of the disintegration of substantive reason into various procedurally defined moments. With the rationalization of the lifeworld, "the substantive reason expressed in religious and metaphysical worldviews falls apart into moments that are held together only procedurally, that is, through the form of argumentative justification. . . . Traditional problems are divided up under the specific viewpoints of truth, normative rightness, and authenticity or beauty, and are dealt with respectively as questions of knowledge, justice, or taste. . . ."[41] Corresponding to this we find a differentiation of the cultural value spheres of science, morality, and art. This means that scientific discourse, studies in moral and legal theory, and aesthetic production and art criticism are institutionalized as the affairs of experts. The cultural tradition is dealt with by professionals under just one aspect at a time. This abstract, professionalized treatment is necessary for the emergence of cognitive-instrumental, moral-practical, and aesthetic-expressive complexes of knowledge.[42] Thus, for Habermas, the emergence of specialized value spheres represents both a learning process and a potential source of pathology.

The second type of pathological tendency arises from the fact that, in consequence of this increasing professionalization, the distance between the so-called expert cultures and the general public grows ever wider. Learning processes *within* each of the specialized value spheres do not automatically flow back into everyday communicative practice but remain cut off from it. This leads to a drying up of vital traditions, to the impoverishment of everyday practice.[43]

But why has this happened? Why has the rationalization of the lifeworld apparently led not just to an uncoupling of the administrative and economic subsystems from the lifeworld but also to an uncoupling and an encapsulation of expert cultures? Why has it not permitted the reconnection of modern culture to an impoverished everyday practice, which is dependent on traditions that bestow meaning if it is not to dry up? Beyond suggesting the need for a Marxian explanation, Habermas does not give any clear answer to this. It is obvious that he believes that the impoverishment of the lifeworld is connected with its colonization by imperatives of the economic and administrative subsystems; nonetheless, although he suggests a connection between cultural impoverishment and the fragmentation of consciousness (which in late capitalist societies, he claims, is a functional equivalent for ideology), he provides no argument to show that either of these phenomena results from the colonization of the lifeworld.

Habermas argues that the pacificatory mechanisms of the welfare state are accompanied by a fragmentation of consciousness, which is a "functional equivalent for ideology."[44] Habermas agrees with the thesis of "the end of ideology"[45] to the extent that he maintains that the rationalization of the lifeworld has left no room for what Marx meant by ideologies. Although we can distinguish between first and second generations of ideologies,[46] all forms of ideology take the form of totalizing conceptions of order. It is precisely this form of a global interpretation of the whole that has broken down under the pressure of the rationalization of the lifeworld. Ideologies relied for their success on at least some categories of belief remaining immune to the corrosive effects of rational scrutiny. However, as we have seen, with the extension of processes of communicative action to more and more areas of social life, rational scrutiny is turned on more and more beliefs. This growth in transparency means that ideologies have no longer anywhere to hide: "The communicative practice of everyday life no longer affords any niches for the structural violence of ideologies."[47]

If it is true that, in accordance with its rationalization, the lifeworld loses its structural possibilities for ideology formation, then one would expect that the conflict between social and system integration (and presumably also the causes of the impoverishment of the lifeworld) would be openly recognized. Since this does not appear to have happened in late capitalist societies, Habermas suggests that such societies have found a functional equivalent for ideology formation. Instead of positively producing ideologies to meet the need for interpretation in a given society, they function negatively to prevent interpretations of the whole from coming into existence in the first place. Everyday knowledge remains diffuse and below the level of articulation at which it might be accepted as valid according to the standards of cultural modernity. Everyday consciousness loses its power to grasp the whole; it becomes fragmented. We can see that this is directly connected with the splitting off of the cultural value spheres from everyday communicative practice. Once again, the metaphor of colonization is appropriate; like colonial masters, the imperatives of the economic and administrative subsystems make their way into the lifeworld and force a process of assimilation upon it.[48] The fragmentation of everyday consciousness prevents the coordination necessary to rebel against this and to create "institutions of freedom" which would harness the colonizing power of the market and the administrative apparatus. The protest reactions that Habermas discerns in the emergence of new social movements merely confirm the metaphor of colonization: Colonial masters may take over modes of social existence, but they are unlikely to be able to suppress them indefinitely. The idea of fragmentation suggests the metaphor of "divide and conquer" to accompany the metaphor of colonization. At the same time, it should be noted that Habermas does not argue this explicitly. There is an implication that the fragmentation of consciousness deriving from the splitting off of expert cultures from everyday practice is the result of the encroachment of system integration into the lifeworld, but this is not worked out systematically. The causes of cultural impoverishment, as a specific pathology of modernity, remain underdeveloped in Habermas's writings.[49]

2

Where does communicative rationality fit into all this? Can it provide a yardstick against which the pathologies of modernity might be measured? As we have seen, Habermas identifies two kinds of rationalization process in modern societies; but even if his diagnosis and his explanation of tendencies within modern societies are correct, it is not yet clear why these developments should be regarded as *pathologies*. The claim that the rationalization processes of modern societies either are in themselves pathological or lead to pathologies within the life-world might be given some empirical support if it could be shown that the new social movements are best characterized as protests against the developmental trends of modern societies. At the same time, this can hardly bear the full weight of Habermas's thesis. Moreover, as Habermas himself argues, the fragmentation of consciousness that accompanies these rationalization processes means that their effects are, as a rule, not perceived as pathologies—indeed, as a rule, their effects are not perceived at all.

Can the notion of communicative rationality provide standards that would enable us to criticize the development of modern societies as pathological? More specifically, can it provide standards that would allow us to denounce the infiltration of modes of system integration into more and more domains of the lifeworld and also to call for the reconnecting of knowledge arrived at by specialists in the three cultural spheres of value with the impoverished lifeworld?

It seems to me that the concept of communicative rationality can be used as a means of criticizing both the encroachment of mechanisms of functional (system) integration into the communicatively structured lifeworld and the cultural impoverishment of the lifeworld only in conjunction with other arguments. Moreover, it is worth noting that it can do so only indirectly: It can permit a critique of the developmental tendencies of modern societies only to the extent that it permits criticism of deformations of the lifeworld that can be shown to result from these tendencies. The pathological nature of the latter is shown through the demonstration of the pathological nature of their *effects* within the lifeworld: Only these effects are susceptible to critique through appeal to the notion of communicative rationality. Obviously, the burden of proof here is a double one. If Habermas is to argue that the development of modern rationalization processes is pathological, he will have to show that it gives rise to certain effects in the lifeworld and he will have to suggest standards that would allow us to reject these effects as pathological. It is important to be clear about precisely where the notion of communicative rationality has relevance as a yardstick for measuring pathologies, for Habermas himself is often confusing in this regard. What is particularly confusing is that Habermas uses the term "social pathology" to refer both to the developmental trends of modernity (colonization of the lifeworld and cultural impoverishment) and to the effect of these on the lifeworld (of which loss of meaning, anomie, and psychopathologies are examples). I want to argue that the concept of communicative rationality is *directly* applicable only to the latter—although, of course, criticizing the effects of rationalization processes is a perfectly adequate way of criticizing the processes themselves. Habermas, however, sometimes suggests that the concept of communicative rationality permits us to criticize not just the effects of the rationalization processes of modern societies within the lifeworld but also the uneven development of these processes.

On the basis of remarks scattered throughout his writings, Habermas appears to suggest two main ways in which the concept of communicative rationality can function as a yardstick for assessing and criticizing the pathologies of modernity. First, it provides a model for the free interplay of the three dimensions of reason which he believes have been differentiated out historically. Second, it rests on certain idealizations implicit in our everyday practices, that permit us to criticize actual communicative practices (and perhaps also actual beliefs and normative judgements) for their failure to live up to those idealizations.

What does the first of these two ways look like? As we know, Habermas regards the development of rationalization processes in modern societies as selective or uneven (unbalanced). He criticizes the predominance of imperatives of the subsystems of power and money over the communicative action of the lifeworld in modern societies, and he calls for a new balance between the integrative mechanisms of the subsystems and the integrative mechanisms of the lifeworld.[50] He repeatedly expresses the notion of a balanced or nonselective pattern of rationalization in terms of a harmonious interplay of the three cultural value spheres in which no one sphere would predominate and all three spheres would be anchored institutionally in the lifeworld.[51] The yardstick he appeals to for the assessment of one-sided rationalization and the predominance of one complex of rationality (the cognitive-instrumental) at the expense of the other two (moral-practical and aesthetic-expressive) is: "the idea of the free play of the cognitive-instrumental with the moral-practical and with the aesthetic-expressive within an everyday practice in which cognitive interpretations, moral expectations and expressions and evaluations would interpenetrate in an *uninhibited* and *balanced* way."[52]

As we have seen, for Habermas this notion of a free and harmonious interplay of the cultural value spheres expresses the idea of the unity of reason under conditions of modernity. It is given a formal-pragmatic underpinning by the thesis that, in everyday communicative action, the speaker with every speech act makes reference to three mutually irreducible dimensions of validity simultaneously. In chapter 3 above I found the substance of this thesis to be justified and suggested the need for no more than minor qualifications. Habermas clearly wants to appeal to this notion in order to criticize the selectivity of modern rationalization processes—that is, the predominance of the spheres of influence of the subsystems of money and power over those of the lifeworld in modern societies. He can do so, however, only to the extent that he correlates the economic and administrative subsystems with the dimension of cognitive-instrumental rationality. However, as has been indicated in section 1 of the present chapter and section 2 of chapter 1, the rationality characteristic of the subsystems of money and power is not cognitive-instrumental but *functionalist*.

Functionalist rationality is not the same as cognitive-instrumental rationality. In focusing on functionalist reason as opposed to instrumental reason or purposive-rational (*zweckrational*) activity, Habermas breaks decisively not only with the first generation of critical theory (Horkheimer, Adorno et al.)[53] but also with his own earlier writings. In his earlier work, Habermas proposed a fundamental distinction not between the system and the lifeworld (and, correspondingly, functional integration and social integration) but between purposive-rational and communicative action (as two analytically distinguishable and mutually irreducible categories of human activity).[54] His shift in perspective is presented systematically for the first time in *The Theory of Communicative Action* (recall the subtitle of the second volume: *Lifeworld and System: A Critique of Functionalist Reason*). Although Habermas does not always spell this out clearly, he now makes a distinction between instrumental rationality (or purposive-rational action) and functionalist reason. As we have seen, strategic action is an example of the former but not of the latter to the extent that it (in contrast to functionalist reason) does not bypass the consciousness of the agents concerned.

Strategic action is a type of instrumental action to the extent that participants in action instrumentalize one another as a means for their respective success. Nonetheless, although what is expected of agents in media-steered interaction is strategic action (an objectivating attitude toward the action situation and an ability to affect the decisions of others in a purposive-rational (*zweckrational*) manner),[55] the economic and administrative subsystems are systems not of instrumental rationality but of functionalist reason, for the *system itself* acts as the transmittor of the system-maintaining imperatives. The agents' (strategic) goals become the means of system maintenance. This inverts the relationship between ends and means that is characteristic of instrumental action.[56] The result, as Habermas has now acknowledged, is that "media-steered interactions no longer embody instrumental but rather functionalist reason."[57] If this is the case, then the functionalist rationality characteristic of the media-steered subsystems cannot straightforwardly be equated with the cultural value sphere of cognitive-instrumental rationality. At the very least, the claim that it can would have to be argued far more forcefully. For this reason, and as things stand, the idea of a free and harmonious interplay of the three value spheres cannot serve as a yardstick for measuring the selectivity of modern rationalization processes; it is merely a possibly dubious metaphor that indicates the need for balance in a very general way.

Nor can the concept of communicative rationality be used in this way as a standard for the critique of the second pathology of modernity identified by Habermas: the cultural impoverishment of the lifeworld.[58] Whereas colonization is an attack on the lifeworld from *outside* it, cultural impoverishment is a pathological development that takes place *within* the lifeworld.[59] However, once again we see that, when it comes to criticizing this phenomenon, the idea of achieving a balance between various dimensions of rationality is not particularly helpful.

The idea of the unity of reason, expressed in terms of the free and harmonious interplay of the three (or more)[60] dimensions of rationality to which everyday communicative action makes reference, cannot

provide a normative standard for the critique of cultural impoverishment. According to Habermas, everyday communicative practice
becomes impoverished as, increasingly, the knowledge produced by
experts in their various fields remains encapsulated in the specialist
cultures. The problem here, however, is one not of imbalance but of
dessication, and this occurs more or less equally in all three domains
of the lifeworld. Habermas acknowledges this, pointing out that the
question of how the moments of reason retain their unity within differentiation has nothing to do with the question of how the knowledge produced in expert cultures can be mediated with everyday
practices (or with that of how we can find an equivalent for the mean-
ing-bestowing power of traditional worldviews).[61]

Although the idea of communicative rationality as the free and harmonious interplay of various dimensions of reason turns out to be of
very limited usefulness as a yardstick for measuring societal pathologies, this does not mean that the concept of communicative rationality
cannot be used to criticize both the loss of freedom and the loss of
meaning that have been produced by the one-sided development of
the rationalization processes of modernity. However, it cannot do so
by appealing to the idea of the free and harmonious interplay of the
three cultural value spheres; it can do so only by reference to the
idealizations implicit in everyday communicative practice. Further, it
cannot be applied directly to criticize the developmental trends of
modern societies; it can be applied directly only to the effects of these
trends within the lifeworld. At most it can provide standards for the
critical evaluation of deformations within the lifeworld that have been
shown to be the results of the steady encroachment of mechanisms of
functional integration into more and more domains of the lifeworld.
Identifying such deformations and explaining their origins is thus a
necessary first step in the process of criticism. For this reason, other
arguments are necessary before the notion of communicative rationality can be employed as a standard for criticizing the loss of freedom and the loss of meaning.

3

As we know, the reproduction of the lifeworld takes place in three
domains: cultural reproduction, social integration, and socialization.

If we combine these with the three structural components of the life-world (culture, society, and personality), we arrive at a schema (figure 23 in *The Theory of Communicative Action*[62]) that shows the contributions that the individual processes of reproduction make toward maintaining the structural components of the lifeworld. Figure 23 represents the contribution made by social reproduction processes in a society in which the lifeworld has been rationalized to the extent that these processes rely on postconventional modes of action oriented toward understanding.[63] Corresponding to this, Habermas suggests a schema (figure 22) to represent disturbances in the processes of reproduction.[64] This schema shows nine possible manifestations of disturbance (pathologies). It highlights, in the domain of culture, the *loss of meaning* that results from a disturbance in cultural reproduction;[65] in the domain of society, the *anomie* that results from a disturbance in the process of social integration; and in the domain of personality, the *mental illnesses* (psychopathologies) that result from a disturbance in the process of socialization.

If Habermas can show that the pathologies mentioned result from the colonization of the lifeworld, it must then be possible to use the concept of communicative rationality as a yardstick for the assessment of these disturbances. Habermas contends that he can do this by providing a formal pragmatic account of systematically distorted communication.[66] However, apart from occasional suggestive remarks, he has not attempted to work this out in any detail. To give this task the attention it deserves would be beyond the scope of the present study; nonetheless, it is worth taking a brief look at what Habermas means by "systematically distorted communication."

Habermas applies this term to communicative action that violates its own necessary presuppositions. In the essay "Überlegungen zur Kommunikationspathologie," published in 1974, he attempted to give an account of such distorted communication in terms of a disturbance of the validity basis of speech. As we know, in the everyday communicative use of language there is a connection between meaning and validity, a connection between meaning and intention, and a connection between speaking and acting. This is what Habermas refers to as "the internal organization of speech."[67] Systematically distorted communication violates this internal organization. Habermas sees this as the result of overwhelming pressure exerted on the internal organization by the external organization of speech; the latter has to do with the regulation of the normative context in which discussion takes place; it regulates who is allowed to participate in which discussion, who can initiate topics, who can bring the discussion to a close, who can contribute and in which order, how the topics are ordered and how the scope of the discussion is determined, etc.[68] Habermas has continued to maintain that social pathologies can be interpreted as manifestations of systematically distorted communication.[69] However, he has not made any serious attempt to work out such a theory, either with regard to the idea of the violation of the internal organization of speech or in the light of his critique—developed since the 1974 essay—of functionalist reason. In the light of the latter he would have to show, in particular, how the increasing infiltration of modes of functional (system) integration into the communicatively structured domains of the lifeworld exerts irresistible pressure on the internal organization of speech. With regard to the former, the idea of a disconnection between meaning and validity, a disconnection between meaning and intention, and a disconnection between speaking and acting would need to be worked out in much more detail.[70] Habermas himself has not seriously pursued this task; however, James Bohman has taken up his idea of systematically distorted communication, and attempts to use it as a basis for a new theory of ideology.[71] Bohman gives an interesting account of what disruptions of the internal organization of speech might look like. He argues that we can speak of ideology where the connections between meaning and validity, between meaning and intention, and between speaking and acting are used to maintain relations of domination:

A promise, say of equality, is not ideological when it is simply violated, as much as when it is left standing and yet does not bind those with power in their subsequent interaction. In the opposite direction, an expression of desire becomes ideological when it cannot effectively bring into public discourse the needs and desires of the poor, the oppressed and the colonized. The theory of ideology identifies such pragmatic mechanisms for distorting the structure of meaningful speech in the service of power.[72]

Bohman also suggests a possible example of what "disconnections" between meaning and validity might look like. While agreeing with Habermas that the cognitive function represents a problem area for the theory of distorted communication "because there is no violation of the validity claim to truth that would be symptomatic for systematically distorted communication,"[73] Bohman contends that this is due to a misunderstanding on Habermas's part of what such "disconnections" amount to. In Bohman's view, the critique of ideology must focus not on *what* is said but on *how* it is said—for instance, on the manner in which a claim is redeemed in discourse. Consequently, discourses in which certain semantic contents are withdrawn from discursive testing can be denounced as ideological.[74]

While this is illuminating with regard to what Habermas might mean by "disturbances in the internal organization of speech," Bohman's account of "disconnections" between the structural components of speech acts clearly must look elsewhere for its normative force. We might ask, for example, why all expressions of desire *should* be given an equal hearing in public discourse. This suggests that an account of systematically distorted communication in terms of "disconnections" between the structural components of speech acts must be accompanied by an account of normative standards that would permit criticism of these "disconnections." In other words, the theory of systematically distorted communication requires the assistance of the concept of communicative rationality.

4

As we have seen, the idea of a harmonious interplay of various dimensions of rationality is not a useful basis for such a concept of communicative rationality. However, this does not exhaust the notion of communicative rationality. In the concluding pages I want to suggest that the real critical thrust of the concept of communicative rationality lies in the idealizing suppositions to which everyday communicative action necessarily refers. This brings me back to the idea of communicative rationality as a nondefeatist conception of reason. In chapter 2 I indicated some ways in which communicative rationality could be understood as a nondefeatist (that is, stubbornly critical) conception of reason. I want now to take another look at these in the light of the subsequent chapters.

The notion of communicative rationality is nondefeatist to the extent that it rests on certain idealizations which are built into everyday processes of communicative action and which lend to validity claims a potentially context-transcendent power. In chapter 2 I suggested three ways in which we might interpret this idea of the context-transcendent power of validity claims. On the first interpretation, on the presupposition of a post-traditional everyday communicative practice in which postconventional forms of communicative action are embedded, it resided in the idealizing supposition of argumentation (in postconventional forms of communicative action) that no argument is exempt in principle from critical evaluation in argumentation. Validity claims have a subversive power in such contexts because they are based on a subversive, continually flexible potential of disputable reasons.[75] Because validity claims are based on "a potential of" reasons that are always in principle disputable, they have the power to call into question and go beyond what is accepted as valid in any particular local context. The discussion in chapter 4 lent weight to this thesis to the extent that it affirmed a connection (at least for certain sorts of societies) between linguistic understanding and the critical and open intersubjective evaluation of validity claims. However, as I pointed out in chapter 2, this kind of subversive power is too diffuse to permit concrete critical assessment of the validity of actual beliefs and practices. Equally, it is too undefined to provide a standard for the measurement of social pathologies such as loss of meaning, anomie, and pyschological disorders.

As we know from chapter 2, Habermas attributes to both truth claims and moral claims a special context-transcendent power over and above this subversive potential. This derives from their connection with the idealizing supposition that everyone would agree to the universal validity of an agreement reached regarding them in a process of argumentation. The critical thrust of truth claims and moral claims resides in the tension between this notion of universal agreement (in a double sense of "universal") and the non-universality of the prevailing consensus as to the validity of a given claim. This idea becomes clearer if we take a brief look at Habermas's accounts of the justification of claims to moral validity and of claims to propositional truth; these accounts are known, respectively, as his theory of moral discourse (or justice)[76] and his theory of theoretical discourse (or truth).

At the center of Habermas's theory of moral discourse is the claim that the justification of moral norms and principles is conceptually tied to the notion of a discursively reached agreement as to their validity.

We should note that within the greater category of practical questions[77] Habermas distinguishes *moral, pragmatic,* and *ethical* questions. He defines moral questions (in the strict sense) on the basis of their internal connection with the idea of universal agreement (in a double sense of "universal"); they thus include only those norms and principles that embody a generalizable interest. Pragmatic questions (defined negatively through reference to moral questions) make up the class of practical questions on which no universal agreement is possible, but at best only a fair compromise. For Habermas, ethical questions of the good life are context-specific[78] practical questions that are concerned with the self-realization of specific individuals and groups.[79] For our present purposes, only those claims referred to by Habermas as moral claims are the subjects of moral discourses and have the relevant context-transcendent power.

As we saw in chapter 2, the strong idealizations to which moral discourses make implicit reference include the ideas of "universal moral respect" and "egalitarian reciprocity"[80]; over and above this, they make reference to an idea of universal validity (in a double sense of "universal"). In the context of his moral theory, Habermas refers to this idea as the principle U:

[that] *All* affected can accept the consequences and side effects its *general* observance can be anticipated to have for the satisfaction of *everyone's* interests (and these consequences are preferred to those of known alternative possibilities for regulation).[81]

Principle U has been criticized as too indeterminate, or too complex, or too counterfactual.[82] In this regard I am inclined to agree with Seyla Benhabib, who argues that U is not only confusing and implausible but—even more important—unnecessary. In her view, the discourse-ethical principle, "D" (together with the principles of universal moral respect and egalitarian reciprocity) is quite sufficient to serve as the only test of universalizability.[83] Principle D states that

only those norms can claim validity which could meet with the approval of all concerned in their capacity as participants in a practical discourse.[84]

In the following, I follow Benhabib in preferring D to U as the most convincing formulation of the idea of universal validity (in a double sense of "universal") to which moral argumentations make reference. However, since Habermas in *Faktizität und Geltung* proposes a new and more general formulation for the discourse principle D, to avoid confusion it might be advisable to refer to what used to be D as "U[1]."[85]

If we leave aside problems of formulation and terminology, Habermas's basic position seems to be that only those moral norms that express the general interest of everyone are valid, whereby the general interest is the agreement reached by participants in a moral discourse. Accordingly, in Habermas's theory of justice, a discursively reached agreement as to the validity of moral norms or principles is a *criterion* of their truth.

In consequence, the idea that the only moral norms and principles that are valid are those that express the general interest (where this is the product of a moral discourse) provides a standard by which we can criticize existing moral norms for their failure to embody the general interest. Of course, it only does so to the extent that we accept that participation in postconventional processes of moral argumentation requires us to make reference to the "strong idealizations" of universal moral respect and egalitarian reciprocity as well as to the other idealizing suppositions implicit in all forms of communicative action.

But how useful is this really? Habermas's discourse ethics has been attacked from many angles, but most frequently because its requirement of consensus in the face of the multiple value perspectives that characterize modern democracies would make moral judgement impossible to achieve.[86] Habermas's response to such criticism makes clear that he still sees rationally motivated consensus—moreover, consensus achieved in actual discourses—as central to the very notion of a discourse ethics; at the same time, he has acknowledged that the plurality and irreconcilability of value standards in contemporary societies means that the norms and principles on which it is possible to reach universal agreement in discourse will become more and more abstract and that the set of questions which can be answered rationally from the moral point of view will become smaller and smaller.[87] As I have indicated, Habermas maintains that not all practical questions are capable of being redeemed discursively. The general set of practical questions must be divided further into pragmatic questions (which are not concerned with general interests and on which the best we can hope for is a fair compromise) and evaluative questions of the good life (which are concerned with interests specific to individual life histories and which are, by their very nature, not generalizable).[88] Nonetheless, Habermas's acknowledgement that the set of questions on which it is possible to reach universal agreement is getting smaller and smaller raises questions about the usefulness of his discourse theory.[89] It could be argued that if we accept the substance of Habermas's discourse theory as an account of what constitutes the validity of a moral norm or judgement, the class of moral norms and judgements becomes so small that the part played by moral reason in dealing with the practical questions[90] of everyday life shrinks alarmingly. One could argue that Habermas's account of moral judgement, even if it can be maintained, has nothing to say about the most pressing practical problems confronting individuals and groups in everyday life; that the discourse theory of moral reason, even if valid, would have to be complemented by another theory dealing with all the practical questions excluded from Habermas's narrowly defined sphere of strictly moral questions; and indeed, that all the truly interesting and important practical questions are excluded from this sphere.[91] I think there are some grounds for such an argument, although I can do no more than suggest it here. For our present purposes it is sufficient to note the following: The assertion that moral validity claims have a special context-transcendent power deriving from their connection with the idea of universal agreement loses its relevance in proportion as the class of moral validity claims shrinks in modern societies. Thus, the idea that only those moral norms that express the general interest are valid may indeed provide a critical standard for the assessment of existing moral norms, but it is a standard that is increasingly inapplicable in the everyday practical affairs[92] of modern pluralist societies.

Habermas also attributes a special context-transcendent power to empirical and theoretical truth claims. As a brief look at his account of truth makes clear, truth claims, too, make reference to the idea that everyone would accept the universal validity of the agreement reached with regard to a disputed claim. However, on closer inspection, we find that Habermas acknowledges an important difference between truth claims and moral claims in this regard. This difference has implications for his attribution to truth claims of a special context-transcendent power.

The difference between truth claims and moral claims has to do with their respective connection with the idea of a universal agreement (in a double sense of "universal"). Whereas moral validity claims, as we have seen, are internally connected with the idea of discursively achieved universal agreement, truth claims are internally connected only with the idea of universal agreement. In contrast to moral claims, the link between truth claims and agreement reached in argumentation is not a *constitutive* one. Whereas the validity of moral claims is conceptually bound to actual processes of argumentation, the validity of claims to propositional truth is not. In contrast to his earlier position with regard to propositional truth, Habermas now argues that agreement reached in discourse is not a criterion of truth; it merely explicates the meaning of the idea of truth.[93]

I take Habermas to be making two points here. The first is the fallibilist point that every agreement—even one reached in a process of argumentation that comes very close to satisfying the strong idealizations I have mentioned—is tensed and relative to a context. For this reason, the possiblity of new evidence and arguments that would challenge this consensus can never be excluded in principle. Thus, all actual agreements—no matter how well founded—are always in principle subject to revision in the light of possible new evidence and arguments. For this reason, although we can regard a validity claim as well founded or *justified* if agreement as to its validity has been reached in discourse, its well-foundedness is always conditional. The idea of truth, in contrast, contains a moment of unconditionality that transcends all spatio-temporal contexts. Truth is an regulative idea[94]: "the anticipation of an infinite rational consensus."[95] It is part of the idea of truth that if we hold a claim to be true we hold that every rational person who is aware of the relevant arguments and evidence must accept it as true, not just now but also at any conceivable time in the future.[96] I take Habermas here to be affirming Putnam's point that "truth is supposed to be the property of a statement that cannot be lost, whereas justification can be lost."[97] Putnam gives the example that the view that "the earth is flat" was very likely justified (supported by a well-founded agreement) 3,000 years ago, but it is not justified today. Yet it would be wrong to say that "the earth is flat" was *true* 3,000 years ago, for that would mean that the earth has changed its shape. To this extent, the idea of truth contains a transcendent moment—a moment of unconditionality—and is a regulative idea. It is interesting to note that Habermas wants to reserve the notion of a regulative idea for the idea of truth, and that he wants to avoid the use of this notion in connection with the unavoidable presuppositions of communication (the "strong idealizations") because these have to be satisfied to a sufficient degree if argumentation is to be possible at all (and thus undermine the classical opposition between regulative and constitutive).[98]

The second point that I take Habermas to be making is that, in contrast to an earlier position, he no longer maintains that the discursive redemption of propositional truth claims is a criterion of their truth.[99] One of the reasons that such an assertion is implausible is that it neglects the importance of evidence in grounding empirical truth claims. The claim "There are tigers in Africa," if true, is not true *because* it is the result of a process of theoretical discourse in which agreement was reached as to the validity of the claim; it is true, if true, if there are tigers in Africa and if conclusive evidence for this can be produced by empirical research. In establishing truth claims of this kind, argumentation does not play any *constitutive* role. At the same time, it is part of the very meaning of truth that, if the claim "There are tigers in Africa" is true, all persons would have to agree to its universal validity if they were to participate in a theoretical discourse. To this extent, the idea of a rationally motivated consensus *explicates* (in part) the idea of truth[100]—"in part" because what is missing is the dimension of unconditionality to which I have already referred. To provide a fuller explication of the meaning of the idea, we would have to say: If a claim is true, all persons would have to agree to its universal and *infinite* validity in their capacity as participants in a theoretical discourse.

The fact that the truth of propositional truth claims is not constituted through theoretical discourse (which merely explicates their meaning) marks a point of distinction between such claims and moral validity claims. Theoretical discourses are not a criterion of the validity of (at least a significant number of) truth claims, whereas practical discourses are a criterion of the validity of moral validity claims. This has implications for the notion that validity claims have a context-transcendent power. As we have seen, in the case of moral validity claims, the notion of a discursively achieved agreement provides a standard for the critique of actual moral claims; but because this notion merely *explicates* the meaning of truth claims, it cannot fulfil the same function in the case of the latter. We cannot criticize an actual truth claim as false on the ground that it is not the product of a discursively achieved agreement. We can say that if an actual truth claim is false it would not be agreed to by the participants in a theoretical discourse; but this assertion is no more than an explication of the notion of propositional falsity, and it has, at best, only a very weak critical (context-transcendent) power.

Given that the context-transcendent (in the sense of subversive) power of validity claims is too *diffuse*, the special context-transcendent power of truth claims *too weak* and the special context-transcendent power of moral validity claims too *restricted*, we shall have to look elsewhere for the critical thrust of the concept of communicative rationality. I have suggested that there is a third sense in which validity claims are context-transcendent. Once again, this has to do with the connection between validity claims and argumentation. This time, however, what is at issue is not the validity or lack of validity of *claims* but the way in which argumentation is conducted and the actions and dispositions of those who participate in it. On this interpretation, the critical power of the notion of communicative rationality resides in the tension between the normative promise contained in the strong idealizations implicit in the very notion of argumentation and what happens in actual empirical practices of argumentation. Here we should bear in mind the distinction between those strong idealizations that are implicit in, respectively, conventional and post-conventional forms of argumentation.

As we have seen, all forms of argumentation are guided by the idealization that participants are motivated only by a concern for the better argument. This necessary presupposition allows us to criticize those who, by virtue of their very participation in discussion, must profess to but do not in fact share this motivation. This amounts to a standard for the critique of latently strategic action. Indeed, latently strategic action could be defined as action that fails to satisfy the necessary presupposition of an orientation toward the better argument in even the most minimal way. As we know from chapter 1, Habermas allows for both conscious and unconscious forms of latently strategic action. In the case of conscious latently strategic action, one of the participants in interaction deceives the other with regard to her orientation toward reaching understanding. In the case of unconscious latently strategic action, in contrast, at least one of the parties is deceiving herself.[101]

In addition, all forms of argumentation make reference to the idealizing supposition that the participants in discussion regard one another as accountable (*zurechnungsfähig*) and as willing to participate in the process of reaching understanding (*verständigungsbereit*).[102] Moreover, all forms of argumentation also make reference to the idea that participants act in an accountable way and show willingness to reach understanding. The discussion in chapters 3 and 4 has thrown light on what it is to be accountable. According to Habermas, a participant in communicative action is accountable to the extent that she acknowledges her obligation to support the claims raised with a given utterance, if challenged. But what counts as a violation of this presupposition? Here we can distinguish between (a) the failure to regard the other participant(s) as accountable and (b) the failure to be accountable. Both failures are susceptible to criticism as violations of the presupposition of accountability.

Failure (a) results from a failure to recognize the distinction between action oriented toward understanding and action oriented toward success; in modern societies this can be traced back to various pyschological disturbances, which in turn can have various causes. Recall Habermas's contention that the rationalization of the lifeworld is characterized by an increasingly clear demarcation between communicative and strategic action[103]; as communicative action is progressively freed from particular value orientations, participants begin increasingly to recognize the difference between these two types of action. In the case of participants in postconventional forms of communicative action, therefore, confusion between action oriented toward success and action oriented toward understanding is presumably a sign of pyschological regression. Of course, only the *unjustified* attribution to others of a strategic attitude can be regarded as a violation of this presupposition.

In contrast, failure (b) is not the result of a categorial confusion but results from the (deliberate or nondeliberate) pursuit of action oriented toward success within a context of action oriented toward understanding. We can see this if we look more closely at what it would mean to lack accountability—at what would count as a violation of the presupposition that one is acting as an accountable agent. We see that failure to provide convincing reasons in support of a validity claim raised need not count as a violation, for the presupposition of accountabilty has to do not with the validity of the claim raised but with the speaker's *undertaking of a warranty* (*Gewähr*) to provide reasons if challenged. It requires not that participants raise only valid claims but that they assume a certain kind of responsibility. This assumption of responsibility can be tested only through the speaker's *willingness* to enter into discussion with regard to the validity of the claims in question, whereby the sole aim of this discussion must be reaching understanding. Thus, the presupposition of accountability must be combined with the presupposition of willingness to reach understanding (*Verständigungsbereitschaft*) if it is to allow us to criticize a speaker who turns out not to be willing to enter into such a discussion, or to criticize a discussion in which the participants do not have this willingness. Lack of willingness to reach understanding is—in most cases, at least—likely to be the result of a strategic attitude. In most cases, therefore, lack of accountability and willingness to reach understanding can be said to amount to the replacement, whether deliberate or nondeliberate, of an attitude oriented toward understanding with an orientation toward success. The absence of accountability and willingness to reach understanding is, once again, simply a case of (conscious or unconscious) latently strategic action.

It is interesting to note that lack of accountability and willingness to reach understanding takes on a special significance in postconventional forms of communicative action. In forms of communicative action that are guided by the idealizing supposition that no argument is in principle exempt from critical evaluation in argumentation, this presupposition implies that participants must be willing to engage in genuinely open processes of intersubjective critical evaluation of validity claims. This allows us to criticize actual processes of argumentation on the basis of the participants' lack of willingness to consider new perspectives and their lack of openness to new arguments. To this extent, in postconventional forms of communicative action the idea that participants must be willing to reach understanding adds a new dimension to the critique of latently strategic action. Whereas in conventional forms of communicative action the presupposition of willingness to reach understanding amounts to no more than a concern for the force of the better argument, in postconventional forms it goes beyond this: participants here must be willing (in principle) to consider *any* argument and to continue the discussion indefinitely. Moreover, if we draw out the implications of this, we see that in postconventional forms of communicative action this presupposition implies that participants must be willing (in principle) to consider the arguments of *everyone*, no matter how poorly they are articulated, and to attach (in principle) equal weight to all these arguments. This, in turn, implies that participants in argumentation possess not just certain grammatical and logical skills but also "virtues" (such as a sense of justice and honesty in their dealings with themselves and others). If participants in such forms of communicative action must seriously consider (in principle) all arguments, no matter who puts them forward or how they are put forward, the presupposition of willingness to reach understanding must include the presupposition of willingness to face the possibility of self-deception and to avoid lack of truthfulness in dealing with others, as well as a willingness to treat all partners in discussion fairly. This means, on the one hand, a recognition of everyone's equal entitlement to introduce new topics into discussion and to express needs and desires and, on the other, a willingness to confront the arguments of others in a fair and unbiased way. In addition, since argumentation can work in favor of those who are practiced in the skills of argumentation and against those who lack these skills, willingness to reach understanding also presupposes a willingness not just to listen to what the other participants actually say but also to be sensitive to what they might want to say as well as an awareness of the danger of imposing categories and concepts on the needs and desires of others. Willingness to reach understanding requires a genuine openness not just to new arguments but also to the needs, desires, anxieties, and insecurities—whether expressed or unexpressed—of the other participants; at times this will require a special sensitivity and a willingness to look beyond explicit verbal expressions and deficiencies in argumentative skills.[104]

Thus, if we draw out the implications of the presupposition of accountability in postconventional forms of communicative action, we see that it amounts to a willingness to participate in open and critical discussions in which no argument is immune (in principle) to critical scrutiny, from which nobody is excluded (in principle), and in which everyone's arguments carry (in principle) equal weight. We might also say that such forms of argumentation are guided by the idealizing suppositions of "universal moral respect" and "egalitarian reciprocity." [105] This suggests—contrary to what Benhabib implies—that these principles do not refer exclusively to moral argumentation but are necessary presuppositions of all postconventional forms of argumentation. At the same time, we should recall Benhabib's insistence that they are presuppositions of argumentation only for the members of modern ethical communities for whom the theological and ontological bases of inequality among humans have been radically called into question. [106]

The third suggested interpretation of the context-transcendent power of validity claims thus appears to provide the most fruitful basis for a nondefeatist conception of communicative rationality. The tension between the normative promise contained in the various idealizing suppositions that guide (in particular, postconventional) communicative action and what actually happens in specific contexts of communicative action permits us to criticize participants and practices on the basis of their failure to fulfil this normative promise. At the same time, the limitations of such a position should be recognized. Interpreted in this way, communicative rationality allows us to criticize not arguments themselves but only the way in which they are conducted. The basis for criticism is not the validity or lack of validity of reasons but the way in which reasons are discussed. Judgements cannot be criticized on the basis of the knowledge they embody; they can be criticized only on the basis of the way in which they are reached. [107] Those—including Habermas—who wish to maintain a cognitive basis for the criticism of validity claims may be concerned by the relative weakness of such a position. We should recall, however, that the foregoing discussion has shown not that there is *no* possibility of criticism on the basis of cognitive content but only that this possibility is much more limited that Habermas's writings imply. The discussion has, for instance, allowed that there may be an internal connection between discursively reached universal agreement (in a double sense of "universal") and moral validity claims; it has also allowed that this connection may provide a standard for the criticism of such claims on the basis of the knowledge they embody. However, as I pointed out, even Habermas himself acknowledges that such claims constitute an increasingly small category in modern pluralist societies; consequently, if the critical thrust of the concept of communicative rationality were to be confined to cognitive justification, it would be very restricted indeed. For this reason, a noncognitive but broader basis for criticism that allows us to criticize actual practices of argumentation is an important complement to a critical approach that focuses on cognitive content. Some may be disappointed by the perceived weakness of this conclusion, but it could be argued that this is precisely where its strength lies. It avoids asserting an implausibly strong connection between language and validity by acknowledging that, of the multiple kinds of validity claims that characterize everyday communicative practice, only some—in certain sorts of society—are internally connected with the idea of agreement reached in discourse; at the same time, it refuses to see this as a ground for defeat, for the pragmatic presuppositions of argumentation themselves provide an alternative basis for criticism that does not require proof of a link between validity claims and consensus (which is often problematic). Indeed, the conception of communicative rationality that has emerged from the foregoing is a reassuringly modest one.

5

The concept of communicative rationality has a utopian content to the extent that it points toward a vision of a rationalized lifeworld where cultural traditions would be reproduced through processes of intersubjective evaluation of validity claims, where legitimate orders would be dependent on critical and open argumentative practices for establishing and justifying norms, and where individual identities would be self-regulated through processes of critical reflection. I have already dealt with a number of common objections to this vision.[108] Some of these turned out to be based on misunderstandings: For instance, the objection that the rationalization of the lifeworld purports to tell us which beliefs are true or which values are right misunderstands the purely formal character of Habermas's utopian projection; and the objection that this is a projection of the necessary developmental dynamics of modern societies neglects Habermas's distinction between the logics and dynamics of development. However, it seems to me that even a sympathetic interpretation of the notion of communicative rationality that does not succumb to these and other misunderstandings must have reservations about some aspects of Habermas's vision. I see grounds for unease with regard to the utopian projection of a rationalized lifeworld in all three of its constitutive domains. Although none of these reservations implies that we should abandon the concept of communicative rationality, they do suggest the need for modification and caution.

In the first domain, Habermas projects the vision of a lifeworld in which cultural traditions would be reproduced through the critical and open intersubjective assessment of validity claims. My main reservation here is that Habermas's vision fails to take sufficiently seriously the inadequacy of a communicative socialization in which only the mechanism of reaching understanding in argumentation (*Verständigung*) is available. As I pointed out in chapter 1, communicative action cannot itself generate the semantic potentials on which human well-being depends.[109] I argued that increasing reflexivity (in the sense of increasingly open and critical scrutiny of validity claims) may lead to the progressive erosion of the traditional interpretations and practices which have hitherto been a source for human attempts to understand themselves in their relation to society and history. It is far from clear that the specialized knowledge generated in the so-called expert cultures of science, law and morality, and art could provide a substitute for the semantic potentials generated by tradition *even if* the thorny problem of feedback from these expert cultures to the lifeworld could be resolved. That Habermas does not sufficiently acknowledge the seriousness of this problem may be connected with his neglect of the world-articulating and world-disclosing dimensions of everyday language.[110] Certainly any attempt to address this question would have to rectify this neglect. However, Habermas's failure to take this problem sufficiently seriously may also be symptomatic of his concern with freedom (in the sense of self-determination) rather than happiness. Perhaps there is a need to readdress the question of whether emancipation without happiness or fulfilment is really desirable. At any rate, the limitations of this vision of cultural reproduction would have to be explicitly acknowledged.[111] What may be required here is a more modest understanding of the connection between the emancipatory power of communicative rationality and human well-being.

In the second domain, Habermas projects the vision of a lifeworld in which legitimate orders would be reproduced and regulated through critical and open processes of discursive will and opinion formation; furthermore, and connected with this, the bonds that join the members of such a lifeworld would be based on a common concern with question of legal, political, and moral right rather than on a shared commitment to common substantive notions of the good life. This projection of a rationalized lifeworld thus conceives solidarity as the mirror image of justice: The solidarity between members of such a rationalized lifeworld is founded on their common concern with the good of a society based on self-determination and equal respect, as manifested through a commitment to discursive procedures of will and opinion formation.[112] This, surely, is the vision that has been at the heart of Habermas's theoretical enterprise, at least since *Transformation of the Public Sphere*.[113] It is the vision of a public realm in which individuals gather to take part in open discussions, to which everyone has equal access and in which everyone participates on an equal basis. It is also the vision of a democratic state in which public issues are regulated through discussion and collective decision making.

While acknowledging the power of Habermas's vision and its importance in the context of the development of modern democracies, I have reservations about some aspects of it. My main concern is not that this vision prioritizes questions of right but that it neglects questions of the good. In particular, Habermas's account of solidarity as the bond that joins the members of a democratically self-regulated lifeworld is unconvincing. Indeed, it is so abstract that it is not recognizable as a conception of solidarity. Solidarity is not just a point of view; it is a feeling. It has affective as well as cognitive dimensions. It is difficult to see how a common concern for freedom (in the sense of self-determination) and for norms and principles that are in the general interest could provide the required affective basis.[114] Although Habermas is no doubt justified in deploring the lack of solidarity in his sense in modern pluralist and self-professed democratic societies and in seeing it as a resource that is under threat,[115] it could be argued that what is also lacking is a sense of solidarity that, while based on recognition of shared traditions and common interpretations of the good life, does not succumb to chauvinism and exclusivity. While the question of whether it is possible to work out such a conception of solidarity is still open—and it is conceivable that no such conception of solidarity is possible in modern pluralist societies—the limitations of Habermas's account of solidarity must be acknowledged. Once again, what is required here is modesty; a recognition that the extension of processes of intersubjective critical evaluation to more and more areas of (political and public) will and opinion formation does not in itself amount to a solution of the problem of social integration.

In the third domain, Habermas projects the vision of a lifeworld in which individuals would regulate their identities through processes of intersubjective critical evaluation. My main reservation here is Habermas's reliance on a model of transparent subjectivity. Although Habermas may not be claiming that the development of the individual subject takes place in and through processes of intersubjective critical evaluation, he does appear to be implying that full knowledge of the self to itself is desirable and that it is possible in principle.[116] He appears to see consciousness as (in principle) rationally—and thus also linguistically—retrievable. He allows for no gap (in principle) between subjectivity and interpretations of subjectivity—between what I *am* and what I and others see me to be. This could be viewed as part of a more general tendency to "linguistify" experience and action: It could be argued that Habermas "linguistifies" human experience and action and fails to take sufficient account of their nonlinguistic and prelinguistic dimensions.[117] Although I cannot conduct such an argument here, I believe it could be shown that a problematic adherence to an ideal of communicative transparency permeates Habermas's theory and has implications for the ideals of lifeworld rationalization in each of the three domains.[118] However, I also believe it can be shown that this problematic adherence to an ideal of communicative transparency is intimately connected with Habermas's emphasis on agreement as the telos of rational discussion[119]; a severing or a loosening of the link between validity and consensus can help us to avoid this problem.[120] The concept of communicative rationality that has emerged from the foregoing takes a step in the right direction to the extent that it looks more toward the pragmatic presuppositions of *practices* of argumentation and less toward the *results* of such argumentations. Once again, what is required is a more modest conception of communicative rationality—one that acknowledges the importance of the pre- and nonlinguistic dimensions of human experience and action.

Although there may be grounds for unease with regard to some aspects of Habermas's utopian projection of a rationalized lifeworld, we should be wary of losing sight of Habermas's achievements. Over the years, from *Transformation of the Public Sphere* to *Faktizität und Geltung*, Habermas has kept alive the vision of a self-regulating, deliberative political and public realm as central to the very project of a critical social theory. Nothing in the foregoing discussion has called this vision into question—at most, I have suggested on occasion that it may not be enough. In addition, Habermas is one of the few contemporary thinkers to have seriously addressed the question of normative standards in a world in which universally shared notions of the good life no longer seem to be possible. Since Habermas looks to language in the attempt to find normative standards for the critique of social pathologies, of the injustice of norms and of social practices, and of failures in the development of personal identity, those who reject his linguistic approach are faced with the problem of finding generally acceptable alternative bases for criticism. While the question of possible alternative bases for criticism must remain open, it may be that we abandon Habermas's notion of communicative rationality at our peril. Moreover, the foregoing discussion should allay some worries with regard to Habermas's linguistic approach to the extent that the concept of communicative rationality that has emerged is an unassuming one, both in its critical scope and as regards its self-understanding: It acknowledges that it has little to say about the cognitive content of judgements and norms, that it does not provide a complete account of human experience and action, and that it is not a sufficient condition for human well-being. I thus suggest, in conclusion, that Habermas's concept of communicative rationality merits a third attribute: What Habermas has extracted from the validity bases of everyday linguistic activity is not just a postmetaphysical yet nondefeatist concept of communicative rationality but also a self-consciously modest one. Perhaps we should see in this its distinctive modernity.

Notes

Chapter 1

1. See, in particular, *Erkenntnis und Interesse* / *Knowledge and Human Interests*.

2. See, e.g., Wellmer, "Reason, Utopia and the Dialectic of Enlightenment."

3. For a comprehensive and reliable discussion of Habermas's work up to the mid 1970s see McCarthy, *The Critical Theory of Jürgen Habermas*.

4. In the sense of reflection on the constraints to which a given subject succumbs in the process of self-formation.

5. Ibid.

6. See *TCA*, 2, 399 / *TKH*, 2, 584; in addition, this idea is the main concern of Habermas's essay "Die Philosophie als Platzhalter und Interpret" / "Philosophy as Stand-In and Interpreter," in *Moralbewußtsein und kommunikatives Handeln* / *Moral Consciousness and Communicative Action*.

7. *TCA*, 1, 138 / *TKH*, 1, 199.

8. W. E. Connolly, quoted by Habermas in "Reply," 239f.

9. *Faktizität und Geltung*, 9.

10. Ibid., 21.

11. *TCA*, 1, 318 / *TKH*, 1, 426; see also "Entgegnung"349f. / "A Reply," 230f.

12. *TCA*, 2, 400f. / *TKH*, 2, 587.

13. Habermas's theory of formal pragmatics is complemented *inter alia* by a theory of social evolution in which the development of societies is examined from the point of view of their general logic. This is the diachronic complement to his synchronic analysis of everyday language. See, e.g., *Communication and the Evolution of Society*.

14. Although the terms "universal" and "formal" appear to be used interchangeably by Habermas, the notion of "universal" pragmatics suggests that the results of his investigations into language hold universally and not just for the communicative practices of members of certain sorts of societies. For this reason I prefer the more modest connotations of "formal pragmatics," and I shall opt for this formulation in the following. In his more recent writings Habermas most frequently speaks of "formal" rather than "universal" pragmatics, although he has not, to my knowledge, specified why.

15. "Quasi-transcendental" to the extent that Habermas retains the universalist line of questioning of transcendental philosophy while detranscendentalizing the mode of procedure and the conception of what is shown. See "Reply" for more on this theme.

16. The term *Verständigung* is discussed below.

17. *TCA*, 1, 328 / *TKH*, 1, 440.

18. "Entgegnung," 353ff. / "A Reply," 233ff. and below, esp. chapter 4.

19. The subtitle of volume 1 is "Reason and the Rationalization of Society"; the subtitle of volume 2 is "Lifeworld and System: A Critique of Functionalist Reason."

20. "Remarks," 175.

21. "Remarks," 151.

22. Bernstein, *Habermas and Modernity*, 20.

23. Habermas criticizes Max Weber, for instance, for conceiving all social actions as derivatives of one basic type—purposive-rational action.

24. "Entgegnung," 379 / "A Reply," 252.

25. I will have more to say about this in the next section.

26. As we shall see, Habermas also refers to strategic action as a mode of action coordination *within* the lifeworld. This is a mode of lifeworld integration to the extent that it relies on the action orientations of individual agents. However, Habermas argues that it is secondary to communicative action as a mode of lifeworld integration (see chapter 1, section 4).

27. This term will be clarified in the next section.

28. *TCA*, 2, 375ff. / *TKH*, 2, 549ff. Habermas here appears to use the term "modern" in a more restricted sense than that discussed on pp. 9–14 below.

29. *TCA*, 2, 330 / *TKH*, 2, 487.

30. For Habermas's critique of Marx see *TCA*, 2, 334ff. / *TKH*, 2, 491ff.

31. "Entgegnung," 377 / "A Reply," 250.

32. See the contributions, in particular, of T. McCarthy, H. Joas, and H. Schnädelbach in *Kommunikatives Handeln* / *Communicative Action*, ed. Honneth and Joas. Habermas replies to his critics and clarifies his position in his "Entgegnung" / "A Reply" in the same volume.

33. "Entgegnung," 377ff. / "A Reply," 250ff.

34. "Reply," 234.

35. Although I will suggest a difference in emphasis between the two in chapter 4, for present purposes they can be taken as equivalent.

36. For an overview see Piaget, *The Principles of Genetic Epistemology*.

37. T. McCarthy, "Reflections on Rationalization in *The Theory of Communicative Action*," in Bernstein (ed.), 178.

38. "Questions," 208.

39. Ibid.

40. Ibid. (tr. J. Bohman). Habermas bases his theory on "reflections in the theory of meaning" (see chapters 3 and 4 below).

41. Ibid., 209. At least I take this to be what Habermas means by "moralism" and "aestheticism"; in fact, his characterization of both of these is inconsistent with his characterization of "objectivism": Whereas we are warned of the dangers of "objectivism" when all three "worlds" are related to in an objectivating attitude, we are warned of "moralism" and "aestheticism" when, in the respective forms of argumentation, elements of the other worlds are not brought into play. But this is a different charge and requires a quite different kind of justification.

42. Indeed, he suggests that it is desirable to do so; see chapter 3, section 7.

43. *TCA*, 1, 444 / *TKH*, 1, 442, note 84; "Reply to Skjei," 108f. I take a closer look at this idea in section 7 of chapter 3.

44. See section 4 below.

45. I deal with Habermas's theory of validity claims in detail in chapter 3.

46. *TCA*, 1, 66ff. / *TKH*, 1, 102ff.

47. "Remarks," 163.

48. See below.

49. "Entgegnung," 366 / "A Reply," 241.

50. But see my objections in chapter 2, section 4.

51. I have more to say about this in section 3 of chapter 3.

52. Although Habermas does not take adequate account of this distinction, he does acknowledge it on occasion—for instance, in *Faktizität und Geltung* (395), where he admits that dogmatic worldviews and rigid patterns of individual identity formation can form a barrier to a discursive mode of socialization.

53. *Nachmetaphysisches Denken*, 178 / *Postmetaphysical Thinking*, 138.

54. *TCA*, 1, 66ff. / *TKH*, 1, 102ff.

55. *TCA*, 2, 74 / *TKH*, 2, 114; also "Reply," 235. In section 1 of chapter 2 I deal with the concept of "discourse."

56. Habermas acknowledges the former point (see "Reply," 236) but not the latter—at least, not explicitly.

57. "Remarks," 165.

58. *TCA*, 1, 70 / *TKH*, 1, 107.

59. "Remarks," 164.

60. *Nachmetaphysisches Denken*, 95ff; "Remarks," 167f.

61. See below.

62. Habermas, too, refers to the destructive effects of communicative action; but, as I make clear below, he is concerned primarily not with damage to the fabric of the life-world through the exhaustion of semantic potentials but with the possibly destabilizing effects of the threat of dissensus that accompanies increasingly reflective forms of communicative action.

63. See chapter 5 below.

64. *Diskurs*, 397 / *Discourse*, 343.

65. Ibid.

66. Ibid., 401 / 346.

67. Ibid., 402 / 347. The term "post-traditional" is not used by Habermas here, but I think it captures the thrust of his meaning.

68. *Diskurs*, 390ff. / *Discourse*, 336ff.; *Moralbewußtsein und kommunikatives Handeln*, 24ff. / *Moral Consciousness and Communicative Action*, 17ff.

69. *Moralbewußtsein und kommunikatives Handeln*, 25f. / *Moral Consciousness and Communicative Action*, 18f.; *Diskurs*, 240ff. / *Discourse*, 204ff.

70. "Entgegnung," 341 / "A Reply," 225.

71. We can find no more than a few hints that this may be a problem in his writings. See "Questions," 209; *Nachmetaphysisches Denken*, 240f. / *Postmetaphysical Thinking*, 199f.; *Texte und Kontexte*, 47f.; and his essay on Benjamin cited below.

72. "Consciousness-Raising or Redemptive Criticism—The Contemporaneity of Walter Benjamin," 57 (tr. P. Brewster and C. H. Buchner).

73. This is Habermas's formulation. The question is, presumably, not "safe" to the extent that it undermines Habermas's emphasis on freedom rather than (and possibly at the expense of) happiness.

74. In the sense of increasing critical scrutiny and openness to the arguments of others.

75. For example, in *Nachmetaphysisches Denken*, 84f., and in *Faktizität und Geltung*, 23f. and 39ff.

76. Indeed, he speaks of a "maelstrom of problematization" (ibid.).

77. See "Entgegnung," 371 / "A Reply," 246.

78. In his most recent work, Habermas also draws attention to the stabilizing and regulatory functions of modern law, specifically the institution of subjective rights (*Faktizität und Geltung*, 43ff.).

79. *TCA*, 1, 288 / *TKH*, 1, 388; "Remarks," 169.

80. Rasmussen, *Reading Habermas*, 26, note 23.

81. Ibid.

82. A. Honneth, for instance, criticizes Habermas's exclusion of power-based relationships from the internal structures of the lifeworld in *Kritik der Macht*, (307ff., esp. 330f.). Habermas replies to Honneth on this point ("Entgegnung," 371f. / "A Reply,"246f.).

83. "Entgegnung," 372f. / "A Reply," 247f.

84. *TCA*, 1, 101 / *TKH*, 1, 150f.; "Entgegnung," 364 / "A Reply," 241.

85. See section 3 above.

86. See my warning above about different senses of "reflective" in Habermas's writings.

87. "Entgegnung," 364 / "A Reply," 241.

88. *TCA*, 1, 331f. / *TKH*, 1, 444. In sections 5 and 6 of chapter 3 I deal with Habermas's claim that the indirect mode of language use is parasitic on the communicative mode (see esp. chapter 3, note 79).

89. *TCA*, 1, 288 / *TKH*, 1, 388f.

90. "Entgegnung," 362f. / "A Reply," 239f.

91. *Nachmetaphysisches Denken*, 71f.

92. Habermas makes use of a conception of illocutionary success in a "broader" and a "narrower" sense. In the narrower sense it refers simply to successful (linguistic) understanding; in the broader sense, it includes the hearer's acceptance of the speech-act offer. See "Entgegnung," 362 / "A Reply," 239f.; *Nachmetaphysisches Denken*, 71.

93. *Nachmetaphysisches Denken*, 73f.

94. Although in "Entgegnung," (361f. / "A Reply," 239) the very same example of a "pure" (power-based) imperative is described as a "borderline case" (*Grenzfall*) of manifestly strategic action.

95. In "Entgegnung" (362 / "A Reply," 239) Habermas simply states that the bank robber's "Hands up!" is a parasitic use of language—there is no attempt to work out an

argument. Moreover, in the relevant section of the more recent *Nachmetaphysisches Denken* (73f.), with the same example, he does not speak of it being parasitic at all.

96. *TCA*, 1, 294 / *TKH*, 1, 396.

97. "Diskursethik—Notizen zu einem Begründungsprogramm" / "Discourse Ethics—Notes on a Program of Philosophical Justification," in *Moralbewußtsein und kommunikatives Handeln / Moral Consciousness and Communicative Action.*

98. *Moralbewußtsein und kommunikatives Handeln*, 110ff. / *Moral Consciousness and Communicative Action*, 99ff.

99. Recall the distinction between conventional and postconventional communicative action—see section 3 above.

100. *Moralbewußtsein und kommunikatives Handeln*, 112 / *Moral Consciousness and Communicative Action*, 100.

101. Habermas claims that this is an empirical question ("Reply," 281; *TCA*, 2, 313 / *TKH*, 2, 461). See also section 1 of chapter 5 below.

Chapter 2

1. In the following I use the terms "utterance" and "speech act" interchangeably to refer to the smallest unit of linguistic communication. To the extent that the communicative mode of language use is the original mode of language use (see chapter 1), utterances raise validity claims by definition.

2. See chapter 1, section 3.

3. *Nachmetaphysisches Denken*, 55 / *Postmetaphysical Thinking*, 47.

4. Ibid. See also *Faktizität und Geltung*, esp. 33ff.

5. Habermas borrows the term "performative contradiction" from K. O. Apel to describe the idea of unavoidable or necessary presuppositions of communication: strong idealizations to which we have to make reference when engaging in communicative action if we are to be able to give a coherent account of what we are doing. See *Moralbewußtsein und kommunikatives Handeln*, 99ff. / *Moral Consciousness and Communicative Action*, 76ff. Since it is in my view questionable whether the term "contradiction" is appropriate here, I do not use the term "performative contradiction" in the following. It is worth noting that, in his recent work, Habermas himself rarely uses the term, preferring to speak of "necessary presuppositions" or "strong idealizations."

6. *Moralbewußtsein und kommunikatives Handeln*, 99f. / *Moral Consciousness and Communicative Action*, 76f.

7. Benhabib, *Situating the Self*, 32.

8. For example, "Wahrheitstheorien," 211ff.; but see also *TCA*, 1, 42 / *TKH*, 1, 71.

9. Although Habermas used it as recently as in *TCA*, by 1983 there is already some evidence of his unease with the term and his present position is that he regrets ever having used it, as it is too "concretist" ("Ein Interview mit der *New Left Review*," 229)

and "too concretist and open to misinterpretation" (*Die nachholende Revolution*, 131f.) In *Faktizität und Geltung* (392) he warns against "essentialist" misunderstandings of the notion of the ideal speech situation.

10. *TCA*, 1, 42 / *TKH*, 1, 71.

11. I have used this term here because Habermas uses it, although I in fact believe it to be inaccurate. For reasons I shall make clear in chapter 3, I prefer to speak of normative validity claims or, more specific, claims to moral validity.

12. In *TCA*, 1, 42 / *TKH*, 1, 71 Habermas includes claims to the comprehensibility or well-formedness of symbolic expressions in the class of universal validity claims (as defined above). Since he does not develop this point, it need not concern us further here. See note 87 to chapter 4.

13. Habermas's reference to universal validity claims is often confusing because he does not make this double aspect clear. Moreover, the situation is complicated by the fact that Habermas uses the term "universal validity claim" with regard to the claims to truth, normative rightness, and truthfulness to indicate that they are *present* in every speech act (e.g. *TCA*, 1, 311 / *TKH*, 417f.). See section 7 of chapter 3 below.

14. Habermas distinguishes, within the greater class of moral-practical claims, between moral claims, pragmatic claims, and ethical claims. Only moral claims are the subject of practical discourses (see chapter 5, section 4).

15. In "Realizing the Postconventional Self" I argue that Habermas fails both to distinguish adequately between a "double" and a "singular" sense of context-specificity and to make clear in which sense ethical questions are context-specific.

16. In *TCA*, 1, 41f. / *TKH*, 1, 70f.

17. Ibid.

18. *Erläuterungen*, 100ff.

19. "Reply," 235 (tr. T. McCarthy).

20. Benhabib implies that these principles are necessary presuppositions only of postconventional moral discussions; however, in section 4 of chapter 5 below I suggest that they may in fact be necessary presuppositions of all forms of postconventional communicative action.

21. In section 4 of chapter 5 I draw attention to the weaker and more restricted but nonetheless critical power that derives from idealizations implicit in all forms of communicative action.

22. In section 4 of chapter 5 I suggest that if we draw out the implications of this necessary presupposition we see a connection between it and the principles of universal moral respect and egalitarian reciprocity.

23. I argue in section 3 of chapter 1 that Habermas does not make the context-specificity of communicative rationality sufficiently clear.

24. *Nachmetaphysisches Denken*, 55 / *Postmetaphysical Thinking*, 47.

25. Ibid.

26. This particular interpretation of "context-transcendent" is stressed in *Faktizität und Geltung* (see esp. 30ff.).

27. Indeed, latently strategic action (see chapter 1, section 4) could be described as communicative action that fails to satisfy the necessary presupposition of an orientation toward the better argument in even the most minimal way (see also chapter 5, section 4).

28. See the critique of Benhabib in Cooke, "Habermas and Consensus."

29. "Entgegnung," 338 / "A Reply," 222. (This point does not come across clearly in the translation, which substitutes "non-separatist" for "non-defeatist.")

30. See *Nachmetaphysisches Denken* / *Postmetaphysical Thinking*.

31. *TCA*, 1, 8ff. / *TKH*, 1, 25ff.

32. "Reply," 227f.

33. See "Die Philosophie als Platzhalter und Interpret" / "Philosophy as Stand-In and Interpreter," in *Moralbewußtsein und kommunikatives Handeln* / *Moral Consciousness and Communicative Action*.

34. *Nachmetaphysisches Denken*, 178f. / *Postmetaphysical Thinking*, 139.

35. Ibid.

36. See section 3 of chapter 1 above. For an account of the differentation processes in question see esp. the second volume of TCA, section V, chapters 2 and 3.

37. "Reply," 235 (tr. T. McCarthy).

38. *Nachmetaphysisches Denken*, 155 / *Postmetaphysical Thinking*, 117.

39. *TCA*, 2, 398 / *TKH*, 2, 586.

40. *Erläuterungen*, 118. Habermas raises this problem specifically with regard to the question of the unity of practical reason, but it is equally relevant to our discussion here.

41. Ibid.

42. He concludes the essay "Vom pragmatischen, ethischen und moralischen Gebrauch der praktischen Vernunft" (in *Erläuterungen*, 100ff.) with the tantalizing remark that moral theory must leave open the question of the unity of practical reason and pass on the problem to legal theory since the unity of practical reason in some way depends on the institutionalization in a given society of rational processes of collective will-formation among citizens (ibid., 118).

43. "Questions," 194.

44. The exception is the power to criticize argumentative practices as dishonest.

45. *Nachmetaphysisches Denken*, 185f. *Postmetaphysical Thinking*, 145f.; "Reply," 227f.

46. See chapter 1, section 3.

47. *TCA*, 2, 153ff. / *TKH*, 2, 219ff.; *Diskurs*, 396f. / *Discourse*, 341f.

48. In section 5 of chapter 5 I express some reservations of my own with regard to some aspects of Habermas's utopian vision.

49. *Nachmetaphysisches Denken*, 180 / *Postmetaphysical Thinking*, 140.

50. Ibid.

51. "Moralbewußtsein und kommunikatives Handeln," 189ff. / "Moral Consciousness and Communicative Action," 178ff.

52. It could be argued that ethical questions, although context-specific in one sense, are connected with the idea of universal agreement to the extent that, if they are valid, everyone would have to agree that they are valid (but only for a particular individual in the context of that individual's life history). There is some evidence that this may now be Habermas's position: See Cooke, "Realizing the Postconventional Self." However, this does not affect the point at issue in the present instance, which is that Habermas allows for a plurality of possibly conflicting ethical choices and views.

53. *TCA*, 2, 149 / *TKH*, 2, 224.

54. See chapter 5, section 4.

55. See, for instance, Lacan, *Ecrits*.

56. See Cooke, "Realizing the Postconventional Self."

57. It makes no difference in this instance whether the "everyone" is taken to mean "everyone capable of speech and action" or "everyone who shares a particular substantive evaluative horizon."

58. I have argued this in "Realizing the Postconventional Self."

59. Not all ethical claims are concerned primarily with interpretations of inner nature. Some are concerned in the first instance with the validity of the "strongly evaluative interpretations" (in Charles Taylor's sense) that inform the self's self-interpretations (see Cooke, "Realizing the Postconventional Self"). My point in the present instance is simply that the idealizing supposition of agreement makes no sense in the case of certain kinds of ethical judgement once we give up the idea of transparent subjectivity.

60. See esp. sections 4 and 5 of chapter 5 below.

61. See Cooke, "Habermas, Autonomy and the Identity of the Self."

62. The notion of rational accountability will become clearer in the following chapters and will be dealt with explicitly (if briefly) in section 4 of chapter 5. For a more detailed discussion see Cooke, "Habermas, Autonomy and the Identity of the Self."

63. I have argued this in more detail in "Habermas, Autonomy and the Identity of the Self" and in "Habermas and Consensus." However, in "Realizing the Postconventional Self" I have also argued that the self seeks more than just recognition of rational ac-

countability in her project of self-realization—although rational accountability is one element of this.

64. See *Nachmetaphysisches Denken*, 210ff. / *Postmetaphysical Thinking*, 171ff.

65. See Cooke, "Habermas, Autonomy and the Identity of the Self."

66. Ibid.

67. Ibid.

68. However, the idea of the self as unique and distinct from all others must surely go beyond this. See Cooke, "Realizing the Postconventional Self," and Taylor, *The Ethics of Authenticity*.

69. *TCA*, 2, 382f. / *TKH*, 2, 561f.

Chapter 3

1. See section 4 of chapter 1. Although I have questioned whether Habermas has shown this, in the following I assume that he has. Thus, in examining his respective theories of validity claims and meaning, I confine myself to the communicative use of language. For this reason, the term "speech act" in the following is shorthand for "communicatively used speech act."

2. Of course, this is not to say that Habermas's interpretations of other theorists and approaches should not be examined and criticized for what they neglect or distort—or that it would not be helpful to him in his overall project to do so. It would, however, be beyond the scope of the present discussion.

3. See chapter 1.

4. As I have already indicated, I, like Habermas, use "utterance" and "speech act" interchangeably.

5. For a more detailed criticism of intentionalist approaches to meaning, see *Nachmetaphysisches Denken*, 136ff.

6. *TCA*, 1, 274ff / *TKH*, 1, 372ff; *Nachmetaphysisches Denken*, 105ff. / *Postmetaphysical Thinking*, 57ff.

7. Bühler, *Sprachtheorie*.

8. *Nachmetaphysisches Denken*, 105 / *Postmetaphysical Thinking*, 57.

9. *TCA*, 2, 63 / *TKH*, 2, 99.

10. *TCA*, 2, 62 / *TKH*, 2, 97.

11. "Whenever it is used in constative speech acts, the sentence with propositional content takes the form of a propositional sentence (*Aussagesatz*). In its elementary form, the propositional sentence contains: (i) a name or a referring expression, with the aid of which the speaker identifies an object about which he wants to say something; (ii) a predicate expression for the general determination that the speaker wants to grant or

deny to the object. In non-constative speech acts, the propositional content is not stated but mentioned; in this case, propositional content co-incides with what is usually called the unasserted proposition." ("What Is Universal Pragmatics?" (tr. T. McCarthy), 36)

12. "This sentence is formed in the present indicative, affirmative, and has as its logical subject the first person and as its logical (direct) object the second person; the predicate, constructed with the help of a performative expression, permits in general the particle 'hereby'." (ibid.)

13. "The latter is constructed with the first-person pronoun (as subject expression) and an intentional (in Husserl's sense) verb (with a predicative function), while the place of the logical object is occupied either by an object (e.g. 'I love T') or by a nominalized state of affairs ('I fear that p')." (*TCA*, 2, 98 / *TKH*, 2, 62).

14. *Nachmetaphysisches Denken*, 106 / *Postmetaphysical Thinking*, 58.

15. *TCA*, 1, 277 / *TKH*, 1, 375.

16. Austin, *How to Do Things with Words;* Searle, *Speech Acts.*

17. "What Is Universal Pragmatics?" 44ff.; *Nachmetaphysisches Denken*, 118ff. / *Postmetaphysical Thinking*, 69ff.

18. *TCA*, 1, 323 / *TKH*, 1, 431f. (tr T. McCarthy).

19. Ibid.

20. *TCA*, 1, 277 / *TKH*, 1, 375.

21. Of course, we must bear in mind that this holds, if at all, only for the communicative use of language (see note 1 above).

22. Compare this notion of illocutionary force with that put forward by Grice.

23. Habermas explains the historical emergence of the binding and bonding force of speech acts through his thesis of "the linguistification of the sacred." In the course of the historical process of linguistification, the spellbinding power (*bannende Kraft*) of the sacred is replaced by the binding and bonding power (*bindende Kraft*) of validity claims (see *TCA*, 2, 77ff. / *TKH*, 2, 119ff.).

24. See, for example, *TCA*, 2, 73 / *TKH*, 2, 113.

25. Habermas's theory of validity claims also allows for an intersubjectively criticizable claim to efficacy within this first dimension of validity; however, since it does not occupy a central place in his theoretical edifice and will merely complicate the discussion, in the following I refer only to a claim to propositional truth.

26. Habermas's schema originally contained four validity claims. In addition to the three mentioned here he asserted a "claim to intelligibility" (*Verständlichkeit*), in which the speaker claims that what is said is comprehensible ("What Is Universal Pragmatics?" 2). For reasons that will become clearer in chapter 4, this is at odds with his pragmatic account of meaning; presumably for this reason, only three types of validity claims are identified in TCA. (See *TCA*, 1, 288ff. / *TKH*, 1, 386ff.) See also note 87 to chapter 4 below.

27. *TCA*, 2, 62ff. / *TKH*, 97ff., and see above.

28. For example, *TCA,* 1, 306 / *TKH,* 1, 411; "Reply to Skjei," 110.

29. See Strawson, *Logico-Linguistic Papers.* See also Searle, *Speech Acts.*

30. "What Is Universal Pragmatics?" 55f.

31. "Reply to Skjei," 111.

32. I have more to say about this in section 4 of chapter 5.

33. Of course, it is also striking that in this respect Habermas's view is quite close to that of analytic philosophers who see truth and falsity as properties of propositional assertions.

34. In chapter 2 above.

35. Indeed, Habermas is always at pains to emphasize that it is their detachment from the contexts of everyday life that distinguishes moral claims from ethical claims. (See, for example, *Moralbewußtsein und kommunikatives Handeln,* 188ff. / *Moral Consciousness and Communicative Action,* 176ff.)

36. See section 4 of chapter 5 below.

37. The fact that such claims are bound to specific contexts, however, would seem to exclude them by definition from the class of moral claims as defined by Habermas.

38. "What Is Universal Pragmatics?" 53ff.

39. In chapter 4.

40. *TCA*, 1, 296ff. / *TKH*, 398ff.

41. *TCA,* 1, 303 / *TKH,* 1, 407f. Again, it is worth remembering that Habermas is referring only to the communicative mode of language use (on which, he claims, the strategic mode is parasitic).

42. I have more to say about this in section 7 of the present chapter.

43. This is an analytic distinction. In the actual situations of everyday communicative practice, the two often overlap.

44. Habermas recognizes this: see "What Is Universal Pragmatics?" 56f.

45. This remains to be shown (see section 3 of chapter 4).

46. What I am attempting here is no more than an analytic distinction. I suggest that it is possible to distinguish between a rational obligation and a moral obligation, while acknowledging that in many instances the two overlap; in particular, there will often be moral reasons as to why I should act in a rational way.

47. Of course, this depends on the particular circumstances. In many cases there will also be moral reasons for why I ought not to damage my health (for instance, the well-being of others may depend on my good health, or I may stand accused of giving bad

example to others); however, circumstances in which there are no moral reasons for acting rationally are, at least, conceivable.

48. I have acknowledged that there are many instances in which there are moral reasons as to why I should act in a rational way. Nonetheless, as a general rule, I have a moral obligation to act rationally (in the sense of consistently) only where I have committed myself to behaving in a certain way, i.e., in paradigmatic regulative speech acts such as promises. Merely giving other people reason to believe that I will act in a certain way does not morally oblige me to. Giving burglars reason to believe that I will not be at home over the weekend does not morally oblige me not to be at home.

49. I do not attach a great deal of importance to this conclusion. The main point of my argument in this chapter is to suggest that there are no compelling reasons for asserting precisely three categories of speech act (rather than 23 or 53) and that, if minimalism is preferred, then there are more arguments for asserting two rather than three categories. Rather than argue for an expanded category of constative speech act, I could just as easily have argued for the creation of many new categories to accommodate aesthetic claims, evaluative claims, normative validity claims, grammatical claims, etc. Nothing in the subsequent discussion turns on my argument for the former rather than the latter.

50. Although it is arguable that they make reference to an idea of universal agreement in a "singular" sense of universal: see Cooke, "Realizing the Postconventional Self"; see also section 4 of chapter 2 above.

51. See note 49 above.

52. "What Is Universal Pragmatics?" 57f.

53. The fact that the same linguistic expression can take on various meanings depending on the context is often a cause of confusion. The sentence "I love you" may often be a disclosure, but sometimes it is an expression of commitment (a promise) and thus not an expressive but a regulative speech act. Habermas himself recognizes this; see "Reply to Skjei," 108.

54. It is not even necessary to the argument that everyday language fulfils functions of individual socialization. In order to show this, Habermas has to show that every speech act functions (also) to express the speaker's subjectivity. As I discuss in section 7 of the present chapter, the idea of a "universal" claim to truthfulness is sufficient in this respect; the demonstration of a separate *category* of expressive speech acts is not required (see note 99 below).

55. *TCA*, 1, 16f. / *TKH*, 1, 36f.

56. *TCA*, 1, 16, / *TKH*, 1, 36.

57. "Entgegnung," 336 / "A Reply," 221.

58. "Questions" (tr. J. Bohman), 203f.

59. Wellmer, "Wahrheit, Schein, Versöhnung," in *Zur Dialektik von Moderne und Postmoderne*.

60. Habermas often refers to "aesthetic-expressive" rationality (see, e.g., *TCA*, 2, 326 / *TKH*, 2, 481). Furthermore, in *TCA*, in his correlation of validity claims with the

cultural spheres of value in modern societies, he correlates the claim to truthfulness with the sphere of art and art criticism (see, e.g., *TCA*, 1, 238 / *TKH*, 1, 326, figure 11).

61. "Remarks," 152, 164.

62. In *Social Action and Power,* F. Crespi directs a different kind of criticism against Habermas's conception of action. He argues that Habermas ignores the negative dimensions of consciousness and consequently fails to acknowledge the limits of the symbolic order. The result is a problematic identity between action and language. Although I have considerable sympathy with this line of criticism, it is not directly relevant to my present concern (but see chapter 5, section 5).

63. *TCA*, 1, 101 / *TKH*, 1, 150f.; see also "Entgegnung," 364f. / "A Reply," 240f.

64. *TCA*, 1, 186 / *TKH*, 1, 128.

65. Habermas does admit the possibility of "special cases." In such special cases, the orientation toward understanding is split off from its normal connection with contexts of action. One such special case is conversation (*TCA*, 1, 327 / *TKH*, 1, 438; "Entgegnung," 401 (note 62) / "A Reply", 291 (note 62)); presumably another is the "virtualized" position of the social scientist in processes of "Verstehen" (*TCA*, 1, 113f. / *TKH*, 1, 167).

66. "Entgegnung," 336 / "A Reply," 221.

67. See note 65 above.

68. *TCA*, 1, 113f. / *TKH*, 1, 167 (T. McCarthy's translation).

69. See note 65 above.

70. *Diskurs*, 236 / *Discourse*, 201.

71. See also *Diskurs*, 240 / *Discourse*, 204.

72. Thompson, *Critical Hermeneutics*, 140f.

73. Pratt, *Toward a Speech Act Theory of Literary Discourse*, esp. 232ff.

74. "I refer to the eminent American socio-linguist William Labov, whose work on the oral narrative of personal experience may well be the only body of data-based research dealing with aesthetically structured discourse which is not, by anyone's, definition, literature." (Pratt, *Toward a Speech Act Theory*, 39)

75. Ibid., 135.

76. Taylor, *Philosophical Papers*, esp. vol. 1.

77. M. Seel, "Am Beispiel der Metapher," manuscript, Konstanz, 1988.

78. As I have said, it is important to bear in mind that the subjective experience of the speaker does not necessarily represent the final instance in the validation of such claims.

79. Here we should recall Habermas's insistence that the "indirect" (e.g. the figurative, the symbolic) mode of language use is parasitic on the communicative mode (*TCA*, 1,

331f. / *TKH*, 1, 444). My discussion in this chapter has undermined his thesis to the extent that it has suggested that certain kinds of "indirect" language use can be characterized in terms of intersubjectively criticizable validity claims and should be accommodated within the category of action oriented toward understanding.

80. Quite apart from anything else, Pratt emphasizes that the question of the speaker's truthfulness is often not relevant to our evaluative reception of acts of verbal displaying; indeed, she argues that we usually expect elaboration, embellishment, and exaggeration.

81. See section 5, above.

82. See, for example, *TCA*, 2, 120 / *TKH*, 2, 184.

83. *TCA*, 1, 306 / *TKH*, 1, 411.

84. One difficulty here is that Habermas makes use of a concept of illocutionary success in a "broader" and a "narrower" sense ("Entgegnung," 362 / "A Reply," 239f). In the narrower sense it refers to understanding; in this sense, a speech act is successful when the hearer undertands what the speaker says. In the broader sense it refers to the hearer's acceptance of the speech act offer; in this sense, a speech act is successful if agreement is reached between speaker and hearer with regard to (all three) claims raised. To simplify matters in the present chapter I presume that Habermas's thesis refers to illocutionary success in the broader sense; in the next chapter it will become clearer whether his thesis also extends to illocutionary success in the narrower sense (that is, whether understanding an utterance requires understanding all three claims it raises).

85. *TCA*, 1, 311 / *TKH*, 1, 417.

86. *TCA*, 1, 306 / *TKH*, 1, 411.

87. Ibid.

88. *TCA*, 1, 311 / *TKH*, 1, 417.

89. See chapter 2 above.

90. "Überlegungen zur Kommunikationspathologie," 249.

91. See, e.g., Zimmermann, *Utopie–Rationalität–Politik*, 375.

92. Wellmer, *Ethik und Dialog.* 144f.

93. Grice, "Logic and Conversation."

94. Pratt, *Toward a Speech Act Theory*, 134.

95. *TCA*, 1, 311 / *TKH*, 1, 418.

96. Obviously there are exceptions and borderline cases. Persistent irrelevance may well be a moral transgression.

97. We can distinguish existential presuppositions, normative presuppositions, and the presupposition that the speaker is genuinely oriented toward understanding.

98. I consider it misleading to the extent that in normal linguistic usage "raising a claim" is used to refer to the speaker's thematization of a given propositional content. Only utterances in the (expanded) category of constative speech acts raise claims in this sense. In the other instances where Habermas speaks of "raising claims," he appears to mean "aspects of validity under which an utterance can be contested."

99. It is not at all clear that the idea of a universal claim to truthfulness is the best way of arguing that language fulfils functions of individual socialization. Indeed, the argument discussed above (chapter 2, section 4) that (in postconventional forms of communicative action) the very act of raising a validity claim is an act of individuation seems to me to present a more promising strategy. Furthermore, even if the idea of an universal claim to truthfulness is useful in this regard, it should be noted that it is not dependent in any way on the existence of a separate *category* of expressive speech acts.

100. See chapter 2 above.

101. *TCA*, 2, 75f. / *TKH*, 2, 115f.

102. See chapter 1, section 3.

103. See *TCA*, 1, 330 / *TKH*, 1, 441f.; "Entgegnung," 343 / "A Reply," 226.

104. See chapter 2, section 3.

105. In section 3 of chapter 2 I drew attention to Habermas's reservations concerning the idea that what is required is some sort of Aristotelian practical judgement and his preference for the idea of a "sorting ability."

106. "Entgegnung," 343 / "A Reply," 226.

107. Habermas sometimes identifies the idea of transition between validity dimensions with the idea of "intermodal invariances of validity" ("Entgegnung," 343 / "A Reply," 226; *TCA*, 1, 444 / *TKH*, 1, 442, note 84 and figure 17). This area of the logic of speech acts attempts to explain, e.g., why we can infer the validity of a constative speech act ("Peter loves Frances") from the validity of an expressive speech act ("I (Peter) love Frances") and vice versa. However, the plausibility of the above transfer is the result of a cleverly selected example; it works only because the two supposedly different categories of speech act mentioned here have the same mode of validation. But what expressive speech act would correspond to the constative utterance "Bern is the capital of Switzerland"? Habermas himself recognizes that intermodal validity transfer is impossible from regulative to constative speech acts and vice versa, or from expressive to regulative and vice versa. In view of this, it seems so rare as to be uninteresting for our present purposes.

108. *TCA*, 1, 311 / *TKH*, 1, 417f. This should not be confused with his thesis that truth claims and moral claims are universal validity claims (see above, chapter 2, section 1).

Chapter 4

1. *TCA*, 1, 297 / *TKH*, 1, 400; "Remarks," 175. See also "Entgegnung," 353ff., esp. 383ff. / "A Reply," 233ff., esp. 255ff.

2. *TCA*, 1, 297 / *TKH*, 1, 400. (Compare T. McCarthy's translation, where *entfernt* (distant) is wrongly translated as *distinct*.)

3. More accurate, it should be seen as a development of Dummett's development of truth-conditional semantics. As is well known, and as will become clear in the following, Dummett replaces the idea of "truth conditions" with that of "assertibility conditions"; Habermas applauds this move.

4. *Nachmetaphysisches Denken,* 127 / *Postmetaphysical Thinking,* 77; "Entgegnung," 353ff. / "A Reply," 233ff.

5. In contrast to "intentionalist" (*Nachmetaphysisches Denken,* 136). See chapter 3, section 1.

6. *TCA,* 1, 298f. / *TKH,* 1, 400f. / "Remarks," 175; "Entgegnung," 353ff., esp. 383ff. / "A Reply," 233ff., esp. 255ff.

7. "Entgegnung," 354f. / "A Reply," 234f.

8. D. Davidson, "Truth and Meaning," in *Synthese* (1967), quoted by Habermas in "Entgegnung," 400, note 50 / "A Reply," 290, note 50.

9. Wittgenstein, *Philosophical Investigations,* paragraph 242.

10. "Entgegnung," 353ff. / "A Reply," 233ff.

11. Ibid.

12. *TCA,* 1, 317f. / *TKH,* 1, 424f. (tr. T. McCarthy).

13. As I explain below, we can interpret this either as the objection that Dummett fails to take account of the internal connection between truth and argumentation or as the objection that Dummett does not pay adequate attention to the fact that what counts as a good reason is never immune in principle to critical evaluation by others in argumentation.

14. I argue below that Habermas's position here may be problematic.

15. I argue below that we can distinguish between the objection that the validation conditions cannot be produced according to a "monological" procedure (an objection which is problematic, at least in certain cases) and the objection that Dummett's assertibility conditions are not construed in a dialogical-fallibilist way.

16. *TCA,* 1, 316f. / *TKH,* 1, 424f.

17. *TCA,* 1, 297f. / *TKH,* 1, 400f.

18. *TCA,* 1, 298f. / *TKH,* 1, 401f.

19. *TCA,* 1, 298 / *TKH,* 1, 401.

20. Ibid.

21. *TCA,* 1, 302 / *TKH,* 1, 406.

22. *TCA,* 1, 302 / *TKH,* 1, 405f.

23. See chapter 3, section 2.

24. This commitment refers, as we saw in chapter 3, to a moral obligation to give an account of why one failed or was unable to be at home: to justify, explain, excuse—or accept the blame.

25. As an example of a hearer's negation of a speaker's claim to normative rightness raised with an act of promising, Habermas suggests the following: "No, you were always unreliable in such matters." (*Nachmetaphysisches Denken*, 78) In this instance the hearer challenges the speaker's competency as a moral agent. However, we can also imagine cases where the hearer challenges the speaker's right to make that promise.

26. *TCA*, 1, 303 / *TKH*, 1, 407.

27. Ibid.

28. Ibid.

29. We saw this in section 3 of chapter 3.

30. More precise, they do not give rise to moral obligations to act in a certain way but only (at most) to rational ones (see chapter 3, section 3). Since the content of the notion of a "rational obligation" is difficult to specify, it would be implausible to suggest that knowledge of what it would mean to fulfil such an obligation could be part of what it is to understand an utterance.

31. *TCA*, 1, 303 / *TKH*, 1, 407.

32. See Wellmer, "Was ist eine pragmatische Bedeutungstheorie?"

33. For instance, simple predicative sentences.

34. "Entgegnung," 358 / "A Reply," 237.

35. See also, *Nachmetaphysisches Denken*, 127 / *Postmetaphysical Thinking*, 77.

36. *Nachmetaphysisches Denken*, 79f. (my emphasis).

37. *TCA*, 1, 317f. / *TKH*, 1, 425. See also Putnam, *Realism and Reason*, xvi–xviii.

38. "Entgegnung," 350 / "A Reply," 231.

39. Ibid.

40. See below, chapter 5, section 4.

41. Habermas's reply to his critics in "Entgegnung" ("A Reply") might possibly support this interpretation.

42. *TCA*, 1, 318 / *TKH*, 1, 426. Compare McCarthy's (usually very reliable) translation, which obscures Habermas's point here.

43. Ibid.

44. "Entgegnung," 350f. / "A Reply," 231f. On occasion Habermas has used the term *Begründung* (translated as "grounding") to refer to the proof of the existence of states of affairs (*TCA*, 1, 39f. / *TKH*, 1, 66f).

45. Ibid.

46. Ibid.

47. I shall have more to say about this in section 4 of chapter 5.

48. Wittgenstein, *Philosophical Investigations.*

49. Putnam, *Realism and Reason,* 185f.

50. In "Überlegungen zur Kommunikationspathologie" (233), Habermas explicitly draws attention to its dynamic aspect. He refers to *Verständigung* as a process—as the bringing about of a consensus (*Einverständnis*).

51. For instance, in describing communicative action as action oriented toward *Verständigung*, he appears to use it interchangeably with *Einverständnis*. (See chapter 1, section 3.)

52. However, although it may well be absurd to suppose that participants in argumentation could aim at disagreement, it is far from absurd to suppose that they aim not at agreement but at the articulation and clarification of certain viewpoints and perspectives. In section 4 of chapter 2 I argued that the asserted connection between agreement and validity is problematic in at least certain kinds of discussion to the extent that it depends on a model of transparent subjectivity (see also Cooke, "Habermas and Consensus").

53. *Nachmetaphysisches Denken,* 128 / *Postmetaphysical Thinking,* 78.

54. *Nachmetaphysisches Denken,* 127 / *Postmetaphysical Thinking,* 77. It should be noted that Habermas suggests that this holds for every single speech act; the discussion in the foregoing has indicated that this would need to be qualified. Furthermore, it is worth pointing out that a holistic theory of meaning does not have to be a pragmatic one; see Fodor and LePore, *Holism: A Shopper's Guide.*

55. This thesis is implied in *TCA,* 1, 316f. / *TKH,* 1, 424f.

56. For example by McCarthy in "Reflections on Rationalization in *The Theory of Communicative Action*" and by Schnädelbach in "Transformation der kritischen Theorie" / "The Transformation of Critical Theory."

57. If this is an accurate reconstruction of Habermas's position here, then it seems to tie in most closely with the thesis that the very concept of a reason is internally linked to argumentation—a thesis which, as we saw, does not hold without qualification, even in postconventional forms of communicative action.

58. See chapter 1, section 4. At one stage Habermas seemed to be suggesting some sort of moral obligation to enter into argumentation (for instance, his reference to "moral-practical obligations" in "What is Universal Pragmatics?" and in the first "Intermediate Reflection" of *TCA,* vol. 1). However, he seems to have abandoned this problematic notion in favor of the idea of grave existential consequences.

59. In "Entgegnung," 371 / "A Reply," 245, Habermas points out that there is broad room within communicative action for dealing with disagreement—from "costly" (in terms of time and energy) argumentation to everyday repair work (patching things up), various forms of leaving things be, deliberate ambiguities, etc.

60. "Entgegnung," 348 / "A Reply," 229f.; "Questions," 205; *TCA*, 1, 115 / *TKH*, 1, 169.

61. McCarthy, "Reflections on Rationalization," 184f.

62. "Questions," 204f. (tr. J. Bohman).

63. "Entgegnung," 348 / "A Reply," 229f.

64. Ibid.

65. "Entgegnung," 360 / "A Reply," 238; *Nachmetaphysisches Denken*, 76.

66. "Entgegnung," 362 / "A Reply," 239. See note 84 to chapter 3, above.

67. This lends support to my interpretation (chapter 3, section 7) of Habermas's thesis that three validity claims are raised with every utterance. There I suggested that we take this not as a thesis about what it is to understand an utterance but as a thesis about what it is for a speech act to be successful (in the broader sense).

68. "Entgegnung," 360 / "A Reply," 238.

69. Tugendhat, "Habermas on Communicative Action."

70. Zimmermann, *Utopie–Rationalität–Politik*, 373.

71. "Entgegnung," 360 / "A Reply," 238.

72. This is Habermas's response ("Entgegnung," 360f. / "A Reply," 239); however, I think it is misleading to the extent that it implies that a hearer would have to know this particular reason to understand this particular utterance. This seems to me to be counter-intuitive. It surely must be possible to understand a specific utterance without knowing anything specific about the specific normative context in which it is spoken.

73. Ibid.

74. In the expanded sense I have suggested in chapter 3.

75. *Diskurs*, 231f. / *Discourse*, 196f; *Nachmetaphysisches Denken*, 78.

76. "What Is Universal Pragmatics?" 35f.

77. Ibid., 34ff.

78. "What Is Universal Pragmatics?" 41ff.

79. *TCA*, 1, 297 / *TKH*, 1, 400.

80. "What is Universal Pragmatics?" 39.

81. Ibid and *TCA*, 1, 330 / *TKH*, 442f. Although Habermas refers to what the speaker "means with his speech act," we know from our discussion in section 1 of chapter 3, that Habermas rejects any intentionalist interpretation of utterance meaning; for this reason, what the speaker "means with his speech act" must be defined in terms of the relevant conditions of validation (and in some cases, satisfaction).

82. *TCA*, 1, 328ff. / *TKH*, 1, 440ff.

83. *TCA*, 1, 329f. / *TKH*, 1, 440f.

84. *TCA*, 1, 335ff. / *TKH*, 1, 449ff.; *Nachmetaphysisches Denken*, 86ff.

85. *TCA*, 1, 335 / *TKH*, 1, 449.

86. *TCA*, 1, 298 / *TKH*, 1, 401 (see also note 43 to this "Intermediate Reflection"). Habermas also mentions general contextual conditions that have to be satisfied if understanding is to be possible—for instance, the condition typically presupposed for promises that a speaker cannot promise to do what she is expected to do in any case (*TCA*, 1, 441 / *TKH*, 1, 401, note 43). This appears to be a notion he has taken over from Searle and seems to me to be problematic to the extent that it prioritizes the use of expressions in "standard contexts" (see J. Derrida's provocative critique of Searle in "Limited Inc. abc").

87. The notion of grammatical well-formedness appears to replace Habermas's original formulation of a "claim to intelligibility" as a fourth validity claim raised with every speech act ("What is Universal Pragmatics?" 2).

88. *TCA*, 1, 310 / *TKH*, 1, 416.

89. The utterance mentioned violates the condition of grammatical well-formedness only if it is interpreted as an act of promising. As an act of assurance or reassurance, for instance, it is grammatically entirely in order.

90. In *TCA*, 1, 310 / *TKH*, 1, 416 Habermas refers to "well-formedness" as a *presupposition* of communication. By this he may mean, not that it is a condition that has to be met if understanding is to be possible, but that it is a "strong idealization" implicit in everyday communicative action (and thus, presumably, comparable to the presupposition of consistency of meaning—see section 1 of chapter 2 above). It seems to me, however, that even this is debatable.

91. Compare D. Davidson's discussion of the question of how we are generally able to understand malapropisms in "A Nice Derangement of Epitaphs."

92. Indeed, Habermas himself has recognized this on occasion—for instance, in referring to "intelligibility" (see note 87 above) as a claim that merely has to be sufficiently satisfied if communication is to be successful ("Überlegungen zur Kommunikationspathologie," 247).

93. *Nachmetaphysisches Denken*, 65.

94. This is Habermas's "weak" interpretation of Searle's "principle of expressibility": "only those expressions that can be expanded into explicit speech acts come into consideration" ("Reply," 270). See also "What Is Universal Pragmatics?" 240.

95. *Nachmetaphysisches Denken*, 76.

96. *Nachmetaphysisches Denken*, 86. Habermas borrrows the term "unthematic knowledge" from Husserl, but he gives it his own distinctive interpretation.

97. *Nachmetaphysisches Denken*, 87.

98. Ibid., 89.

99. MacIntyre, *After Virtue*, 195f.

100. Ibid., 195.

101. Admittedly, this is a rather unfortunate example as the very "tellability" (see chapter 3) of the assertion that it is snowing in California would appear to render it immediately intelligible even in the most unusual circumstances.

102. Ibid.

103. *TCA*, 1, 336 / *TKH*, 1, 450. See also Searle, *Expression and Meaning*.

104. Habermas mentions the need for a situation-specific background knowledge and a topic-dependent contextual knowledge for the first time in *Nachmetaphysisches Denken*. In *The Theory of Communicative Action* he refers merely in a general way to the background knowledge of the lifeworld.

Chapter 5

1. "Entgegnung," 368 / "A Reply," 243f.

2. *Die nachholende Revolution*, 84.

3. Ibid.

4. Habermas presents the former as an interpretation of what Max Weber meant by the "loss of freedom" in modern societies and the latter as an interpretation of what Weber meant by the "loss of meaning" (*TCA*, 2, 301f. / *TKH*, 2, 447f.) See also note 28 to chapter 1.

5. See chapter 1, section 3.

6. See chapter 3, section 5.

7. *TCA*, 2, 150 / *TKH*, 2, 226.

8. *TCA*, 2, 117 / *TKH*, 2, 179.

9. *TCA*, 2, 117 / *TKH*, 2, 179. "Non-normative" may be confusing; the economic and administrative subsystems also make use of communicative action which is embedded in a normative framework. Habermas's thesis is that functional (system) integration is not in the final instance based on the potential for social integration of communicative actions (see "Entgegnung," 386 / "A Reply," 256f.).

10. *TCA*, 2, 180f. / *TKH*, 2, 268f.

11. Habermas often speaks of the "system" in contrast to the "lifeworld." It is not at all clear, however, what the "system" actually is. Its main point of distinction from the lifeworld is as a mode of action coordination, and it makes most sense when used in this way. On the other hand, Habermas's use of the term "subsystem" is more straightforward, to the extent that economic and administrative subsystems are more easily identifiable in contemporary societies (see "Entgegnung," 377f. / "A Reply," 250f.).

12. This is Habermas's formulation (see note 11 above), which I take to mean the colonization of modes of social coordination by modes of system integration.

13. *TCA*, 2, 329 / *TKH*, 2, 486.

14. *TCA*, 2, 183 / *TKH*, 2, 272.

15. *TCA*, 2, 181 / *TKH*, 2, 269. In *Faktizität und Geltung* Habermas also describes modern law as a relief mechanism.

16. Habermas takes Talcott Parsons' media theory as his starting point in developing this notion. See Habermas's discussion of Parsons in section vii of the second volume of TCA.

17. *TCA*, 2, 390 / *TKH*, 2, 572f.

18. Writing and the printing press are further examples of generalized forms of communication (*TCA*, 2, 184 / *TKH*, 2, 274).

19. Ibid.

20. *TCA*, 2, 185 / *TKH*, 2, 275. See note 9 above.

21. See note 11 above.

22. Ibid. (tr. T. McCarthy).

23. *TCA*, 2, 328 / *TKH*, 2, 485.

24. *TCA*, 2, 328 / *TKH*, 2, 484.

25. *TCA*, 2, 328ff. / *TKH*, 2, 485ff.

26. *TCA*, 2, 350 / *TKH*, 2, 515.

27. *TCA*, 2, 393 / *TKH*, 2, 578.

28. White, *The Recent Work of Jürgen Habermas*, 124.

29. "Dialektik der Rationalisierung," 195. For more criticism along these lines, see the questions asked by Knödler-Bunte and Honneth in ibid., 194ff.

30. Ibid., 195f.

31. The Republic of Ireland is currently one of these. Figures for the past several years show a steady economic growth rate (over 8% in the year ending 1991) accompanied by an unemployment rate of around 20%.

32. *TCA*, 2, 351 / *TKH*, 2, 515f.

33. "Juridification" refers to the extension of formalized legal relations to hitherto communicatively structured domains of social life, such as the family and the educational system. Habermas argues that the expansion and intensification of formal law originally meant emancipation from premodern relations of dependency but that it has created new forms of dependency between the agent and the administrative apparatus

(*TCA*, 2, 356ff. / *TKH*, 2, 522ff.). Against this, in *Faktizität und Geltung* Habermas draws attention to the positive functions that modern law takes on in its capacity as a relief mechanism. However, he has not yet made clear how this affects his juridification thesis (see Dews, "Agreeing What's Right").

34. See Luke and White, "Critical Theory, the Informational Revolution and an Ecological Modernity."

35. *TCA*, 2, 386ff. / *TKH*, 2, 567ff.

36. "Reply," 281. Compare *TCA*, 2, 313 / *TKH*, 2, 461. See also the final pages of section 4 of chapter 1 above.

37. "Ein Interview mit der *New Left Review*," 242.

38. "Dialektik der Rationalisierung," 194. In support of this, it could be argued that communicative action in the three consitutive domains of the lifeworld is functionally necessary to its reproduction (see above, chapter 1, section 4); however, as I pointed out in connection with this argument, we should be aware of its limitations: It is restricted to *modern* societies and it can tell us neither how much nor what sort of communicative action is necessary.

39. Ibid., 189.

40. "Ein Interview mit der *New Left Review*," 242.

41. *TCA*, 2, 326 / *TKH*, 2, 481 (tr. T. McCarthy).

42. Ibid.

43. Ibid. In section 3 of chapter 1, I argued that the problem is not just one of feedback; the internal dynamics of the rationalization of the lifeworld in each of its three consitutive domains may also lead to cultural impoverishment to the extent that postconventional communicative action progressively erodes the fabric on which it depends for its existence. It seems to me, therefore, that the question of whether (and what kind of) semantic renewal is possible from within the lifeworld also has to be addressed.

44. *TCA*, 2, 355 / *TKH*, 2, 521.

45. See Bell, *The Cultural Contradictions of Capitalism.*

46. *TCA*, 2, 353f. / *TKH*, 2, 519f.

47. *TCA*, 2, 354 / *TKH*, 2, 520 (tr. T. McCarthy).

48. *TCA*, 2, 355 / *TKH*, 2, 522.

49. See notes 58 and 65 below.

50. "Die Krise des Wohlfahrtsstaats und die Erschöpfung utopischer Energien," 158.

51. E.g. *TCA*, 1, 240 / *TKH*, 1, 328f.

52. "Entgegnung," 342 / "A Reply," 226.

53. See esp. *TCA*, vol. 1, chapter IV.

54. See "Technik und Wissenschaft als 'Ideologie' " / "Technology and Science as 'Ideology' "; see also McCarthy, *The Critical Theory of Jürgen Habermas*, esp. 16ff.

55. See *TCA*, 2, 265ff. / *TKH*, 2, 395ff.

56. "Entgegnung," 388 / "A Reply," 258.

57. Ibid. Presumably, what Habermas means with "no longer" is that he now recognizes this; earlier he had referred to the economic and administrative subsystems as instrumental orders (see e.g. "Remarks," 155) but he has since amended his position.

58. As described by Habermas (see my comments in chapter 1, section 3).

59. Habermas regards loss of meaning (cultural impoverishment) both as a pathological development that runs parallel to the colonization of the lifeworld and as a social pathology that is caused by colonization of the lifeworld.

60. See chapter 3 above.

61. "Questions," 209.

62. *TCA*, 2, 144 / *TKH*, 2, 217, figure 23.

63. In *TCA*, 2, 142 / *TKH*, 2, 214 Habermas presents a schema (figure 21) that fits societies in which the reproduction of the lifeworld takes place by way of conventional processes of communicative action.

64. *TCA*, 2, 143 / *TKH*, 2, 215, figure 22.

65. As we know, the loss of meaning is just another name for the thesis of cultural impoverishment. Since Habermas here simply asserts—without further argument—that loss of meaning is a pathology that results from the colonization of the lifeworld, this supports my earlier contention that the thesis of cultural impoverishment is underdeveloped in Habermas's writings.

66. "Entgegnung," 342f. / "A Reply," 225–227.

67. "Überlegungen zur Kommunikationspathologie," 242.

68. Ibid.

69. "Entgegnung," 342 / "A Reply," 226.

70. The discussion in "Überlegungen zur Kommunikationspathologie" is suggestive but not always convincing in detail. On a number of occasions Habermas approvingly cites James Bohman's doctoral dissertation (Language and Social Criticism, Boston University, 1985), which he sees as a development of the ideas in his 1974 essay.

71. See Bohman, "Formal Pragmatics and Social Criticism" and "Critique of Ideologies."

72. Bohman, "Critique of Ideologies," 700.

73. "Überlegungen zur Kommunikationspathologie," 252.

74. Bohman,"Formal Pragmatics and Social Criticism," 339.

75. "Entgegnung," 367 / "A Reply," 243.

76. It has more commonly been known as his "theory of practical discourse." However, since Habermas now distinguishes three types of practical discourse (see *Erläuterungen,* 100ff.), it is probably more correct and less misleading to refer to the forum in which moral norms are tested as "moral discourse."

77. Following Habermas, I use the term "practical question" to refer to the three different types of question (pragmatic, ethical, and moral) that are the concerns of practical reason. Practical reason is not, of course, the same as communicative reason; it is no more than a subcategory of this.

78. See note 15 to chapter 2 above.

79. *Moralbewußtsein und kommunikatives Handeln,* 127ff. / *Moral Consciousness and Communicative Action,* 116ff. See *Erläuterungen,* 100ff., for a more recent (but substantially unchanged) clarification of the relevant distinctions.

80. These terms are Benhabib's. See note 7 to chapter 2 above.

81. *Moralbewußtsein und kommunikatives Handeln,* 75f. / *Moral Consciousness and Communicative Action,* 65 (as translated by Lenhardt and Weber Nicholson).

82. See, for instance, the respective critiques of Wellmer, in *Ethik und Dialog,* McCarthy, in *Ideals and Illusions,* and Benhabib, in *Critique, Norm and Utopia.*

83. Benhabib, *Situating the Self,* 37.

84. *Erläuterungen,* 12.

85. In *Faktizität und Geltung* Habermas proposes a new formulation for "D"; this is because he now wants to modify his position in order to distinguish between a moral principle and a principle of democracy. "D" is given a more general formulation: "D: Only those norms of action are valid to which all those possibly affected by them could assent in their capacity as participants in rational discourses" (138). "D" has to be made more specific in various ways before it can function as a principle of democracy and a moral principle. In the latter case it takes on the form of "U," the principle of universalization (140). Since I hold the view that the only nonproblematic interpretation of "U" is as "D" (in its old formulation), and since Habermas's new proposal does not in any way affect my argument, I continue to use "D" in its old formulation, but I suggest that we now refer to it as "U1."

86. See, for example, the criticisms of Habermas on precisely this point in Wellmer, *Ethik und Dialog,* Benhabib, *Critique, Norm and Utopia,* and McCarthy, *Ideals and Illusions.*

87. *Erläuterungen,* 199ff.

88. In *Faktizität und Geltung* Habermas further identifies questions of legal and political right; however, these appear not to constitute new categories of practical questions but to be themselves defined on the basis of their dependence on shifting constellations of moral, pragmatic, and ethical questions.

89. *Faktizität und Geltung* is the first text in which Habermas seriously addresses the questions that are raised by his acknowledgement of the limitations of the universalist point of view. He does this by distinguishing between the moral principle and a principle of democracy (see note 85 above) and recognizing that postconventional morality requires the complementary form of law.

90. See note 77 above.

91. It could be argued that Habermas recognizes this and addresses the problem in *Faktizität und Geltung*. However, although I think Habermas has taken a step in the right direction here, there is nothing in *Faktizität und Geltung* that significantly modifies his view of moral reason. I maintain that his category of moral questions is still too restricted to the extent that there are moral questions which do not fit into this category as he defines it but which, at the same time, are neither ethical questions of the good life nor questions of political or legal right (see Cooke, "Habermas and Consensus").

92. See note 77 above.

93. "Ein Interview mit der *New Left Review*," 228; "Entgegnung," 352 / "A Reply," 232f.

94. *Die nachholende Revolution*, 132.

95. "Entgegnung," 352 / "A Reply," 232f.

96. "Reply," 277.

97. Putnam, *Reason, Truth and History*, 55.

98. *Die nachholende Revolution*, 132.

99. He suggested this in "Wahrheitstheorien," for instance.

100. "Ein Interview mit der *New Left Review*," 228.

101. It is interesting to note that in *TCA* (1, 332 / *TKH*, 1, 445) Habermas refers to unconscious latently strategic action as a manifestation of systematically distorted communication. However, the discussion in section 3 above suggests that it is no more than one such manifestation. See Bohman's articles (cited in note 71 above) for a critique of Habermas's tendency to define ideology in terms of latently strategic action.

102. "Überlegungen zur Kommunikationspathologie," 245.

103. *TCA*, 2, 180f / *TKH*, 2, 268f.

104. This may go some way toward alleviating the (justified) fears of, in particular, feminist critics that the emphasis on argumentation as the forum for discussion of questions of validity may work in favor of those who already occupy socially privileged positions. See, e.g., Fraser, "Toward a Discourse Ethic of Solidarity."

105. See above, chapter 2, section 1.

106. Ibid.

107. In "Habermas and Consensus" I discuss the implications of such a position with reference to Benhabib's attempt (in *Situating the Self*) to put forward a dialogical but nonconsensual theory of justice.

108. In chapter 2, section 4.

109. One could also argue that the mechanism of reaching understanding in argumentation (*Verständigung*) cannot function as the only mechanism of self-organization in modern complex societies, as to do so would be to overburden the capacities of the members of such societies. In *Faktizität und Geltung* Habermas acknowledges this criticism and attempts to overcome it by drawing attention to the ways in which politics and law function as relief mechanisms.

110. See chapter 3, sections 5 and 6.

111. In section 3 of chapter 1 I drew attention to one of the rare occasions on which Habermas acknowledges possible limitations. See also note 71 to chapter 1.

112. *Erläuterungen*, 49ff., esp. 70f.

113. *Strukturwandel der Öffentlichkeit / Transformation of the Public Sphere.*

114. One could put this slightly differently by saying that Habermas reduces the various types of mutual recognition that are necessary for the development of personal identity and for the constitution of social practices to just one kind: recognition of the other's rational accountability (see Cooke, "Habermas, Autonomy, and the Identity of the Self"). Since what is recognized here is a language-based capacity, this supports my contention below that Habermas "linguistifies" human experience and action. For an account of other (prelinguistic or nonlinguistic) forms of mutual recognition, see Honneth, *Kampf um Anerkennung*.

115. See, for instance, *Faktizität und Geltung*, 12.

116. See above, chapter 2, section 4.

117. See Crespi, *Social Action and Power*.

118. See note 113 above.

119. See Cooke, "Habermas and Consensus."

120. Ibid. See also Cooke, "Habermas, Autonomy and the Identity of the Self."

Works by Habermas Cited in the Text (in Chronological Order)

Books

Strukturwandel der Öffentlichkeit (Suhrkamp, 1962) / *The Structural Transformation of the Public Sphere* (MIT Press, 1989)

Erkenntnis und Interesse (Suhrkamp, 1968) / *Knowledge and Human Interests* (Beacon, 1971)

Technik und Wissenschaft als 'Ideologie' (Suhrkamp, 1968)

Legitimation Crisis (Beacon, 1973)

Communication and the Evolution of Society (Heinemann, 1975)

Theorie des kommunikativen Handelns, two volumes (Suhrkamp, 1981) / *The Theory of Communicative Action*, two volumes (Beacon, 1984 and 1987)

Moralbewußtsein und kommunikatives Handeln (Suhrkamp, 1983) / *Moral Consciousness and Communicative Action* (MIT Press, 1990)

Vorstudien und Ergänzungen zur Theorie des kommunikativen Handeln (Suhrkamp, 1984)

Die Neue Unübersichtlichkeit (Suhrkamp, 1985) (Several of the essays in this collection appear in English in *Habermas, Autonomy and Solidarity*, ed. P. Dews (Verso, 1986).)

Der philosophische Diskurs der Moderne (Suhrkamp, 1985) / *The Philosophical Discourse of Modernity* (Polity Press, 1987)

Nachmetaphysisches Denken (Suhrkamp, 1988) / *Post-Metaphysical Thinking* (Polity Press, 1992) (The translation does not include all the essays published in the original. In particular, "Actions, Speech Acts, Linguistically Mediated Interactions and the Lifeworld," and "Remarks on J. Searle's 'Meaning, Communication and Representation" are missing from the English volume. On a number of occasions, therefore, I have not been able to give page numbers.)

Erläuterungen zur Diskursethik (Suhrkamp, 1991) / *Justification and Application: Remarks on Discourse Ethics* (MIT Press, 1993)

Faktizität und Geltung (Suhrkamp, 1992)

Essays and Articles

"Technik und Wissenschaft als 'Ideologie' " / "Technology and Science as 'Ideology,' " in *Technik und Wissenschaft als 'Ideologie'* (Suhrkamp, 1968). The last three essays appear in English in J. Habermas, *Toward a Rational Society* (Heinemann, 1971).

Works by Habermas

"Wahrheitstheorien," in *Wirklichkeit und Reflexion,* ed. H. Fahrenbach (Neske, 1973).

"Überlegungen zur Kommunikationspathologie" (1974), in *Vorstudien und Ergänzungen zur Theorie des kommunikativen Handelns* (Suhrkamp, 1984).

"What Is Universal Pragmatics?" in *Communication and the Evolution of Society* (Heinemann, 1975).

"Consciousness-Raising or Redemptive Criticism—The Contemporaneity of Walter Benjamin." *New German Critique* 17 (1979).

"Modernity versus Postmodernity." *New German Critique* 22 (1981).

"The Entwinement of Myth and Enlightenment." *New German Critique* 26 (1982).

"A Reply to My Critics," in *Habermas: Critical Debates,* ed. J. B. Thompson and D. Held (Macmillan, 1982).

"Remarks on the Concept of Communicative Action," in *Social Action,* ed. G. Seebaß and R. Tuomela (Reidel, 1985) / "Erläuterungen zum Begriff des kommunikativen Handelns," in *Vorstudien und Ergänzungen zur Theorie des kommunikativen Handelns* (Suhrkamp, 1984).

"Was macht eine Lebensform 'rational'?" in *Rationalität,* ed. H. Schnädelbach (Suhrkamp, 1984).

"Question and Counterquestions," in *Habermas and Modernity,* ed. R. Bernstein (Polity Press, 1985).

"Reply to Skjei." *Inquiry* 28 (1985).

"Dialektik der Rationalisierung," in *Die Neue Unübersichtlichkeit* (Suhrkamp, 1985).

"Die Krise des Wohlfahrtsstaates und die Erschöpfung utopischer Energien," in *Die Neue Unübersichtlichkeit* (Suhrkamp, 1985).

"Ein Interview mit der *New Left Review,*" in *Die Neue Unübersichtlichkeit* (Suhrkamp, 1985).

"Gerechtigkeit und Solidarität," in *Zur Bestimmung der Moral,* ed. W. Edelstein and G. Nunner-Winkler (Suhrkamp, 1986).

"Moralität und Sittlichkeit," in *Moralität und Sittlichkeit,* ed. W. Kuhlmann (Suhrkamp, 1986).

"Entgegnung," in *Kommunikatives Handeln,* ed. A. Honneth and H. Joas (Suhrkamp, 1986) / "A Reply," in *Communicative Action,* ed. A. Honneth and H. Joas (Polity Press, 1991). The latter should not be confused with "A Reply to My Critics," which is cited as "Reply" (see above).

For a bibliography of Habermas's works prior to 1981, see René Görtzen, *Jürgen Habermas: Eine Bibliographie seiner Schriften und der Sekundärliteratur 1952–1981* (Suhrkamp, 1982). See also R. Görtzen and F. van Gelder, "A Bibliography of Works by Habermas, with Translations and Reviews," in T. McCarthy, *The Critical Theory of Jürgen Habermas* (Polity Press, 1984). For a bibliography of Habermas's *Theory of Communicative Action,* see R. Görtzen, "Bibliographie zur *Theorie des kommunikativen Handelns,*" in *Kommunikatives Handeln,* ed. A. Honneth and H. Joas (Suhrkamp, 1986).

Bibliography

Alexy, R. "Eine Theorie des praktischen Diskurses," in *Materialien zur Normendiskussion,* ed. W. Oelmüller, vol. 2 (Schöningh, 1978).

Apel, K.-O. *Towards a Transformation of Philosophy* (Routledge & Kegan Paul, 1980).

Austin, J. L. *How to Do Things with Words* (Blackwell, 1962).

Barwise, J., and J. Perry. *Situations and Attitudes* (MIT Press, 1983).

Baurmann, M. "Understanding as an Aim and Aims of Understanding. Comments on Jürgen Habermas," in *Social Action,* ed. G. Seebaß and R. Tuomela (Reidel, 1985).

Baynes, K., "Rational Reconstruction and Social Criticism: Habermas's Model of Interpretive Social Science." *Philosophical Forum* 21, no. 1–2 (1989–90).

Baynes, K., J. Bohman, and T. McCarthy, eds. *After Philosophy* (MIT Press, 1987).

Bell, D. *The Cultural Contradictions of Capitalism* (Basic Books, 1976).

Benhabib, S. *Critique, Norm and Utopia* (Columbia University Press, 1986).

Benhabib, S. "Modernity and the Aporias of Critical Theory." *Telos,* no. 49 (1981).

Benhabib, S. "Philosophy at the Crossroads" (review of Bernstein's *Beyond Objectivism and Relativism*). *Praxis International* 5 (1985–86).

Benhabib, S. *Situating the Self* (Routledge, 1992).

Benhabib, S., and D. Cornell. *Feminism as Critique* (University of Minnesota Press, 1987).

Benhabib, S., and F. Dallmayr, eds. *The Communicative Ethics Controversy* (MIT Press, 1990).

Bernstein, R. *The Restructuring of Social and Political Theory* (Blackwell, 1976).

Bernstein, R. *Beyond Objectivism and Relativism* (Blackwell, 1983).

Bibliography

Bernstein, R., ed. *Habermas and Modernity* (Polity Press, 1985).

Bohman, J. F. Language and Social Criticism. Ph.D. dissertation, Boston University, 1985.

Bohman, J. F. "Formal Pragmatics and Social Criticism: The Philosophy of Language and the Critique of Ideology in Habermas's *Theory of Communicative Action*." *Philosophy and Social Criticism* 11, no. 4 (1986).

Bohman, J. F. "Critique of Ideologies," in *Sprachphilosophie / Philosophy of Language / La Philosophie du Langue*, ed. M. Dascal, D. Gerhardus, K. Lorenz, and G. Meggle (W. de Gruyter, 1992).

Bohman, J. F. "Emancipation and Rhetoric: The Perlocutions and Illocutions of the Social Critic." *Philosophy and Rhetoric* 21, no. 3 (1988).

Bübner, R. "Habermas's Concept of Critical Theory," in *Habermas: Critical Debates*, ed. J. B. Thompson and D. Held (Macmillan, 1982).

Bühler, K. *Sprachtheorie* (Fischer, 1934).

Cavell, S. *Must We Mean What We Say?* (Scribner, 1989).

Cavell, S. *The Claim of Reason* (Clarendon, 1979).

Cole, M., and J. L. Morgan, eds. *Syntax and Semantics,* vol. 3 (Academic Press, 1974).

Cooke, M. "Habermas, Autonomy and the Identity of the Self." *Philosophy and Social Criticism* 18, no. 3/4 (1992).

Cooke, M. "Habermas and Consensus." *European Journal of Philosophy* 1, no. 3 (1993).

Cooke, M. "Realizing the Postconventional Self." *Philosophy and Social Criticism,* 20, no. 1/2 (1994).

Crespi, F. *Social Action and Power* (Blackwell, 1992).

Culler, J. *On Deconstruction* (Cornell University Press, 1982).

Culler, J. "Communicative Competence and Normative Force." *New German Critique* 35 (1985).

Dallmayr, F. *Beyond Dogma and Despair* (University of Notre Dame Press, 1981).

Dallmayr, F. *Polis and Praxis* (Cambridge University Press, 1984).

Dallmayr, F., and T. McCarthy, eds. *Understanding and Social Inquiry* (University of Notre Dame Press, 1977).

Davidson, D. *Inquiries into Truth and Interpretation* (Clarendon, 1984).

Davidson, D. "A Nice Derangement of Epitaphs." In *Truth and Interpretation,* ed. E. Le Pore (Blackwell, 1986).

Derrida, J. "Signature Event Context." In *Glyph* 1 (Johns Hopkins University Press, 1977).

Derrida, J. "Limited Inc. abc." In *Glyph* 2 (Johns Hopkins University Press, 1977).

Dews, P. *Logics of Disintegration* (Verso, 1987).

Dews, P. "Agreeing What's Right" (review of Habermas's *Faktizität und Geltung*). *London Review of Books* 15, no. 9 (May 1993).

Dews, P., ed. *Habermas, Autonomy and Solidarity* (Verso, 1986).

Dummett, M. "What Is a Theory of Meaning? II." In *Truth and Meaning,* ed. G. Evans and J. McDowell (Clarendon, 1976).

Dummett, M. "Can Analytic Philosophy Be Systematic and Ought It to Be?" In *After Philosophy,* ed. K. Baynes et al. (MIT Press, 1987).

Edelstein, W., and G. Nunner-Winkler, eds. *Zur Bestimmung der Moral* (Suhrkamp, 1986).

Evans, G., and J. McDowell, eds. *Truth and Meaning* (Clarendon, 1976).

Fahrenbach, H., ed. *Wirklichkeit und Reflexion* (Neske, 1973).

Fodor, J., and E. LePore. *Holism: A Shopper's Guide* (Blackwell, 1991).

Forester, J., ed. *Critical Theory and Public Life* (MIT Press, 1985).

Fraser, N. "Toward a Discourse Ethic of Solidarity." *Praxis International* 5, no. 4 (1986).

Fraser, N. "What's Critical about Critical Theory?" in *Feminism as Critique,* ed. S. Benhabib and D. Cornell (University of Minnesota Press, 1987).

Gadamer, H.-G. *Wahrheit und Methode* (Mohr, 1986) / *Truth and Method* (Crossroad, 1985).

Giddens, A. "Reason without Revolution? Habermas's *Theorie des kommunikativen Handelns,*" in *Habermas and Modernity,* ed. R. Bernstein (Polity Press, 1985).

Goodman, N. *Ways of Worldmaking* (Harvester, 1978).

Grandy, R. E., and R. Warner, eds. *Philosophical Grounds of Rationality* (Clarendon, 1986).

Gregg, B. "Modernity in Frankfurt" (review of Benhabib's *Critique, Norm and Utopia*). *Theory and Society* 16, no. 1 (1987).

Grice, H. P. "Logic and Conversation," in *Syntax and Semantics,* vol. 3, ed. M. Cole and J. L. Morgan (Academic Press, 1974).

Gripp, H. *Jürgen Habermas: Und es gibt sie doch. Zur kommunikationstheoretischen Begründung von Vernunft bei J. Habermas* (Schöningh, 1984).

Haferkamp, H. "A Critique of Habermas's *Theory of Communicative Action,*" in *Social Action,* ed. G. Seebaß and R. Tuomela (Reidel, 1985).

Hesse, M. "Science and Objectivity," in *Habermas: Critical Debates,* ed. J. B. Thompson and D. Held (Macmillan, 1982).

Bibliography

Holub, R. *Jürgen Habermas: Critic in the Public Sphere* (Routledge, 1991).

Honneth, A. *Kritik der Macht* (Suhrkamp, 1985) / *The Critique of Power* (MIT Press, 1991).

Honneth, A. *Kampf um Anerkennung* (Suhrkamp, 1992).

Honneth, A. "Communication and Reconciliation." *Telos* 39 (1979).

Honneth, A., and H. Joas, eds. *Kommunikatives Handeln* (Suhrkamp, 1986) / *Communicative Action* (Polity Press, 1991).

Honneth, A., T. McCarthy, C. Offe, and A. Wellmer, *Zwischenbetrachtungen.* (Suhrkamp, 1989).

Ingram, D. *Habermas and the Dialectic of Reason* (Yale University Press, 1987).

Jay, M. *Marxism and Totality* (University of California Press, 1984).

Jay, M. "Habermas and Modernity," in *Habermas and Modernity*, ed. R. Bernstein (Polity Press, 1985).

Kohlberg, L. *The Philosophy of Moral Development* (Harper & Row, 1981).

Kohlberg, L., D. R. Boyd, and C. Levine. "Die Wiederkehr der sechsten Stufe," in *Zur Bestimmung der Moral,* ed. W. Edelstein and G. Nunner-Winkler (Suhrkamp, 1986).

Kuhlmann, W., ed. *Moralität und Sittlichkeit* (Suhrkamp, 1986).

Lacan, J. *Ecrits: A Selection* (Tavistock, 1975).

Le Pore, E., ed. *Truth and Interpretation* (Blackwell, 1986).

Luke, T. W., and S. K. White. "Critical Theory: The Informational Revolution and an Ecological Modernity," in *Critical Theory and Public Life,* ed. J. Forester (MIT Press, 1985).

Lukes, S. "Of Gods and Demons: Habermas and Practical Reason," in *Habermas: Critical Debates,* ed. J. B. Thompson and D. Held (Macmillan, 1982).

MacIntyre, A. *After Virtue* (Duckworth, 1981).

McCarthy, T. *The Critical Theory of Jürgen Habermas* (Polity Press, 1984).

McCarthy, T. *Ideals and Illusions* (MIT Press, 1991).

McCarthy, T. "Rationality and Relativism: Habermas's 'Overcoming' of Hermeneutics," in *Habermas: Critical Debates,* ed. J. B. Thompson and D. Held (Macmillan, 1982).

McCarthy, T. "Reflections on Rationalization in *The Theory of Communicative Action,*" in *Habermas and Modernity,* ed. R. Bernstein (Polity Press, 1985).

Mendelson, J. "The Habermas-Gadamer Debate." *New German Critique* 18 (1979).

Misgeld, D. "Critical Theory and Hermeneutics: The Debate between Habermas and Gadamer," in *On Critical Theory,* ed. J. O'Neill (Heinemann, 1977).

Nunner-Winkler, G. "Ein Plädoyer für einen eingeschränkten Universalismus," in *Zur Bestimmung der Moral*, ed. W. Edelstein and G. Nunner-Winkler (Suhrkamp, 1986).

Oelmüller, W., ed. *Materialien zur Normendiskussion*, three vols. (Schöningh, 1978).

O'Neill, J., ed. *On Critical Theory* (Heinemann, 1977).

Parkinson, G. H., ed. *Marx and Marxisms* (Cambridge University Press, 1982).

Pettit, P. "Habermas on Truth and Justice," in *Marx and Marxisms*, ed. G. H. Parkinson (Cambridge University Press, 1982).

Piaget, J. *The Principles of Genetic Epistemology* (Routledge and Kegan Paul, 1977).

Platts, M. ed. *Reference, Truth and Reality* (Routledge & Kegan Paul, 1980).

Polanyi, M., and H. Prosch. *Meaning* (University of Chicago Press, 1975).

Pratt, M. L. *Toward a Speech Act Theory of Literary Discourse* (Indiana University Press, 1977).

Puka, B. "Vom Nutzen und Nachteil der Stufe 6," in *Zur Bestimmung der Moral*, ed. W. Edelstein and G. Nunner-Winkler (Suhrkamp, 1986).

Putnam, H. *Meaning and the Moral Sciences* (Routledge & Kegan Paul, 1978).

Putnam, H. *Reason, Truth and History* (Cambridge University Press, 1981).

Putnam, H. *Realism and Reason: Philosophical Papers, vol. 3* (Cambridge University Press, 1983).

Rajchman, P., and C. West, eds. *Post-Analytic Philosophy* (Columbia University Press, 1985).

Rasmussen, D. *Reading Habermas* (Blackwell, 1990).

Roderick, R. *Habermas and the Foundations of Critical Theory* (Macmillan, 1986).

Rorty, R., ed. *Essays on Aristotle's Ethics* (University of California Press, 1980).

Rorty, R. "Habermas and Lyotard on Postmodernity," in *Habermas and Modernity*, ed. R. Bernstein (Polity Press, 1985).

Rosenberg, J, and C. Travis, eds. *Readings in the Philosophy of Language* (Prentice-Hall, 1971).

Schnädelbach, H., ed. *Rationalität* (Suhrkamp, 1984).

Schnädelbach, H. "Transformation der kritischen Theorie" / "The Transformation of Critical Theory," in *Kommunikatives Handeln* (Suhrkamp, 1986) / *Communicative Action* (Polity Press, 1991), ed. A. Honneth and H. Joas.

Searle, J. *Speech Acts* (Cambridge University Press, 1969).

Searle, J. "Reiterating the Differences," in *Glyph 2* (Johns Hopkins University Press, 1977).

Searle, J. *Expression and Meaning* (Cambridge University Press, 1979).

Searle, J. "Meaning, Communication, and Representation," in *Philosophical Grounds of Rationality*, ed. R. E. Grandy and R. Warner (Clarendon, 1986).

Seebaß, G., and R. Tuomela, eds. *Social Action* (Reidel, 1985).

Seel, M. *Die Kunst der Entzweiung* (Suhrkamp, 1985).

Seel, M. "Die Zwei Bedeutungen kommunikativer Rationalität," in *Kommunikatives Handeln* (Suhrkamp, 1986) / *Communicative Action* (Polity Press, 1991), ed. A. Honneth and H. Joas.

Seel, M. Am Beispiel der Metapher. Manuscript, Konstanz, 1988.

Skjei, E. "A Comment on Performative, Subject and Proposition in Habermas's Theory of Communication." *Inquiry* 28 (1985).

Smart, B. *Modern Conditions, Postmodern Controversies* (Routledge, 1992).

Strawson, P. F. *Logico-Linguistic Papers* (Methuen, 1971).

Sullivan, B. "The Rationality Debate and Gadamer's Hermeneutics: Reflections on *Beyond Objectivism and Relativism.*" *Philosophy and Social Criticism* 11, no. 1 (1985).

Taylor, C. *Philosophical Papers*, two vols. (Cambridge University Press, 1985).

Taylor, C. "Die Motive einer Verfahrensethik," in *Moralität und Sittlichkeit*, ed. W. Kuhlmann (Suhrkamp, 1986).

Taylor, C. "Sprache und Gesellschaft," in *Kommunikatives Handeln* (Suhrkamp, 1986) / *Communicative Action* (Polity Press, 1991), ed. A. Honneth and H. Joas.

Taylor, C. *The Ethics of Authenticity* (Harvard University Press, 1992).

Thompson, J. B. *Critical Hermeneutics* (Cambridge University Press, 1981).

Thompson, J. B. *Studies in the Theory of Ideology* (Polity Press, 1984).

Thompson, J. B. "Universal Pragmatics," in *Habermas: Critical Debates*, ed. J. B. Thompson and D. Held (Macmillan, 1982).

Thompson, J. B., and D. Held, eds. *Habermas: Critical Debates* (Macmillan, 1982).

Tugendhat, E. *Vorlesungen zur Einführung in die sprachanalytische Philosophie* (Suhrkamp, 1976).

Tugendhat, E. *Probleme der Ethik* (Reclam, 1984).

Tugendhat, E. "Habermas on Communicative Action," in *Social Action*, ed. G. Seebaß and R. Tuomela (Reidel, 1985).

Wellmer, A. *Zur Dialektik von Moderne und Postmoderne* (Suhrkamp, 1985).

Wellmer, A. *Ethik und Dialog* (Suhrkamp, 1986).

Bibliography

Wellmer, A. "Communications and Emancipation: Reflections on the Linguistic Turn in Critical Theory," in *On Critical Theory*, ed. J. O'Neill (Heinemann, 1977).

Wellmer, A. "Reason, Utopia and the Dialectic of Enlightenment," in *Habermas and Modernity*, ed. R. Bernstein (Polity Press, 1985).

Wellmer, A. "Was ist eine pragmatische Bedeutungstheorie?" in *Zwischenbetrachtungen*, ed. A. Honneth et al. (Suhrkamp, 1989).

White, S. K. *The Recent Work of Jürgen Habermas* (Cambridge University Press, 1988).

White, S. K. "On the Normative Structure of Action: Gewirth and Habermas." *Review of Politics* 44, no. 2 (1982).

Whitebook, J. "The Problem of Nature in Habermas." *Telos* 40 (1979).

Whitebook, J. "Reason and Happiness: Some Psychoanalytic Themes in Critical Theory," in *Habermas and Modernity*, ed. R. Bernstein (Polity Press, 1985).

Wiggens, D. "Deliberation and Practical Reason," in *Essays on Aristotle's Ethics*, ed. R. Rorty (University of California Press, 1980).

Wittgenstein, L. *Philosophical Investigations* (Blackwell, 1958).

Wood, A. W. "Habermas's Defence of Rationalism." *New German Critique* 35 (1985).

Zimmermann, R. *Utopie–Rationalität–Politik* (Karl Alber, 1985).

Zimmermann, R. "Emanzipation und Rationalität: Grundprobleme der Theorien von Marx und Habermas." *Ratio* 26, no. 2 (1984).

Index

Index

Jürgen Habermas, *Postmetaphysical Thinking: Philosophical Essays*

Jürgen Habermas, *The Structural Transformation of the Public Sphere: An Inquiry into a Category of Bourgeois Society*

Jürgen Habermas, editor, *Observations on "The Spiritual Situation of the Age"*

Axel Honneth, *The Critique of Power: Reflective Stages in a Critical Social Theory*

Axel Honneth and Hans Joas, editors, *Communicative Action: Essays on Jürgen Habermas's* The Theory of Communicative Action

Axel Honneth, Thomas McCarthy, Claus Offe, and Albrecht Wellmer, editors, *Cultural-Political Interventions in the Unfinished Project of Enlightenment*

Axel Honneth, Thomas McCarthy, Claus Offe, and Albrecht Wellmer, editors, *Philosophical Interventions in the Unfinished Project of Enlightenment*

Max Horkheimer, *Between Philosophy and Social Science: Selected Early Writings*

Hans Joas, *G. H. Mead: A Contemporary Re-examination of His Thought*

Reinhart Koselleck, *Critique and Crisis: Enlightenment and the Pathogenesis of Modern Society*

Reinhart Koselleck, *Futures Past: On the Semantics of Historical Time*

Harry Liebersohn, *Fate and Utopia in German Sociology, 1887–1923*

Herbert Marcuse, *Hegel's Ontology and the Theory of Historicity*

Gil G. Noam and Thomas E. Wren, editors, *The Moral Self*

Guy Oakes, *Weber and Rickert: Concept Formation in the Cultural Sciences*

Claus Offe, *Contradictions of the Welfare State*

Claus Offe, *Disorganized Capitalism: Contemporary Transformations of Work and Politics*

Helmut Peukert, *Science, Action, and Fundamental Theology: Toward a Theology of Communicative Action*

Joachim Ritter, *Hegel and the French Revolution: Essays on the* Philosophy of Right

Alfred Schmidt, *History and Structure: An Essay on Hegelian-Marxist and Structuralist Theories of History*

Dennis Schmidt, *The Ubiquity of the Finite: Hegel, Heidegger, and the Entitlements of Philosophy*

Carl Schmitt, *The Crisis of Parliamentary Democracy*

Carl Schmitt, *Political Romanticism*

Carl Schmitt, *Political Theology: Four Chapters on the Concept of Sovereignty*

Gary Smith, editor, *On Walter Benjamin: Critical Essays and Recollections*

Michael Theunissen, *The Other: Studies in the Social Ontology of Husserl Heidegger, Sartre, and Buber*

Ernst Tugendhat, *Self-Consciousness and Self-Determination*